ESSENTIAL PROJECT INVESTMENT GOVERNANCE AND REPORTING

Preventing Project Fraud and
Ensuring Sarbanes-Oxley Compliance

Steven C. Rollins, PMP
Richard B. Lanza, CPA, CFE, PMP

Copyright ©2005 by J. Ross Publishing, Inc.

ISBN 1-932159-26-6

Printed and bound in the U.S.A. Printed on acid-free paper
10 9 8 7 6 5 4 3 2 1

Library of Congress Cataloging-in-Publication Data

Rollins, Steven C., 1950-
    Essential project investment governance and reporting : preventing project
fraud and ensuring Sarbanes-Oxley compliance / by Steven Rollins and Richard
Lanza.
        p. cm.
    ISBN 1-932159-26-6 (hardcover : alk. paper)
    1. Project management—United States—Accounting 2. Corporate
governance—Law and legislation—United States. 3. Corporations—Corrupt
practices—United States. I. Lanza, Richard. II. Title.
    HF5686.C7R65 2004
    657'.7—dc22

                                                            2004020322

Phone: (561) 869-3900
Fax: (561) 892-0700
Web: www.jrosspub.com

Table of Contents

Preface

Some may ask, "Why write this book?" To answer, we first felt it imperative to get groups of professionals to work together: auditors, fraud examiners, and project managers. All have similar traits and many times carry out the same tasks (probably without even knowing it). There are even a few people who have mastered all of the requisite skills. While this may be the case, we see a need for a cross-pollinization of knowledge, with project managers learning more about auditing and examining for fraud, while everyone can learn more about project management. Therefore, until this book, the key professional group roles have never been formalized, and as such, they may have never considered what was right under their noses.

That something is the existence of project fraud, which we define for purposes of this book as the misrepresentation of a project's mission or progress to secure project financing, misuse of project resources, and/or improper dealings with project vendors for personal enrichment. It is rampant on projects, inhibits transparent reporting of organizational activity, and inappropriately siphons funds that could have been used more effectively in company investments. It is a subset of the fraud classification system developed by the Association of Certified Fraud Examiners, and until now, the tools were never highlighted to fight its existence. There is great topical importance, especially now that project work is becoming the norm in the corporate world, while fraud is becoming a disease that must be eradicated as quickly as it is found for corporate survival.

This book, therefore, is a first step toward fighting project fraud by providing numerous tools to the appropriate professional groups. To that end, the book is organized as follows:

xiv   Essential Project Investment Governance and Reporting

- *Chapters 1 and 2* provide the current corporate reporting setting, high-lighting the need for improved corporate governance and transparent financial reporting.
- *Chapters 3 and 4* define project fraud while showing how it may have played out in a case study.
- *Chapters 5 and 6* identify the impacts of project fraud to the organization and how it may be identified most readily.
- *Chapters 7 and 8* explain the elements of internal control and auditing as they relate to the detection of fraud. These chapters provide a base understanding of audit concepts for project managers.
- *Chapters 9 through 12* provide tools for assessing project control, as well as preventing and detecting project fraud.
- *Chapter 12* concludes with the associated roles of each party in ensuring corporate governance around projects.
- *Chapter 13* discusses utilizing the audit function and project management office for fraud prevention and detection while maximizing project investments.
- *Chapters 14 through 25* examine the role of project teams in managing for project fraud prevention and detection and how to best facilitate that skill, leading value accretion and business transformation through change management.

We believe this publication will help to mend the level of trust between companies and their stakeholders by working toward improved financial reporting transparency. It will also provide tools to run project investments better through the integration of audit and project disciplines. Finally, we see this book as a reference guide for all project teams seeking project delivery success and to help manage through project delivery uncertainty.

We hope you enjoy this publication and find it a useful resource for the improved management of your projects, for reduction of negative impacts associated with project fraud, and to help you look like a star within your organization.

About the Authors

Steven C. Rollins, MBA, PMP, PMOP, is a well-known leading global expert in the enterprise program/project management office (PMO) project delivery industry and is President and Founder of the ALLPMO Network™ Inc., featuring www.pmousa.com and seventeen other PMO Internet portals free to the general public.

Mr. Rollins is also the Executive Chair for the Mid America PMO Regional Group that operates as a chapter of the Project Management Institute's (PMI) PMO Specific Industry Group (SIG), Past Knowledge Chair Office for the PMI Metrics Specific Interest Group of more than seven hundred people, and the Acting Chair for the PMI Metrics SIG (www.metsig.org). As the former Knowledge Vice-Chair for the PMI Metrics SIG, he led the framework development and rollout of the first-ever comprehensive project management metrics Knowledge Center in 2002.

Mr. Rollins is author with Gerald Kendall of the best-selling PMO book *Advanced Project Portfolio Management and the PMO: Multiplying ROI at Warp Speed,* published in 2003 by J. Ross Publishing.

J. Ross Publishing will be releasing *Value-Based Metrics for Improving Results: An Enterprise Project Management Toolkit* by Mr. Rollins and Dr. Mel Schnapper. This book will correlate the PMI Project Management Body of Knowledge with project-related metrics that focus a business on delivery speed, change management, and PMO support, all leading toward achieving business transformation. This book will feature more than two hundred metrics for readers' use and will establish, for the first time, a standard for actual project management metrics that help lead businesses everywhere toward prosperity and for others that follow to build on.

Mr. Rollins' background includes more than twenty years of extensive PMO/ project management consultative experience in financial services, healthcare, human resources, information technology, insurance, and telecommunication industries.

Today, this leading PMO/project management subject-matter expert is also a featured speaker at many project management organizational conferences and meetings around the world.

Mr. Rollins can be contacted at Steve@pmousa.com for further inquiries.

Rich Lanza, CPA, CFE, PMP, is a Manager of Internal Audit at a Fortune 200 retailer, where he assists in the Sarbanes-Oxley compliance effort and focuses the remainder of his time using computer-assisted audit tools to improve business intelligence, increase efficiencies, and identify multimillion-dollar bottom-line savings.

As a leading authority on the use of audit and assurance software, Mr. Lanza has devoted himself to providing information on the topic freely, as his mission is to help auditors get recognition for their bottom-line results. To that end, he founded *AuditSoftware.Net* (www.auditsoftware.net), which works to increase organizational benefits from the use of audit software. The free site provides tools, case studies, a vendor discount program, a newsletter, and a discussion area for visitors. The site recently announced project communities, whereby anyone interested can share and collaborate on practical audit software tools and solutions. Mr. Lanza has also written numerous articles, software products, and four test set books on how to apply ACL™ and IDEA™ software practically (http://www.ekaros.ca/publications.html). He has commonly been referred to as "The Johnny Appleseed of the Audit Software Industry."

Mr. Lanza headed the PMO, reporting to the chief operating officer, at the American Institute of Certified Public Accountants (AICPA), where he sewed a culture of project management into the fabric of the organization. On his last major project, he worked to coordinate various fraud-reduction initiatives to maximize their benefit for the AICPA and financial markets. He drafted many of the project standards being used at the AICPA to manage projects, implemented a project portfolio management process, and also established a six-month intense training program for project managers. Prior to his program management work, he was a program/project manager in many Web and technology projects including leading the Y2K project.

Prior to joining the AICPA, Mr. Lanza served as a Vice President-Audit Technology at AuditWatch, where he was an ACL™ and IDEA™ trainer. He was an internal audit manager for Lafarge and Disclosure and served in the audit department at KPMG Peat Marwick. He received his undergraduate degree in public accounting from Pace University, is a past President of the Northern Virginia Chapter of the Institute of Internal Auditors, and is a certified member of both the AICPA and PMI. He currently also maintains the New York/New Jersey PMO Special Interest Group for PMI.

In 2003, Mr. Lanza was awarded the Outstanding Achievement in Commerce Award from the Association of Certified Fraud Examiners for his data analysis work in the area of fraud detection and also won the Second Annual ACL™ Users Challenge. His interests include magic and collecting gadgets.

The author's opinions expressed in this publication are his own and do not necessarily represent the policies or positions of his employer.

Mr. Lanza can be reached by e-mail at questions@richlanza.com, by phone at 973-828-0239, and at www.richlanza.com and www.auditsoftware.net.

Acknowledgments

Steve Rollins

The creation of this book represents a personal fulfillment to bring out the nature and consequences of project fraud in business everywhere. Early in my career, I often had to manage situations that were likely fraudulent. I often wondered if I was the only person having this problem or working in the only company with this problem. The answer soon became obvious and thus provided the motivation to create this work.

Writing this book was the easy part, as the writing was accomplished in record time due to the vast knowledge stores that Rich Lanza and I each possessed. The hardest portion of this work was controlling the passion that came out as I recalled past work experiences. If I only knew then what I know now! Each of these past work events proved further that without people working together for a common cause with common beliefs, achievement would be difficult. To reduce and eliminate project fraud, we must all be together on this. Someone once said: "To know success, one must know failure so they can recognize success once it occurs." The heck with failure! Failure is for those who wait and do nothing.

I am thankful for meeting Rich and gaining the perspective from his experiences in the auditing profession, as well as everything else he has helped me with in the production of this book. To this I say, "Thank you, Rich!"

There are very few good books on managing for Sarbanes-Oxley in today's marketplace. There is only one commonly accepted standard in project management as evidenced by the large membership of the Project Management Institute. PMI has developed the Project Management Body of Knowledge (PMBOK®) that includes ten Areas of Knowledge. It is this standard that we have aligned to the project management portion of our message. To this I say, "Thank you, PMI" for placing a stake in the ground for best project management value and for the potential of continuous improvement as mankind continues its evolutionary march.

The impact of human behavior in the project management space must be harnessed by project management professionals everywhere if businesses that apply project management rigor and discipline are ever to achieve the benefit from the promise of project management — *business prosperity.*

Much of my understanding on human behavior in project management I learned first hand from Dr. Edwards Deming through his Total Quality Management paradigm and Dr. Eli Goldratt through his teachings of the Theory of Constraints paradigm. I am ever so grateful to these men for their contributions so that others like me can leverage their concepts with new ideas toward new and improved techniques.

Finally, I encourage you to consider the value of the project management office (PMO) in helping organizations transform themselves as the business climate changes around them, sometimes every day. If companies are to be competitive, they must understand that invisible value exists all around awaiting their discovery. Measurement systems do lead to "raised visibility," eventually resulting in improved cross-collaboration. Thus, let it be understood that if you cannot measure, you cannot control. If you cannot control, you cannot manage. Thus, if you cannot measure, you cannot manage. This leads us to the ever-present question: "What is your value proposition and how do you know?"

My hope and prayer is that this book will help you find new methods to become more successful in your delivery work. I am interested in your stories. Please send me your thoughts, comments, and stories at Steve@pmousa.com.

Rich Lanza

This publication would not have been envisioned or written without some help along the way. To that end, I express my deepest thanks to:

- The American Institute of Certified Public Accountants for giving me the opportunity to work on its antifraud initiative and see the need to reduce fraud in the marketplace. More specifically, Chuck Landes, Director of Audit Standards, for showing me that fraud is something that needs to be reduced in the marketplace.
- The Association of Certified Fraud Examiners, most particularly Joseph T. Wells and Toby Bishop, for being the vanguards in the fight against fraud.

- The Committee of Sponsoring Organizations for its critical definitions and framework of internal control.
- Mort Goldman for his assistance in many engagements where he helped me identify, quantify, and mitigate project risk.
- Steve Rollins for driving me to completion on this project and making sure it was the best we could make it.
- Most importantly, my family and friends for their support throughout the writing of this finished publication.

Web
Added
Value

Free value-added materials available from
the Download Resource Center at www.jrosspub.com

At J. Ross Publishing we are committed to providing today's professional with practical, hands-on tools that enhance the learning experience and give readers an opportunity to apply what they have learned. That is why we offer free ancillary materials available for download on this book and all participating Web Added Value™ publications. These online resources may include interactive versions of material that appears in the book or supplemental templates, worksheets, models, plans, case studies, proposals, spreadsheets and assessment tools, among other things. Whenever you see the WAV™ symbol in any of our publications, it means bonus materials accompany the book and are available from the Web Added Value Download Resource Center at www.jrosspub.com.

Downloads available for *Essential Project Investment Governance and Reporting: Preventing Project Fraud and Ensuring Sarbanes-Oxley Compliance* consist of an MS Project PMO roadmap for implementing SOX 404, project fraud and risk assessment checklists, and templates for benefit/cost estimation and decision analysis and for developing project fraud management policy and risk management plans.

Part 1:
New Corporate
Governance
Landscape

The New World of Corporate Governance

1.1 What Happened?

A host of financial disasters, most notably the Enron debacle, led to an uproar in the capital marketplace, as well as impacting the thousands of people working for the affected organizations. The investing public responded with one of the most volatile stock markets in history. A few corporations had tested the level of grayness in their application of generally accepted accounting principles to a point many would say was downright "cooking of books."

Most surprising was that the cast of characters extended beyond a few bad CEOs posting inappropriate journal entries. Rather, the frauds crept from senior executives to the accountants, lawyers, rating agencies, employees, and banks, as well as the "tone at the top" of corporate governance itself: the boards of directors. Even the auditors had something to hide, which was the eventual downfall of one of the leading accounting firms in the world, Arthur Andersen.

Companies at large need to rebuild trust between the shareholders and the organization. This can be done through transparent reporting and solid corporate governance as explained in this chapter. Trust is then synthesized into written form through a new attestation report provided by the company's external auditor on the organization's control design and effectiveness. This report is one component (Section 404) of the Sarbanes-Oxley Act.

1.2 It Is All About Trust

The world's capital markets depend on trust between:

■ Shareholders or financial institutions and corporations' financial reporting
■ Managers
■ Corporate reporting

This trust leads to efficiency and, thus, reduced costs to all parties. For example, improved trust between financial institutions and corporations leads to improved debt ratings and, thus, lower interest rates on debt. Improved trust in business process controls leads to improved trust between an auditor and a corporation relating to their control consciousness and, thus, will lead to a less costly Sarbanes-Oxley attestation.

1.3 Transparent Reporting

The first step in rebuilding trust is to enhance transparent reporting. This can readily be seen as companies provide segment information, sustainability reporting, and improved notes to make financial statements easier to understand. Some companies are going beyond regulatory requirements to provide the investor with an improved picture, such as through detailing forward-looking information. The desire to hold this transparency has many motives:

■ *Market expectations* — Companies in danger of not meeting analyst expectations.
■ *Increase shareholder value* — Companies that display a move toward transparency have been known to attract increased marketplace value.
■ *Contractual* — To comply with outside contractual requirements, such as a debt covenant on a loan.
■ *Regulatory* — Companies needing to give an appearance to regulators in order to influence their actions, such as lowering earnings to feign an antitrust lawsuit.
■ *Clean house* — When there is a new incoming management team, there is a tendency to write off questionable balances and blame the previous regime. Not only does this allow for improved reporting in future periods, but no blame is placed on the management at hand.
■ *Doing the right thing* — Aside from the above business-focused motives, some companies just want to make sure they are doing all they can to present an honest and open picture of their current status.

1.4 Corporate Governance

The second step in rebuilding trust is through a solid corporate governance structure. This will not only ensure trust, but also prevent fraud. To do so, an entity should have an appropriate oversight function in place with the following roles and responsibilities:[1]

- *Management* — Management is responsible for overseeing the activities carried out by employees, assessing any fraud that may be committed by employees, and implementing new processes as required by other oversight functions.
- *Audit committee* — The audit committee should evaluate management's identification of fraud risks, implementation of antifraud measures, and creation of the appropriate "tone at the top." An entity's audit committee should also encourage senior management (in particular, the CEO) to implement appropriate fraud deterrence and prevention measures to better protect investors, employees, and other stakeholders.
- *Internal audit* — Internal audits can be both a detection and a deterrence measure. Internal auditors can assist in the deterrence of fraud by examining and evaluating the adequacy and the effectiveness of the system of internal control. Internal auditors may also conduct proactive auditing to search for corruption, misappropriation of assets, and financial statement fraud. The internal auditors should have an independent reporting line directly to the audit committee to enable them to express any concerns about management's commitment to appropriate internal controls or to report suspicions or allegations of fraud involving senior management.
- *External auditor* — External auditors can assist management and the board of directors, including the audit committee, by providing an assessment of the entity's process for identifying, assessing, and responding to the risks of fraud. The board of directors should have an open and candid dialogue with the independent auditors regarding management's risk assessment process and the system of internal control. Such a dialogue should include a discussion of the vulnerability of the entity to fraudulent financial reporting and the entity's exposure to misappropriation of assets.
- *Fraud examiner* — Certified fraud examiners may assist audit committees and boards of directors with aspects of the oversight process either directly or as part of a team of internal auditors or external auditors. Certified fraud examiners can provide extensive knowledge and experience about fraud that may not be available within a corporation. They

can provide more objective input into management's evaluation of the risk of fraud (especially fraud involving senior management, such as financial statement fraud) and the development of appropriate antifraud controls that are less vulnerable to management override. They can assist audit committees and boards of directors in evaluating the fraud risk assessment and fraud prevention measures implemented by management. Certified fraud examiners also conduct examinations to resolve allegations or suspicions of fraud, reporting either to an appropriate level of management or to the audit committee or board of directors, depending on the nature of the issue and the level of personnel involved.

1.5 Regulatory Reaction: Sarbanes-Oxley

To help the process of rebuilding trust, the Sarbanes-Oxley Act was introduced and, most notably, Section 404 was included to require the CEO and CFO to sign an internal control report. The internal control report must articulate management's responsibilities to establish and maintain adequate internal control over financial reporting and management's conclusion on the effectiveness of these internal controls at year-end. Section 302 requires management to conclude an internal control each quarter, but this quarterly report is not reviewed by the external auditors. Therefore, the 404 report must also state that the company's external auditors have attested to and reported on management's evaluation of internal control over financial reporting.

For many companies, the requirements of Section 404 present a challenge. As a result, many directors, certifying executives, other senior managers, and even the auditors themselves have many questions as they work together to facilitate compliance with these requirements. Boards and management may need independent advisors to assist them in addressing these questions. This "working together" enhances the corporate governance of the organization, while an internal review and external reporting of internal controls is a critical component of transparent reporting, all now regulated by the Securities and Exchange Commission and federal government for public companies.

1.6 Does Sarbanes-Oxley Go Far Enough?

Many people believe that the Sarbanes-Oxley Act was a hasty response to the public's desire for corporate reform. While the act focused on changes to the accounting profession board of director makeup, criminal penalties, and the like, the main requirement where the most time is being placed is the assessment of internal controls. This is promulgated in Sections 302 and 404 of the act.

The problem with this assessment is that there is a lack of specific methods and standards for evaluating internal controls for preventing and detecting financial statement fraud. Currently the COSO framework (see next section for a further discussion) is being used, yet this framework is not specific at times, especially when it comes to preventing fraud (one of the key requirements of the Sarbanes-Oxley Act) and stopping management override to "cook the books." Further, auditors generally are inexperienced in dealing with internal controls as they audit account balances and not processes on most of their audits. In addition, until the last few years, fraud was hardly a requirement for auditing a company's books and records.

Given the above, public companies are likely to issue reports claiming that internal control is effective and auditors are likely to endorse such reports, only to find out later in some cases that financial statement fraud took place.[2] Stockholders are likely to look skeptically on those earlier assurances of effective internal control. Based on these new reports, additional litigation against companies, corporate executives, and auditors is predictable.[2] To combat this, companies should look beyond the internal control standards into those for fraud prevention and detection, most notably those promulgated by the Association of Certified Fraud Examiners (www.cfenet.com). Such practices, as later outlined in this book, increase the chance of detecting financial statement fraud and management override, two areas that are generally at the root of every financial disaster.

1.7 A Renewed Emphasis on Internal Control

Companies have long recognized the importance of strong internal controls. Effective internal control can help companies achieve established financial goals, prevent loss of resources, and prepare reliable financial statements. And, as amended in 1977, the Securities Exchange Act requires that companies maintain adequate internal control.

The most commonly used and understood framework for evaluating internal controls over financial reporting is that contained in the report of the Committee of Sponsoring Organizations of the Treadway Commission (COSO). The COSO report, Internal Control — Integrated Framework, established a broad definition of internal control extending to all objectives of an organization. The COSO report established three categories of controls: effectiveness and efficiency of operations, reliability of financial reporting, and compliance with laws and regulations. It also identified five interrelated components that must be present and functioning to have an effective internal control system, and it described the criteria for effective internal control. The COSO report, therefore, contains the most widely accepted definition of internal control, which is the reason why it was selected as a basis for Sarbanes-Oxley Section 404 reporting.

1.8   Lack of Project Focus and Training

As this publication focuses on project fraud, a component of financial statement fraud, it must be noted that financial statement accounts are the focus of an auditor's report on internal controls. The COSO report discussed above makes no mention of reviewing projects as part of their internal control reporting framework. Therefore, management and auditors will focus the majority of their time documenting processes, risks, and controls around key accounts, rather than projects.

However, projects mired in fraud can have a material effect on the financial statements. Projects could affect the fixed asset balances of a company, whereby an asset is capitalized for far more than it is worth. It also could be seen in overstated expenses (payroll or otherwise) that were fraudulently spent by rogue project managers. And, given the focus of companies on accounts, coupled with the fact that most professionals are not trained in project and program management, it can be stated predictably that many companies will go without reporting project fraud until after it is too late.

1.9   Summary

After a wave of financial disasters, companies and investors at large saw the imperative to rebuild trust in financial reporting. The steps to rebuilding this trust include more transparent financial reporting and improved corporate governance. A major step to ensure this trust was the passage of the Sarbanes-Oxley Act, which requires companies to confirm their financial reporting internal controls and to have an external auditor attest to such a reporting. This ushered in a time of reflection on internal controls and the reporting frameworks around such processes. However, project internal controls have yet to be explored in the accounting and audit literature, and this is the key premise of this publication.

Questions

1.1   What are the two major steps toward rebuilding trust between companies and investors?

1.2   What is the Sarbanes-Oxley Act?

1.3   What section of the Sarbanes-Oxley Act requires quarterly reporting on financial reporting internal controls?

1.4   What are the five key motives to transparent reporting?

1.5   What is the COSO report?

1.6   To help the process of rebuilding trust, the Sarbanes-Oxley Act was introduced, and most notably, Section 404 was included in this act to require the CEO and CFO to sign an internal control report. True or false?

1.7   Section 302 requires management to conclude an internal control each quarter, but this quarterly report is not reviewed by the external auditors. True or false?

References

1. American Institute of Certified Public Accountants, Consideration of Fraud in a Financial Statement Audit, Auditing Standards Board, 2002.

2. Bishop, Toby J.F., Sarbanes-Oxley Litigation Trap, Business Crimes Bulletin, 2003.

2

Enabling Compliance with Sarbanes-Oxley

2.1 Overall Requirements of the Act

On July 30, 2002, President George W. Bush signed into law the Sarbanes-Oxley Act of 2002 (Accounting Industry Reform Act). The law of sweeping changes created an oversight board to monitor the accounting industry, toughened penalties against executives who commit corporate fraud, and increased the Securities and Exchange Commission (SEC) budget for auditors and investigators. The law was also intended to restore investor confidence in U.S. markets. This was a landmark event, representing the most dramatic changes in the federal securities laws since the 1930s.

Sections 1 and 2 of the act (see Appendix 1 for a full list of sections) made dramatic changes to the accounting industry and created the Public Company Accounting Oversight Board (PCAOB) to provide industry oversight. The PCAOB is a private-sector, nonprofit corporation to oversee the auditors of public companies in order to protect the interests of investors and further the public interest in the preparation of informative, fair, and independent audit reports. It has the authority to set and enforce auditing, attestation, quality control, and ethics (including independence) standards for auditors of public companies. It is also empowered to inspect the auditing operations of public accounting firms that audit public companies, as well as impose disciplinary and remedial sanctions for violations of the board's rules, securities laws, and professional auditing and accounting standards. The board held its first public meeting in January 2003, is currently staffing to full capacity, and has a $104 million annual budget (for fiscal year 2004).

Sections 3 and 4 of the act mainly focused on company management, the company's responsibilities relative to financial statements, and prohibited activities in relation to the company. Two of the most profound sections of the act are 302 and 404, which are further discussed below. Another key section was Section 9, which focused on increased penalties for white-collar crimes. In particular, Section 906 states that the CFO and CEO can be fined up to $5 million and/or imprisoned up to twenty years for willfully certifying false financial conditions and results of operations.

2.2 Sections 302 and 404

Financial statement certification requirements have been the focal point of the Sarbanes-Oxley Act and relate primarily to representations regarding the fair presentation of financial statements and the effectiveness of disclosure controls and procedures. Sections 302 (focused on the certification) and 906 (focused on the penalties) lay a foundation for restoring investor confidence. Section 404 builds on that foundation by requiring management to file an internal control report with its annual report (SEC filing 10K) articulating management's responsibilities to establish and maintain adequate internal control over financial reporting and management's conclusion on the effectiveness of these internal controls at year-end. The report must also be attested to by the company's external auditor through a written report.

Senior executives expect their companies to pay on average 35 percent more in audit fees to comply with Section 404 of the Sarbanes-Oxley Act alone (http://www.fei.org/news/404costsurvey.xls). Per this study, respondents said that they expect their companies, on average, to spend more than six thousand hours (including internal resources, external resources, and attestation time) and an additional $480,000 on software and IT consulting to comply with Section 404. Hence, Section 404 may be the highest focal point of the act. Further, this section has the highest correlation to project fraud in that companies need to ensure that their project assets and liabilities are properly stated in the financial statements and the associated internal controls around project accounting are well in hand, especially considering that project investments invariably represent the largest and most risky internal investment dollars spent by the organization.

2.3 Roles and Responsibilities for Complying with Sarbanes-Oxley

In any project, there are project sponsors, team members to get it done, and managers to ensure that the whole process works smoothly. Below is a summary of roles/responsibilities for the project stakeholders:

- *Disclosure committee* — The SEC has recommended that reporting companies create a disclosure committee to consider the materiality of information, determine disclosure requirements, identify relevant disclosure issues, and coordinate the development of the appropriate infrastructure to ensure that quality material information is disclosed in a timely manner to management for potential action and disclosure. This committee should include senior management and, more specifically, the certifying officers. In addition to reporting directly to (as well as being accountable to) the certifying officers, the disclosure committee chair should meet periodically with the audit committee to provide reports on the various activities of the disclosure committee, including the quality of the company's filings and other disclosures and any disagreements with the certifying officers or with external experts such as legal counsel or external auditors.

- *Section 404 compliance steering committee* — A separate steering committee should be established for Section 404 given the breadth and depth of its scope, as it affects all portions of the organization supporting the company's financial reporting. The Section 404 compliance steering committee serves to evaluate and approve the project plan, approve major scope decisions, review major project findings, and approve the internal control report. It also needs to provide the project team the necessary resources to ensure timely and quality completion of the project. CFOs are generally taking the lead in these committees as they are the most financially literate in the organization and one of the main certifying officers.

- *Project manager and team* — The project manager is generally an independent function reporting to the Section 404 compliance steering committee and the disclosure committee. The manager is tasked with developing and managing the project plan for the entire compliance effort. He or she has a cross-functional team with dotted-line reporting that should include operating, accounting, and auditing representatives from the company's major business units and foreign operations. Operating and accounting managers should participate in the project, as stipulated by the project plan, especially in the area of documenting and testing risks and controls. Such documentation is associated with Section 404 compliance, which is arguably the critical path of any Sarbanes-Oxley compliance effort.

■ *External auditor* — The committees and project manager should communicate with the external auditor at regular intervals throughout the project. They should validate the approach and requirements with the intention of understanding expectations, professional standards, and other requirements. They should also ascertain whether the "body of evidence" provided by the planned approach is acceptable to the external auditor and provides for an efficient audit. The goal is to plan and execute management's assessment so that the methodologies and frameworks used, the documentation developed, and the material issues addressed are consistent with the external auditor's policies. They should also plan reviews of the documentation and testing of the Section 404 controls so that the project moves toward completion in an orderly fashion.

■ *Internal auditors* — Internal auditors play key roles in the initial response, as well as ongoing modification of processes that support the certifications. In performing this advisory work, auditors should follow the consulting standards of the Standards for the Professional Practice of Internal Auditing. In general, once the initial certification systems are in place, the process owner (management) must take ownership. This will free the internal auditor to complete independent testing of the design and effectiveness of controls associated with Section 404, as well as assess the readiness of the organization toward compliance in other sections.

2.4 Summary

The Sarbanes-Oxley Act, which was signed into law in 2002, represented the most dramatic changes in the federal securities laws since the 1930s and was intended to restore investor confidence in U.S. markets. The main sections of the act affecting companies include Sections 302, 404, and 906, which relate to managements' representations regarding financial statements and internal controls, obtaining attestations to that effect, and criminal penalties for noncompliance, respectively. These sections relate to project fraud in that companies need to ensure that their project assets and liabilities are properly stated in the financial statements and the associated internal controls around project accounting are well in hand, especially considering that project investments invariably represent the largest and most risky internal investment dollars spent by the organization.

Questions

2.1   When was the Sarbanes-Oxley Act signed into law?

2.2   What are the main responsibilities of the PCAOB?

2.3   What does Section 404 require companies to do?

2.4   What is the disclosure committee?

2.5   Who usually takes the lead for Sarbanes-Oxley compliance within the organization?

2.6   The PCAOB is a private-sector, nonprofit corporation to oversee the auditors of public companies in order to protect the interests of investors and further the public interest in the preparation of informative, fair, and independent audit reports. True or false?

2.7   Section 404 has the highest correlation to project fraud in that companies need to ensure that their project assets and liabilities are properly stated in the financial statements and the associated internal controls around project accounting are well in hand. True or false?

Part 2:
The Emergence
of Project Fraud

Project Failure (and Possible Fraud) Case Study

3.1 California State Welfare Automation Project

A great case study to illustrate what can go wrong on a project and how this can potentially transition into project fraud is the California State Welfare Automation Project. What needs to be recognized up front is that fraud may **not** have occurred on this project, as it is difficult to discern the difference between fraud and mismanagement. However, given the combination of misreporting, limited reporting of key facts, and other actions taken by the project team, project fraud is probable. Further, given that this is a state program, it becomes public information for sharing with all interested parties. This is a rarity, as most organizations have no interest in airing their dirty laundry.

The project began as an attempt to automate the California State Department of Social Services welfare system,[1] which provides aid to millions of people within the state. What it became was the largest and most costly system ever undertaken by the state. In 1995, the project was estimated to spend over $1 billion to automate the welfare processing of fourteen counties using a new statewide system. Unfortunately, the system was originally estimated to cost $545 million or close to half of what the current estimates (in 1995) projected. Further, the project started with no strategic plan and, therefore, had no true goals to achieve at the end of its delivery.

3.2 How Did This Project Get Out of the Gate?

Probably the most obvious flaw was the lack of a mission and measurable objectives. Although it may seem unfathomable to have a $1 billion project with no goals, it is entirely possible if the right political pressures are exerted from within the organization. Projects can move ahead at the whim of a corporate CEO who has a vision that needs to be implemented in order for his or her goals to be met in the current fiscal period. Projects can also "crash and burn" when the lack of such success measures leads project teams to wallow in their own muck.

Next came the cost estimates where key activities were simply left out of the calculation. This can invariably occur, as projects are unique and unprecedented, making it difficult to see all costs clearly in the initial budget phases. Yet to overlook key cost estimations, such as conversion of welfare files from a legacy system into the new automated platform, is highly suspect. This oversight cost $46 million and was followed by an additional $36 million due to training that was never planned. Did they expect the system to train the users automatically? The budgetary estimates made no mention of the costs incurred to date to automate the welfare systems and used outdated caseload data to estimate usage/maintenance costs. Again, these oversights may have been incompetence of the project team in dealing with a system project of this size or they may point to larger issues within the project.

No goals, improperly reported costs, and now — an overstatement of the benefits expected from the system. The benefits were based mainly on reducing staff ($66 million) due to automation, but did not factor in the massive reductions in staff already taken by counties. Another large cost-saving category was the reduced hardware and software costs at the county level ($39 million) when the state system was operational, yet many counties needed their computer infrastructure for other systems running within the county. Therefore, these savings never materialized. Lastly, there were expected savings in error rates ($51 million) that may appear one day, but since there were never any valid measures of error rates, it was practically impossible to assess the levels of positive change. Was this by accident? Possibly, but it may have been planned as it is difficult to believe that a dollar estimate was prepared with no valid past benchmark on which to base the cost savings estimation.

And if the above was not enough, through a more technical review of the architecture, it was determined that the system itself may not work due to the following reasons:

- The system was based on a proprietary versus open architecture, which was becoming more prevalent in the computing world. Even stranger was that the California State Department issued a new strategic direction a few years earlier that open architecture was the preferred choice for new development. Note that this proprietary system had few people to program and support it, which would hurt its long-term chances for success.

■ It also required significant overhead and was not as efficient in storing case data given it was optimized to run reports and not process transactions.

■ The system's ability to meet the transaction processing demands of California was unproven to date either at past customers or through any sort of testing.

It is no surprise that the evaluation team for the new computer system only looked at business requirements "superficially" as, per a later report on the project, "an in-depth system-to-system comparison of business functions was not an objective of the system selection process."[1] The technology team involved did not look at the long-term goals of the system, but rather looked at the short-term limited needs of the project in initially automating a select number of counties. Then, when the evaluation team members noted that they were divided as to their preference of selecting a system, the executive summary of the report made no mention of this division. It rather suggested the platform that led to the demise of the project.

3.3 Was There Fraud?

The Association of Certified Fraud Examiners defines occupational fraud as *"the use of one's occupation for personal enrichment through the deliberate misuse or misapplication of the employing organization's resources or assets."*[2] This definition encompasses a wide range of misconduct by employees, managers, and executives. Regardless, all occupational fraud schemes have four key elements in common. The activity (1) is clandestine, (2) violates the perpetrator's fiduciary duties to the victim organization, (3) is committed for the purpose of direct or indirect financial benefit to the perpetrator, and (4) costs the employing organization assets, revenue, or reserves.

It may never be known whether fraud was committed on this California project, but a few things are clear:

■ *Many clandestine activities took place.* In selecting the ultimate platform for the welfare automation system, there were changes to platform evaluation.

- *The activities, taken as a whole, appear negligent* and call into question the fiduciary duties of those responsible.
- *There were many parties who benefited financially.* To the State of California, it may have been a cost overrun, but to an army of consultants, it was a windfall of revenue.
- *Costs to the organization were high* not only in the overages in cost, but also in the limited benefits that ensued.

Therefore, from the above analysis, it is highly possible that some fraud was committed. Only through additional investigation and analysis would such a determination become clear, yet on the surface, something definitely was wrong.

3.4 Summary

The California State Welfare Automation Project is a case study that highlights many of the components of project fraud. Whether fraud was committed may never be known precisely, yet there is a high probability of some wrongdoing. Unfortunately, more case studies like this one are unavailable for review given that they are hidden within the annuls of their companies; the threat of such a leakage may have disastrous effects on the companies and will be discussed in later chapters.

Questions

3.1   What was the purpose of the California State Welfare Automation Project?
3.2   What were three potential frauds that were committed in the definition of the project scope and benefits?
3.3   What is the definition of occupational fraud?
3.4   Given the definition of fraud, was fraud committed?

References

1. California State Auditor, Department of Social Services: The Department's Approach to Welfare Automation Is Too Costly and Unlikely to Succeed, Bureau of State Audits, 1995.
2. Wells, Joseph T., *Occupational Fraud and Abuse,* Hyperion Publishing, 2001.

Project Fraud Defined and Its Many Faces

4.1 Fraud Defined

As noted in Chapter 3, occupational fraud is defined (per the Association of Certified Fraud Examiners) as "*the use of one's occupation for personal enrichment through the deliberate misuse or misapplication of the employing organization's resources or assets.*"[1] Note that the definition states a "deliberate misuse," which is different from an error that is unintentional. This definition encompasses a wide range of misconduct by employees, managers, and executives. Regardless, all occupational fraud schemes have four key elements in common. The activity is clandestine, violates the perpetrator's fiduciary duties to the victim organization, is committed for the purpose of direct or indirect financial benefit to the perpetrator, and costs the employing organization assets, revenue, or reserves.

Using the above definition, at the highest level, fraud can be categorized into the following three areas:

1. *Fraudulent statements* — Involving the falsification of an organization's financial statements. This includes fraudulent statements that are outright lies and earnings management that is a shading of the true picture of the company's health.
2. *Corruption* — When fraudsters wrongfully use their influence in a business transaction in order to procure some benefit for themselves or another person, contrary to their duty to their employer or the rights of another.

3. *Asset misappropriations* — Involving the theft or misuse of an organization's assets.

The above three major areas are further segregated into subcategories (see Figure 4.1). This diagram was developed by the Association of Certified Fraud Examiners and is part of an accompanying publication (*Occupational Fraud and Abuse*, by Joseph T. Wells[1]) that explores the prevention and detection of each fraud type.

4.2 Project Fraud Defined

What is intriguing when reviewing the fraud classification system presented in Figure 4.1 is that projects are not discussed. There is no item identified related to business cases that are falsified or project plans that are misreported. Rather, what may be inferred is that the following related frauds may have a high correlation to projects:

- Fraudulent Statements >> Nonfinancial >> Internal Documents
- Fraudulent Statements >> Financial >> Asset/Revenue Overstatements >> Improper Asset Valuations
- Fraudulent Statements >> Financial >> Asset/Revenue Overstatements >> Concealed Liabilities and Expenses
- Corruption >> Bribery
- Corruption >> Conflicts of Interest
- Asset Misappropriation >> Cash >> Fraudulent Disbursements >> Expense Reimbursement Schemes
- Asset Misappropriation >> Cash >> Fraudulent Disbursements >> Payroll Schemes
- Asset Misappropriation >> Cash >> Fraudulent Disbursements >> Billing Schemes
- Asset Misappropriation >> Inventory and Other Assets >> Misuse

By reviewing the above, do not infer that any type of fraud cannot occur on a project. Rather, the above categories are considered the most likely frauds that could occur on a project. Therefore, based on the above categories, a definition for project fraud can be provided for purposes of this publication:

> *Project fraud* — the misrepresentation of a project's mission or progress to secure project financing, misuse of project resources, and/or improper dealings with project vendors for personal enrichment.

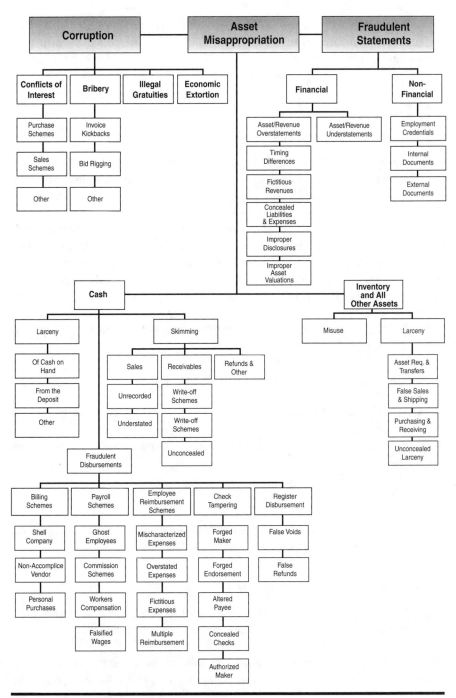

Figure 4.1.   Occupational Fraud and Abuse: Fraud Tree.

Rather than suggest a new category be added for project fraud, it is more logical to explain the set of fraud types identified in the fraud classification system and explain each type.

4.3 Project Fraud Set

4.3.1 Internal Documents

> Fraudulent statements made by employees that have no direct financial statement impact, such as employee credentials or other internal/external documents.

While it may not be as direct as posting an improper general ledger entry to accounts receivable, producing an inappropriate return on investment calculation may lead to the improper valuation of fixed asset balances at year-end. This is further explained in Chapter 6, whereby improper asset valuations may be based on expected cash flows for an investment (that were fabricated from the beginning).

A fairly comprehensive list of fraudulent internal document examples is provided below:

- Overreported and unsubstantiated business case
- Unsubstantiated project decisions
- Underreported initial estimates of project life cycle costs (to get project approved)
- Underreported initial estimates of project maintenance costs (to get project approved)
- Overreported schedule progress
- Overreported quality progress

As you can see, all of the above misrepresent the project's current picture and could lead to improper investment decisions.

4.3.2 Improper Asset Valuations

> Fictitious inflation of asset values or other improper valuations, generally to enhance the appearance of financial statements.[1]

While there are many ways to complete this, including inflating inventory, accounts receivable, and revenue, the most common project financial statement fraud normally transpires from the misreporting of fixed assets, which is the normal reporting position of project dollars:

- *Overstating fixed assets* — The general principle regarding capitalizing project costs is that they are recorded at cost and depreciated over their useful life. If this "life" is no more than one year, the costs are expensed. For example, if the costs are associated with a project that is intended to make a nonworking product for the organization, all associated costs would be expensed. To avoid this negative occurrence, project teams will suggest that the project results will have longer useful lives, and they will also capitalize costs that only benefit the current accounting period. This increases the size of the fixed asset balance associated with a project rather than expensing certain activity. For example, payroll costs to maintain a new building (project result) only benefit the current accounting period and should be expensed. As to a more specific example, financial reporting standard SOP 98-1 requires that all software costs associated with the requirements phase or design phase of the project be expensed. These costs can be a large portion of the project's initial spending. Being aware of the negative effects on the income statement of expensing such costs, the project team may start to "move" more costs into development activities. The team may go so far as to rewrite software contracts with consultants to ensure the capitalization of project costs. For more on software development capitalization, see Appendix 2 for a full explanation of relevant capitalization accounting standards.
- *Understating fixed asset reserves* — As projects begin to **not** meet their intended mission and expected value, these facts may be hidden in order to continue to value the assets at their initial cost (all fixed assets are recorded at cost unless there is a need to downgrade their value). Project teams may report an asset as capitalized given it still provides benefits over and above the initial cost, even when such claims are untrue. This area is further explained in Chapter 6.

4.3.3 Concealed Liabilities and Expenses

Financial statement fraud where liabilities or expenses are excluded in the financial statements.[1]

This type of financial statement fraud normally transpires from not recognizing expenses (unrecognized) or not recognizing expenses (i.e., vendor, payroll, or depreciation) in the current period but rather in later periods (timing).

Any of the above strategies would be used to minimize the expenses associated with a project and, therefore, report an untrue picture of its progress. This can be accomplished through the hiding of invoices or holding of invoices/time reports and associated payments until after the end of a period.

4.3.4 Bribery and Conflicts of Interest

There are four types of improper dealings with external parties that have negative effects on the organization:

1. *Bribery* — Offering, giving, receiving, or soliciting any thing of value to influence an official act[1]
2. *Illegal gratuities* — Similar to bribery, except that there is not necessarily an intent to influence a particular business decision[1]
3. *Economic extortion* — The flip side of a bribery scheme where an employee demands a payment to influence a decision[1]
4. *Conflicts of interest*[1] — Employee, manager, or executive has an undisclosed economic or personal interest in a transaction that adversely affects the company

Many times, project teams are put in difficult positions as they need to work with outside vendors who may use tempting tactics to win their support. Further, the above frauds are difficult to detect as most are "off-the-book" transactions. For example, a vendor may send wine baskets to the project team to influence a project decision indirectly (illegal gratuities). On the other hand, a project team member with a conflicted interest may seek out improper vendor dealings in order to benefit his or her internal interest.

The above type of fraud generally will result in the following negative effects to the organization:

- Not selecting the best vendor for the task at hand
- Kickbacks to the employee rather than project cost reductions
- Fraudulent charging of higher prices that go undetected as they are approved by knowingly influenced internal employees
- Phony invoices charged by the vendor that will be processed by the employee
- Purchasing more inventory, assets, or services than needed; in most cases, any assets associated with these purchases are not used and appropriately written off
- Fraudulent purchasing of poor-quality inventory or services leading to additional purchases or rework, respectively

4.3.5 Expense Reimbursement Schemes

Perpetrator (internal or external to the organization) produces false documents that cause the company to issue a check unknowingly.[1]

Given the magnitude of some projects and the need for employees to process their own expenses (i.e., through expense reporting procedures), the door is left wide open for potential fraud. Also, consider that the project manager and employee may be working together to perpetrate the fraud. In these cases, the employee would submit the expenses and the project manager could approve them. Once paid, the "fruits of their fraud" could be shared under some pre-arrangement. (Note that employee expense reimbursement was cited as the fastest growing fraud scheme in a study by the Association of Certified Fraud Examiners taken between 1996 and 2002.) Schemes fall into the following four categories:

1. *Mischaracterized expenses* — Fraudulent requests for expenses that are personal in nature or would not normally be paid under company policy
2. *Overstated expenses* — The inappropriate inflation of submitted expenses
3. *Fictitious expenses* — An employee fabricates and submits expenses that were never incurred
4. *Multiple reimbursements* — Submitting the same expense on multiple occasions to defraud the company into paying the expenses twice

4.3.6 Payroll Schemes

Perpetrator (internal or external to the organization) produces false documents (sales order, time cards, false employee hiring records) that cause the company to issue a check unknowingly.[1]

The schemes fall into the following two categories, as they relate to projects:

1. *Ghost employees* — Payments to someone on the payroll who does not exist
2. *Falsified hours and salary* — Overpayment of wages due to the falsification of hours, wage rates, or other adjustments

Project managers are in a position to create phony employees and approve such time cards. No one on the project team would know, except maybe for the project accountant (who many times is the project manager). This is especially worrisome given that projects are done in such virtual territory, many times with the project employees never stepping on company premises. In other cases, the employee and project manager could work together to submit (employee) and then approve (project manager) the associated payroll. Once paid, the dollars could be split among the co-conspirators.

4.3.7 Billing Schemes

Billing schemes occur when a fraudster causes the victim organization to issue a payment by submitting invoices for fictitious goods or services, inflated invoices, or invoices for personal purchases.[1] There are three subcategories of billing schemes, defined as follows:

1. *Shell company* — A phony organization on the company's books for use in paying fictitious invoices
2. *Nonaccomplice vendor* — Intentional mishandling of vendor payment in order to make fictitious payment to an employee
3. *Personal purchases* — Purchases using company accounts such as a company procurement card

Since project managers are in a position to submit and approve invoices for a project, they are in a position to create false invoices, mishandle invoices for their personal gain, or use a company credit card inappropriately. Project team members may even do this without the project manager's knowledge.

4.3.8 Inventory and Other Asset Misuse

The borrowing or stealing of inventory/assets from an employer by a perpetrator (internal or external to the organization).[1]

Schemes fall into the following four categories:

1. *Larceny* — Employee takes inventory or other assets from the company premises without attempting to conceal it in the books or records.
2. *Asset transfers* — Employee records an asset transfer from one location to another and takes the inventory or other asset in the transfer process.
3. *Purchasing and receiving schemes* — Receiving employee falsifies records of incoming shipments and misappropriates the assets.
4. *False shipments* — Fraudulent shipments are charged to customers to conceal the taking of inventory.

To perpetrate the above frauds, the project team member needs only to explain that the assets were used in the course of the project. This is especially true if the assets cannot be readily discernible in the project's results (i.e., if fifty I-beams were stolen from a building job site, no one would be able to tell from looking at the finished building). If the assets are easily discernible, it could be noted by the fraudster that they were accidentally destroyed in the course of the project development. The above schemes are normally detected through attempts to conceal the fraud, including writing off assets as obsolete or writing off customer sales (if the asset was fraudulently recorded as sold to the customer).

4.4 Summary

The purpose of this chapter was to define project fraud and align it with the standard thinking in the market. Project fraud is defined as *the misrepresentation of a project's mission or progress to secure project financing, misuse of project resources, and/or improper dealings with project vendors for personal enrichment.* Using this definition, the new fraud type can be aligned to seven major fraud types per the fraud classification system. Given that there has been a great deal of analysis already completed in how to prevent and detect the associated frauds per the fraud classification system, this publication will summarize that body of knowledge for use by its readers.

Questions

4.1   What are the three types of occupational fraud?

4.2   What is the definition of project fraud?

4.3   What asset misappropriation fraud types of the fraud classification system relate to project fraud?

4.4   What financial statement fraud types of the fraud classification system relate to project fraud?

4.5   Illegal gratuities are similar to bribery except that there is not necessarily an intent to influence a particular business decision. True or false?

4.6   An example of "conflicts of interest" is that an employee, manager, or executive has an undisclosed economic or personal interest in a transaction that adversely affects the company. True or false?

4.7   A vendor may send party favors to the project team to influence a project decision indirectly. This is project fraud. True or false?

4.8   Project managers are in a position to create phony employees and approve such time cards. True or false?

4.9   Since project managers are in a position to submit and approve invoices for a project, they are in a position to create false invoices, mishandle invoices for their personal gain, or use a company credit card inappropriately. True or false?

Reference

1. Wells, Joseph T., *Occupational Fraud and Abuse*, Hyperion Publishing, 2001.

Impacts and Motives of Project Failures and Fraud

5.1 Introduction

Project failures and fraud cost money, as well as having various other detrimental effects on the organization such as decreased market value. These costs break down into three major categories: (1) financial statement misstatements, (2) bottom-line impacts, and (3) other detrimental effects. This chapter will highlight these impacts, as well as define the motives for committing project fraud and the benefits of fighting it.

5.2 Financial Statement Misstatements and Financial Accounting Standard 144

Per the most recent and comprehensive study on fraud by the Association of Certified Fraud Examiners, financial statement fraud occurred the least (5.1 percent of cases), but it had the most impact with $4.25 million per scheme. To further define the impact and drivers for financial statement fraud, a study was released in March 1999 by the Committee of Sponsoring Organizations (COSO) entitled *Fraudulent Financial Reporting 1987–1997: An Analysis of U.S. Public Companies.*[1] It analyzed approximately two hundred SEC financial statement fraud actions brought against public companies. Some key statistics that will be explained further in this section were as follows:

- About 50 percent of the fraud instances involved the improper recording of assets (fictitious or overstated). Expense and liability understatements were less frequent.
- In 83 percent of the cases, the CEO, CFO, or both were involved in financial statement fraud.
- Twenty-five percent of the companies did not have an audit committee. Further, when audit committees existed, their substance was often weak; most met only once a year and many lacked directors with financial experience (as broadly defined).
- Some companies that committed financial statement fraud were experiencing net losses or were nearing break-even in the period before the fraud (the median fraudulent company had a net income of $175,000).
- In many cases, stock market pressures may have provided the incentive for fraud.

To summarize the above, pressures were exerted on high-level management to commit fraud, which was accomplished many times through improper capitalization of assets. As seen by the first bullet above, asset valuation was a major factor in financial statement fraud, and projects are just that — assets that are initially valued on the financial statements, depreciated over time, and assessed periodically as to their current value. Let us take the first portion of the above sentence: "assets that are initially valued on the financial statements." It is herein that the potential for project fraud is found as depreciation and later asset valuations occur AFTER the project is completed and the project results are placed into service.

FAS 144 (Accounting for the Impairment or Disposal of Long-Lived Assets) was issued by the Financial Accounting Standards Board and is the most current pronouncement on the valuation of long-term assets (usual results of a project). This is such an important pronouncement for this publication that Chapter 6 has been fully devoted to its explanation. In summary, a project asset on the financial statements is made of all of the capitalizable costs associated with its development. If the project's results, during execution, are deemed impaired per the FAS 144 requirements, one or two things will generally happen:

1. Assets previously capitalized as assets per the balance sheet will be written off as expenses on the income statement.
2. The useful life of the asset may be reduced (say from twenty-five to five years) if the asset is not expected to produce measurable benefits over the originally estimated useful life.

Both of the above effects immediately impact the operating income for the organization and, therefore, the net income and earnings per share (assuming it is a public company).

5.3 Motives for Fraudulent Financial Statement Reporting and Associated Project Statement Reporting

But why would management overreport an assets value and not take into consideration its potential impairment? It is because management is under great pressure to produce favorable statements regarding the performance of the business. These pressures are further categorized below:

- *Market expectations* — Companies in danger of not meeting analyst expectations.
- *Increase shareholder value* — Companies that may not have an expectation, but want to make themselves more attractive in the marketplace.
- *Maintaining status* — Some stock exchanges and other business lists (i.e., Fortune 500) require certain measures to be met.
- *Income smoothing* — To give the appearance of a stable, predictable business by reporting steady earnings.
- *Contractual* — To comply with outside contractual requirements such as a debt covenant on a loan.
- *Regulatory* — Companies needing to give an appearance to regulators in order to influence their actions, such as lowering earnings to feign an antitrust lawsuit.
- *Bonus/profit sharing* — Similar to contractual above, although an internal agreement to provide management with additional earnings.
- *Save a job* — Poor financial performance may lead to the closure of a division, product line, or the entire organization.
- *Greed* — Unfortunately, once greed starts, it is sometimes difficult to stop. Like a bull market, the rush can be intoxicating.
- *Make the budget* — Companies are highly budget conscious and sometimes just making the budget is motive enough.
- *Save my ego* — Executives and management have much at stake when leading organizations and may risk practically anything monetary to save their pride.
- *Clean house* — When there is an incoming management team, there is a tendency to write off questionable balances and blame the previous

regime. Not only does this allow for improved reporting in future periods, but no blame is placed on the management at hand.

- *Big bath/save for a rainy day* — Many times, organizations looking at an eventual write-off or reserve would rather make it larger given that any write-off in the marketplace is viewed negatively. Further, in future years, if any reserve is still on the books and overstated, it can be taken into income.

The above financial statement motives can "trickle down" to the project level where project sponsors and managers may feel pressured to report what is desired versus the true project health. Even if the order does not come from the top (remember that 83 percent of financial statement fraud is committed by either the CEO or CFO), those at the project level may decide it is in their best interests to keep the project out of the "impairment limelight."

5.4 Other Project Impacts

Aside from the financial statement impacts, poorly run or fraudulent projects simply lose money for the organization. Projects are now making over $2.3 trillion in the U.S. economy (25 percent of gross domestic product) according to a recent Project Management Institute study using data from the U.S. Department of Commerce. The Standish Group reports that more than $275 billion relates to application software projects. Over $2.3 trillion in projects ($275 billion for software), yet given their inherent risky nature, projects fail, especially IT projects. In a recent Standish Group survey of technology projects, the following trends were noted:

- Only 16.2 percent of projects are completed on time and on budget.
- 31.1 percent are canceled.
- The average cost overrun was 189 percent of the original time estimate.

The above only shows the project mismanagement costs. Per the most recent and comprehensive study on fraud by the Association of Certified Fraud Examiners, it is estimated that 6 percent of company revenue[2] is lost to fraud each year. This would be for all of the categories of fraud, as explained further in Chapter 4, rather than just those associated with projects. However, applied to the U.S. gross domestic product, this translates to over $600 billion in losses each year. Even if this estimate is 50 percent off, that is still 3 percent of revenues and a great deal to lose for any organization. Note that these estimates are all hampered by the fact that not all fraud is detected or reported.

These are blaringly high trends to overcome and/or ignore, but they tell only half the story. Many times, company morale and customer service suffer when products are not delivered on time, are delivered with minimal functionality, or are delivered with bugs after being poorly tested. A company may also not be able to compete in the marketplace if the associated project deliverables are not borne out in a quality manner. For example, a supply chain management system for a manufacturer that simply does not work may result in orders not getting shipped to customers. If that was not enough, assuming outside vendors are used, there is increased chance of litigation between the companies if the project runs afoul.

5.5 Benefits of Reducing Project Mismanagement and Fraud

Rooting out project mismanagement simply saves money. By increasing the efficiency of the project delivery and gaining transparency to the true status of the endeavor, companies will see benefits mostly in their bottom-line savings. In addition, organizational morale is enhanced, which may sound like a "soft" benefit, yet such attributes can make a good company a great one. Morale would be enhanced through staff seeing the organization as one that CAN complete projects on time and under budget with high quality. Management morale increases when management begins to trust the project reporting system, rather than wasting valuable time checking and rechecking project figures. Furthermore, it is through this improved reporting that management can better assess the next steps, with clarity, for the endeavor. Other general benefits of project management include:

- Replaces an ad hoc process with a *streamlined* one that speeds delivery
- Makes the best use of resources
- Improves communication, coordination, and awareness of project activities for improved decision making

In addition to benefits of project management, there are many benefits to fighting fraud within an organization. Below is a summary:

- *Save 2 to 3 percent of revenues normally lost to fraud* — Per the 2002 Report to the Nation on Occupational Fraud and Abuse (Association of Certified Fraud Examiners),[2] companies lose 6 percent of revenue to fraud. Fraud prevention was found to reduce that figure by between 30 and 48 percent. Therefore, fraud prevention measures could save organizations 2 to 3 percent of revenues. Note that these estimates show only a portion of the true picture as most fraud is never reported.

- *Enhance market value* — A 2002 McKinsey & Company survey[3] indicated that by moving from worst to best in corporate governance, companies could expect to see a 10 to 12 percent increase in their market values. Further, by completing project deliverables in a quality manner, the company has a better competitive advantage, using such deliverables, in the marketplace.

- *Reduce federal penalties* — Under the Federal Sentencing Guidelines, there is a 40 percent reduction in penalties for companies using due diligence in implementing programs to detect and prevent violations of law.

- *Reduce audit fees* — More audit work now required under SAS 99[4] (improved auditing standard working to detect fraud in financial statement audits) generally translates into higher fees. Organizations looking to reduce, or at least hold the line on, audit fees should focus on establishing and managing strong antifraud programs and controls to mitigate fraud risks and provide external auditors a foundation of existing controls for audit planning reliance.

- *Prevent civil lawsuits* — Many times, employees who experience issues in the workplace first try to resolve these issues internally. If their complaints are ignored, employees feel compelled to go to an outside advocate. That could be a private attorney, government regulator, or news agency. Giving employees an internal outlet can solve problems without the event becoming public knowledge or an issue for the courts.

- *Recover more of the loss* — According to a recent study, only 60 percent of organizations carried necessary fraud insurance, and for those that did, 49 percent of them recovered only 0 to 25 percent of the original loss.[2] Prevention, by its nature, would have saved the entire loss.

- *Maintain a positive brand image* — Recent events illustrate the devastating effects to an organization of even the hint of fraudulent financial statement reporting. Through appropriate prevention measures, an organization's image can remain intact.

5.6 Summary

There are various financial and nonfinancial impacts of project fraud to the organization. The key financial impact is based on the accounting for fixed assets associated with the project, given that project deliverables generally translate into fixed assets at the end of the company's reporting period. Other financial impacts may include reduced cash flows or misappropriated assets. Nonfinancial impacts include employee motivation and brand image, which ultimately reflect themselves in the financial statements given the relative company performance. Management is motivated to commit fraud mainly due to maintaining a positive project and financial statement image to stakeholders and the public. Benefits of reducing such fraud include improving the financial performance of the organization and also reducing and/or eliminating any potential legal fallout from the fraud.

Questions

5.1   Why are fixed assets the main result of project activities?

5.2   What financial accounting standard most impacts project deliverables?

5.3   What are five motives of management to commit project fraud?

5.4   What are the nonfinancial impacts of project fraud?

5.5   What are five benefits of reducing project fraud?

5.6   A project asset on the financial statements is made of all of the capitalizable costs associated with its development. True or false?

5.7   The most recent and comprehensive study on fraud by the Association of Certified Fraud Examiners estimates that 6 percent of company revenue[2] is lost to fraud each year. True or false?

5.8   Per the 2002 Report to the Nation on Occupational Fraud and Abuse (Association of Certified Fraud Examiners), companies lose 6 percent of revenue to fraud. Fraud prevention was found to reduce that figure by between 30 and 48 percent. Therefore, fraud prevention measures could save organizations 2 to 3 percent of revenues. True or false?

References

1. Committee of Sponsoring Organizations, Fraudulent Financial Reporting 1987–1997: An Analysis of U.S. Public Companies, Committee of Sponsoring Organizations, 1999.
2. Association of Certified Fraud Examiners, 2002 Report to the Nation on Occupational Fraud and Abuse, Association of Certified Fraud Examiners, 2002.
3. McKinsey & Company, A Premium for Good Governance, McKinsey Quarterly, Number 3, 2002.
4. Lanza, Richard B., What Does New Audit Standard SAS No. 99, Consideration of Fraud in a Financial Statement Audit, Mean for Business and Industry Members? CPA Letter, November 2002.

6

Impairment of Assets

6.1 What Is the Nature of a Long-Lived Asset?

Capitalized assets, otherwise known as fixed or long-lived assets, are the usual results of a project. We build buildings, roads, software, computer networks — tangible and long-living by-products of our projects. To explain what is and what is not capitalizable, the key is to look for organizational costs that have a useful life beyond the current financial reporting period. For example, a building, land purchase, and the costs to develop a new machine would all be capitalized as they are expected to "live" past the current fiscal year. On the other hand, costs such as software requirements gathering, product marketing, and utility costs have been deemed expenses as their benefits only exist in the current financial reporting period. Therefore, these costs impact the company's income statement in the current financial reporting period.

Once a project initiates, the costs of development are accumulated and held as an asset on the books until the project is finished. Therefore, a two-year project would have no current year bottom-line impact if, in fact, the project results have not been put in service. Once placed in service, they are depreciated over the useful life. For example, a project to build a new office space for the organization would be depreciated over the expected life of the building (i.e., twenty-five years).

However, there may be events that happened during the project that caused that asset to be impaired. For example, a wing of the building does not pass state building codes. Now uninhabitable, the costs associated with building that section would need to be written off to the company's operating income…which further trickles to the net income line and earnings per share calculations. Therefore, if an asset is deemed impaired per the Financial Accounting Standard

144 (Accounting for the Impairment or Disposal of Long-Lived Assets) requirements, one or two things will generally happen:

1. Assets previously capitalized as assets per the balance sheet will be written off as expenses on the income statement.
2. The useful life of the asset may be reduced (say from twenty-five to five years) if the asset is not expected to produce measurable benefits over the originally estimated useful life.

6.2   FAS 144: The Basics

FAS 144 is the recognized financial reporting pronouncement for fixed asset accounting. It was issued by the Financial Accounting Standards Board, which, generally speaking, is the keeper of U.S. generally accepted accounting principles (GAAP), the de facto standard for financial reporting. It is effective for financial statements issued for fiscal years beginning after December 15, 2001 and interim periods within those fiscal years. Its main focus is on impairment of an asset's value that shall be tested for recoverability whenever events or changes in circumstances indicate that its carrying amount may not be recoverable.

The following are examples of such events or changes in circumstances:[1]

- A significant decrease in the market price of a long-lived asset
- A significant adverse change in the extent or manner in which a long-lived asset is being used or in its physical condition
- A significant adverse change in legal factors or in the business climate that could affect the value of a long-lived asset, including an adverse action or assessment by a regulator
- An accumulation of costs significantly in excess of the amount originally expected for the acquisition or construction of a long-lived asset
- A current-period, operating, or cash flow loss combined with a history of operating or cash flow losses or a projection or forecast that demonstrates continuing losses associated with the use of a long-lived asset
- A current expectation that, more likely than not, a long-lived asset will be sold or otherwise disposed of significantly before the end of its previously estimated useful life

Of all of the above events/circumstances, the "projection or forecast that demonstrates continuing losses associated with the use of a long-lived asset" is the most common instance of potential impairment in a project. This is because projects are in a developing stage for some time while the project is executing, and it is in that time that the forecasts of future benefits are created and revalued. Proving fraud in these forecasts is difficult since it is usually just a best guess. It is only until the long-lived asset is placed in service that the benefits can be reassessed, using actual experiences of the asset's use and benefits. However, if all facts in that initial "guess" were willfully not presented given they may negatively impact the financial statement value, such actions would support a claim of project fraud.

6.3 How Is Fair Value Calculated?

FAS 144 defines impairment as the condition that exists when the carrying amount of a long-lived asset exceeds its fair value. The fair value of a long-lived asset is the amount at which that asset could be bought or sold in a current transaction between willing parties, that is, other than in a forced or liquidation sale. Quoted market prices in active markets are the best evidence of fair value and should be used as the basis for the measurement, if available. However, in many instances, quoted market prices in active markets will not be available for the long-lived assets produced by a project. In those instances, the estimate of fair value shall be based on the best information available, including prices for similar assets and the results of using other valuation techniques.

A present value technique is often the best available valuation technique with which to estimate the fair value of a long-lived asset. The simplest method is a present value of a single set of estimated cash flows using a single interest rate. Another technique, which is recommended by FAS 144, uses multiple cash flow scenarios that reflect the range of possible outcomes and a risk-free rate is used to estimate fair value. Either present value technique can be used for a fair value measurement. However, for long-lived assets that have uncertainties both in timing and amount, an expected present value technique using the multiple cash flow scenarios will often be the appropriate technique.

Assuming the multiple scenario approach, the first step is to determine the useful life or service potential of the asset. This generally would be based on the number of years that cash flow generation would exist or the length of time an asset would provide physical outputs. Some examples would be:

- Software products that are still being sold
- Office building that is providing space to organizational employees
- Warehouse automation in use to receive and ship company products

Next, the cash flows for each year need to be estimated. These cash flows may be inflows from customers, but could also represent cost savings to the organization for placing the asset in service. Instead of a single cash flow estimate being made for each year, a multiple approach would be taken, translating into a best case, most likely case, and worst case point estimation. For each cash flow estimate, a probability would be assigned that would be multiplied by the various types (best, most likely, and worst) to arrive at a single point estimate for the year. It may be useful when completing this probabilistic estimate to use Monte Carlo software that will iterate the model (using the three scenarios for each point estimate) thousands of times to produce a more accurate and statistical forecast. Regardless of the method used, the point estimate would be stated as the present value (for years two and later) using an interest rate that is estimated conservatively.

The last step is to take the fair value estimate and relate it to the costs expended to date for the project. If the estimate falls below the costs capitalized to date, impairment would exist that would need to be recorded properly in the financial statements.

6.4 How Is an Impairment Reported in the Financial Statements?

An impairment loss recognized for a long-lived asset shall be included in income from continuing operations before income taxes in the income statement. This would then impact the company's net income and associated earnings per share calculations. Further, the following information shall be disclosed in the notes to the financial statements that include the period in which an impairment loss is recognized:[1]

- A description of the impaired long-lived asset and the facts and circumstances leading to the impairment
- If not separately presented on the face of the statement, the amount of the impairment loss and the caption in the income statement or the statement of activities that includes that loss
- The method or methods for determining fair value (whether based on a quoted market price, prices for similar assets, or another valuation technique)
- If applicable, the business segment or division in which the impaired long-lived asset is reported

6.5 Example of a Project Impairment and Financial Statement Fraud

The best way to illustrate the asset impairment concepts of FAS 144 is to provide an example. Assume a company produced a software program add-on to an existing software product line that the company sells to a stable set of customers. The new software add-on, when initially forecasted, was expected to produce the following cash flows. Note that the table below uses the following assumptions:

- Three estimates were used for each annual point estimate (best, most likely, and worst with a 10, 70, and 20 percent probability, respectively).
- The software would be used by 40 percent of the existing customer base and 30 percent of new customers expected to purchase the company's base application.
- The software would have a useful life of three years, at which time the software would need to be replaced entirely by the customer.
- Six percent is the cost of capital that the organization uses given it has a readily available source of cash.
- The cost of the project is expected to be $35 million.

Year		Total Cash Flow Estimate*	Probability	Expected Cash Flows*	Present Value* (6 Percent Interest Rate)
1	Best	28	10%	2.80	
	Most Likely	21	70%	14.70	
	Worst	15	20%	3.00	
				20.50	21.00
2	Best	25	10%	2.50	
	Most Likely	18	70%	12.60	
	Worst	12	20%	2.40	
				17.50	15.57
3	Best	22	10%	2.20	
	Most Likely	14	70%	9.80	
	Worst	10	20%	2.00	
				14.00	11.75
				Asset Fair Value	48.33

* All dollars are stated in millions.

The project was approved and proceeded as there was a projected return on investment of roughly $13 million over a three-year period or a 10 percent return each year. The project was completed slightly over budget at $37 million, but still was expected to provide a positive return to the organization.

Unfortunately, what came to the attention of the product manager halfway through the project was the fact that three of the company's main customers refused to use the product. Apparently, it created a security hole in their computer networks given their unique setups. This information was not revealed to the project sponsors or the project team, but had a significant impact on the expected cash flows from the project as follows:

Year		Total Cash Flow Estimate*	Probability	Expected Cash Flows*	Present Value* (6 Percent Interest Rate)
1	Best	12	10%	1.20	
	Most Likely	8	70%	5.60	
	Worst	6	20%	1.20	
				8.00	21.00
2	Best	10	10%	1.00	
	Most Likely	6	70%	4.20	
	Worst	4	20%	0.80	
				6.00	5.34
3	Best	8	10%	0.80	
	Most Likely	5	70%	3.50	
	Worst	3	20%	0.60	
				4.90	4.11
				Asset Fair Value	30.45

* All dollars are stated in millions.

Given the new estimates, the resulting software asset would need to be written down by roughly $4.5 million that would impact the continuing operations income and reported as a note in the financial statements. The inappropriate reluctance to provide transparency to the true project benefits would be considered fraudulent given that it was apparently done to mask the true value of the project and associated financial statement assets. This action would need to be investigated further, with repercussions to those employees involved based on the policies and procedures within the organization pertaining to fraudulent behavior.

6.6   Summary

Capitalized assets are the likely results of a project and are accounted for mainly through FAS 144. The main focus of this accounting standard is on impairment of an asset's value that shall be tested for recoverability whenever events or changes in circumstances indicate that its carrying amount may not be recoverable. The recoverability is based on the probabilistic cash flows expected over the life of the asset. When this recoverability is questioned, two courses of action will be taken:

1. Assets previously capitalized as assets per the balance sheet will be written off as expenses on the income statement.
2. The useful life of the asset may be reduced (say from twenty-five to five years) if the asset is not expected to produce measurable benefits over the originally estimated useful life, thereby increasing depreciation expense per the income statement.

Questions

6.1   What is the title of FAS 144 and what does GAAP stand for?
6.2   What are three events that may lead to recoverability issues of the asset?
6.3   What is fair value and how is it calculated?
6.4   What must be recorded per the financial statements for assets changing their recoverability status?
6.5   Capitalized assets, otherwise known as fixed or long-lived assets, are the usual results of a project. True or false?
6.6   To explain what is and is not capitalizable, the key is to look for organizational costs that have a useful life beyond the current financial reporting period. True or false?
6.7   Costs such as software requirements gathering, product marketing, and utility costs have been deemed expenses as their benefits only exist in the current financial reporting period. True or false?
6.8   Once a project initiates, the costs of development are accumulated and held as an asset on the books until the project is finished. Therefore, a two-year project would have no current year bottom-line impact if, in fact, the project results have not been put in service. True or false?
6.9   FAS 144 defines impairment as the condition that exists when the carrying amount of a long-lived asset exceeds its fair value. True or false?
6.10   The present value technique is often the best available valuation technique with which to estimate the fair value of a long-lived asset. True or false?

Reference

1. Financial Accounting Standards Board, FAS 144 — Accounting for the Impairment or Disposal of Long-Lived Assets, Financial Accounting Standards Board, 2000.

Part 3:
Overall Responses
to Project Fraud

7

Understanding Internal Control and Using It as a Model for Reviews

7.1 Internal Control Defined

The definition of internal control has come under great fanfare in the last few years with the number of accounting/audit failures coupled with the responding regulations. For example, the Sarbanes-Oxley Act has given new life to the COSO (Committee of Sponsoring Organizations) definition of internal control and expects companies to benchmark themselves to this standard. With this noted, internal control is broadly defined by COSO as:[1]

> a process, effected by an entity's board of directors, management and other personnel, designed to provide reasonable assurance regarding the achievement of objectives in the following categories: effectiveness and efficiency of operations, reliability of financial reporting, and compliance with applicable laws and regulations.

7.2 What Is COSO?

COSO[2] is a voluntary, private-sector organization dedicated to improving the quality of financial reporting through business ethics, effective internal controls, and corporate governance. COSO was originally formed in 1985 to sponsor the National Commission on Fraudulent Financial Reporting, an independent private-sector initiative that studied the causal factors that can lead to fraudulent financial reporting and developed recommendations for public companies and their independent auditors, for the SEC and other regulators, and for educational institutions.

The National Commission was jointly sponsored by the five major financial professional associations in the United States: the American Accounting Association, the American Institute of Certified Public Accountants, the Financial Executives Institute, the Institute of Internal Auditors, and the National Association of Accountants (now the Institute of Management Accountants). The commission was wholly independent of each of the sponsoring organizations and contained representatives from industry, public accounting, investment firms, and the New York Stock Exchange.

One of the major achievements of COSO was the development of the Internal Control — Integrated Framework publication that gave the working definition of this concept and tools to assist in benchmarking an organization. Internal control means different things to different people and causes confusion among businesspeople, legislators, regulators, and others. Problems are compounded when the term, if not clearly defined, is written into law, regulation, or rule. In response, the Integrated Framework publication worked to:

- Establish a common definition serving the needs of different parties
- Provide a standard against which businesses and other entities (large or small, in the public or private sector, for profit or not) can assess their control systems and determine how to improve them

As recently as late 2003, COSO sponsored an Enterprise Risk Management addendum to the Integrated Framework document that provides more guidance in the realm of risk assessment, a key component of internal control. More information on this work can be found on the committee's website at www.coso.org.

7.3 The Internal Control Objectives

The three main objectives being met by the internal control definition are explained in general terms below:

1. *The extent to which an entity's operations objectives are being achieved and awareness of progress* — Relates to an entity's basic business

objectives, including performance and profitability goals, safeguarding of resources, and meeting strategic goals. Essentially, this objective boils down to ensuring the efficiency and effectiveness of meeting company objectives. Effectiveness concerns the quality of controls over the achievement of specific management objectives, while efficiency addresses optimization of resource inputs to producing outputs.

2. *Published financial statements are being prepared reliably* — Relates to the preparation of reliable published financial statements, including interim and condensed financial statements and selected financial data derived from such statements, such as earnings releases.

3. *Applicable laws and regulations are being complied with* — Relates to complying with all associated laws and regulations affecting the organization.

Although the words "audit" and "control" tend to bring negative images to the general businessperson, they are both aimed at improving the organization, not slowing it down. For example, when brakes were placed on an automobile, it was partly done to allow a car to stop, but was mainly done so that a car could go faster. In essence, the better brakes you have, the faster your automobile can travel within safe limits of stopping. Therefore, in business, like the automobile, internal control is working to improve the effectiveness and efficiency of operations while ensuring that the negative impacts of a crime or inappropriate financial reporting are minimized.

7.4 The Internal Control Framework

In meeting the above objectives, internal control is the process utilized, which consists of five interrelated components:[1]

- *Control environment* — The control environment sets the tone of an organization, influencing the control consciousness of its people. It is the foundation for all other components of internal control, providing discipline and structure. Control environment factors include the integrity, ethical values, and competence of the entity's people; management's philosophy and operating style; the way management assigns authority and responsibility, and organizes and develops its people; and the attention and direction provided by the board of directors. See Chapter 9 for a further discussion of this concept.

- *Risk assessment* — Every entity faces a variety of risks from external and internal sources that must be assessed. A precondition to risk assessment is establishment of objectives, linked at different levels and internally consistent. Risk assessment is the identification and analysis of relevant risks to achievement of the objectives, forming a basis for determining how the risks should be managed. Because economic, industry, regulatory, and operating conditions will continue to change, mechanisms are needed to identify and deal with the special risks associated with change. See Chapter 10 for a further discussion of this concept.

- *Control activities* — Control activities are the policies and procedures that help to ensure that management directives are carried out. They help to ensure that necessary actions are taken to address risks to achievement of the entity's objectives. Control activities occur throughout the organization, at all levels and in all functions. They include a range of activities as diverse as approvals, authorizations, verifications, reconciliations, reviews of operating performance, security of assets, and segregation of duties. See Chapters 11 and 12 for further discussions of this concept.

- *Information and communication* — Pertinent information must be identified, captured, and communicated in a form and time frame that enable people to carry out their responsibilities. Information systems produce reports containing operational, financial, and compliance-related information that make it possible to run and control the business. They deal not only with internally generated data, but also information about external events, activities, and conditions necessary for informed business decision making and external reporting. Effective communication also must occur in a broader sense, flowing down, across, and up the organization. All personnel must receive a clear message from top management that control responsibilities must be taken seriously. They must understand their own role in the internal control system, as well as how individual activities relate to the work of others. They must have a means of communicating significant information upstream. There also needs to be effective communication with external parties, such as customers, suppliers, regulators, and shareholders. See Chapters 11 and 12 for further discussions of this concept.

- *Monitoring* — Internal control systems need to be monitored to assess the quality of the system's performance over time. This is accomplished through ongoing monitoring activities, separate evaluations, or a combination of the two. For example, internal audit reviews would be one way to monitor a control system's effectiveness independently. Any internal control deficiencies should be reported upstream, with serious matters reported to top management and the board. See Chapters 11 and 12 for further discussions of this concept.

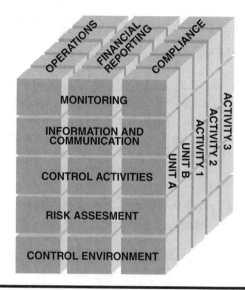

Figure 7.1.   Three Dimensions of COSO Integrated Framework.

The above five components are integrated so that they complement one another in the achievement of each of the three internal control objectives. This can be readily seen in Figure 7.1. Therefore, when looking at the reliability of financial reporting (the key objective being assessed under Section 404 of the Sarbanes-Oxley Act), all of the above five framework components must be present and functioning effectively to conclude reasonably that internal control over operations is effective.

7.5 Limitations of Internal Control

Internal control can help an entity to achieve its performance and profitability targets, to report such performance completely and accurately, and to ensure that laws are not broken.[1] In sum, it can help an entity get to where it wants to go and avoid pitfalls and surprises along the way. It can provide information to management about the entity's progress, or lack of it, toward achieving targets.

But internal control cannot change an inherently poor manager into a good one, and shifts in government policy or programs, competitors' actions, or economic conditions can be beyond management's control. Internal control cannot ensure success or even survival. Therefore, an internal control system, no matter how well conceived and operated, can provide only reasonable and not absolute assurance to management and the board regarding achievement of an entity's objectives. The likelihood of achievement is affected by limitations inherent in all internal control systems including:

- The realities that judgments in decision making can be faulty.
- Controls can be circumvented by the collusion of two or more people.
- Management has the ability to override the system.
- There are resource constraints, and the benefits of controls must be considered relative to their costs.

7.6 Responsibility of Project Stakeholders in Implementing Internal Control

To better understand the elements of internal control, the responsibilities of key project stakeholders is outlined below:[1]

- *Management* — More than any other individual, the chief executive sets the "tone at the top" that affects integrity and ethics and other factors of a positive control environment (one of the elements of the framework). In a large company, the chief executive fulfills this duty by providing leadership and direction to senior managers and reviewing the way they are controlling the business. Senior managers, in turn, assign responsibility for the establishment of more specific internal control policies and procedures to personnel responsible for the unit's functions (setting the control activities, risk assessment, and information and communication channels).
- *Board of directors* — Management is accountable to the board of directors, which provides governance, guidance, and oversight (monitoring). Effective board members are objective, capable, and inquisitive. They also have knowledge of the entity's activities and environment and commit the time necessary to fulfill their board responsibilities.
- *Internal and external auditors* — Internal auditors play an important role in evaluating the effectiveness of control systems and contribute to ongoing effectiveness. Further, external auditors, bringing an independent and objective view, contribute directly through the financial statement audit and indirectly by providing information useful to management and the board in carrying out their responsibilities.
- *All other employees* — Internal control is, to some degree, the responsibility of everyone in an organization and therefore should be an explicit or implicit part of everyone's job description. Virtually all em-

ployees produce information used in the internal control system or take other actions needed to effect control. Also, all personnel should be responsible for communicating problems in operations, noncompliance with the code of conduct, or other policy violations or illegal actions.

7.7 Using the Internal Control Framework as a Model For Project Fraud Reviews

Although not an absolute, internal control does provide reasonable assurance that project fraud is prevented or otherwise detected in the company's operations. Further, given that it is the standard framework adopted by audit and regulatory standards setting organizations, the Internal Control — Integrated Framework developed by COSO will be used in this publication as the basis for developing preventative and detective controls, as well as associated monitoring that these controls are operational.

The project team and/or independent project reviewers can first enact a self-assessment of internal project controls to determine whether there is a need for, and how to proceed with, a broader, more in-depth evaluation. It may be determined that a specific focus will be on the operating efficiency/effectiveness of the project, on financial reporting, or on complying with all associated laws and regulations. It also may be determined to maintain a broad focus to ensure all of these objectives are being met. Regardless, using the Integrated Framework document, a more in-depth discussion of each of the framework components will be completed in this publication as follows:

- Chapter 11 — This chapter will assist in assessing the project control environment and the associated responsibilities of project stakeholders to ensure the maintenance of this environment.
- Chapter 12 — The focus of this chapter will be on completing a project fraud risk assessment of top fraud risks depending on the many faces of project fraud.
- Chapter 13 — This chapter will respond to the key issues found in the control environment and risk assessment procedures by providing preventative and detective control activities, a model for proper communication, and a process for monitoring the internal control structure.

7.8 Summary

This chapter defined a concept that is critical to the controlled operation of a project and to the reduction of any associated fraud. Internal control is a process that provides reasonable assurance that an organization meets company objectives, reports the true financial picture, and complies with associated regulations. It is through the framework activities that a project needs to be assessed so that its environment, risk assessment procedures, and specific procedural controls work to reduce the potential for project fraud.

Questions

7.1   What is the definition of internal control?

7.2   What are the three prime objectives of internal control?

7.3   What are the five sections of the internal control framework?

7.4   What are three most noted limitations of an internal control system?

7.5   What is the role of the CEO in establishing internal control?

7.6   The Committee of Sponsoring Organizations (COSO) is a voluntary, private-sector organization dedicated to improving the quality of financial reporting through business ethics, effective internal controls, and corporate governance. True or false?

7.7   The extent to which an entity's operations objectives are being achieved and awareness of progress relate to an entity's basic business objectives, including performance and profitability goals, safeguarding of resources, and meeting strategic goals. True or false?

7.8   Internal control can help an entity to achieve its performance and profitability targets, to report such performance completely and accurately, and to ensure that laws are not broken. True or false?

7.9   Internal control can change an inherently poor manager into a good one. True or false?

7.10 Internal control is, to some degree, the responsibility of everyone in an organization and therefore should be an explicit or implicit part of everyone's job description. True or false?

References

1. American Institute of Certified Public Accountants, Internal Control — Integrated Framework, Committee of Sponsoring Organizations, 1992.

2. Committee of Sponsoring Organizations website (www.coso.org).

Project Fraud and Statement of Auditing Standard 99

8.1 Audit Standards and Their Relevance to Project Fraud

Audit standards are used by all external auditing firms (i.e., Big 4 firms) so that these organizations may provide an opinion on a company's financial statements. Auditing standards are promulgated by the Auditing Standards Board (for private companies) and the Public Company Accountability Oversight Board (for public companies). The resulting standards go through extensive quality assurance by financial reporting stakeholders prior to issuance.

Such standards are relevant to the review of and protection against project fraud for three key reasons:

1. *Provide a methodology to auditing* — Audit standards provide a much-needed process for completing an audit. Without standards or benchmarks that need to be met in order to sign off on an audit, all would be left to an auditor's judgment, with the probable outcome of lower quality reviews.

2. *Can be used by external auditors* — To a large extent, any work completed under these standards by the company can be used by the external auditors. This not only initiates an immediate fee reduction, but also provides an overall sense to the auditor that the company is taking steps

to ensure a more controlled environment. Also, this "sense" is intangible; it could lead to less costly reviews by the external auditor that are completed more inexpensively internally. For example, a specific internal review of projects for the incidence of fraud may lower audit risk assessment ratings in the planning stages of an external audit, thereby reducing the amount of testwork needed in certain audit areas.

3. *Define programs and controls* — Audit standards, and the one associated with fraud is no exception, generally provide control recommendations that companies can implement to bolster controls, thereby reducing the incidence of project fraud.

8.2 The Effects of SAS 99 on the Audit Industry

SAS 99 (Consideration of Fraud in a Financial Statement Audit[1]), issued in 2002, was part of a broader effort by the CPA profession to reduce the incidences of fraud in financial statements. To do this, the audit standard is expected to improve the likelihood that auditors will unearth material fraud through new audit techniques, improved skills, and increased professional skepticism. Note that this increased effort does not change the auditor's responsibility to detect fraud, namely "a responsibility to plan and perform the audit to obtain reasonable assurance about whether the financial statements are free of material misstatement, whether caused by error or fraud." Although this statement focuses on the auditor's consideration of fraud in an audit of financial statements, it is management's responsibility to design and implement programs and controls to prevent and detect fraud

While carrying the same title as SAS 82, SAS 99 is clearly more far-reaching regarding the procedures an auditor must complete in an engagement. Significant changes in the auditor's approach include:

- An increased focus on professional skepticism.
- A required brainstorming session among the audit team members to discuss the potential for material misstatement due to fraud.
- An increased emphasis on inquiry as an audit procedure along with a consideration of other information, such as client acceptance and continuance procedures, during the information-gathering phase.
- Increased testwork based on a thorough risk assessment. For example, the standard requires expanded use of analytical procedures to gather information used to identify risks of a material misstatement due to fraud.

Given that SAS 99 is the "fraud standard," it will be used throughout this publication to support the work done to prevent and detect project fraud. Each of these new procedures, required under SAS 99, is explained in more depth below.

8.3 Increased Professional Skepticism

Professional skepticism is an attitude, rather than a procedure, that includes a questioning mind and a critical assessment of audit evidence. This attitude is the single most important skill an auditor uses in completing all of his or her audit procedures. An auditor needs to conduct an engagement with a mindset that recognizes the possibility of a material misstatement due to fraud, regardless of any past experience with the entity and regardless of the auditor's belief about management's honesty and integrity. "Joe is a great guy...He would never steal" is a common statement from auditors oblivious to the signs of fraud. Joe may be a great guy, but he may also be pressured to commit fraud by management, financial commitments, or his own rationalization that it is in everyone's best interests for him to commit fraud. Therefore, audit evidence borne from procedures needs to be evaluated closely with a critical and questioning mind.

8.4 Required Brainstorming Sessions

Brainstorming, especially in the early planning stages of the audit, has become so recognized as an audit tool that it was specifically identified as a requirement in the newly enacted fraud audit standard. Brainstorming sessions should allow for open-minded discussion, not be dominated by a few people, and assume that there are no "dumb questions." To maximize the benefits of these sessions, it is generally helpful to:

- Provide every participant in the session with a set of premeeting materials (i.e., financial statement, sample analytical results, key client articles in trade magazines, etc.) so that everyone can prepare appropriately.
- Plan some stated questions to start the flow of ideas (What fraud type could be the most material at this client? What motivation would they have to commit fraud this year?).
- Have a facilitator guide the session, working to best capture the thinking of the group. Many times, these sessions are audiotaped so that they can be synthesized into meeting notes later.

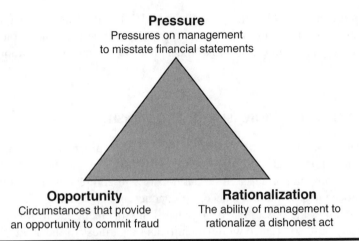

Figure 8.1. Fraud Triangle.

During this session, the engagement team should brainstorm the question, "If someone wanted to perpetrate a fraud, how would they do it?" To answer this question appropriately, the engagement team should keep in mind the three conditions that are present with all frauds:

1. Incentives or pressures on management to commit fraud (see Chapters 5 and 12 for a list of these motives)
2. Opportunity, such as management's ability to override controls (see Chapter 12 for more on these opportunities)
3. Attitude or someone's rationalization of why the fraud is acceptable behavior

These points are illustrated in Figure 8.1.

8.5 Increased Inquiries

Forensic experts have noted that often there are employees in an organization who would alert the auditor or blow the whistle if only the auditor would ask. Prior auditing standards did not require the audit team to simply ask management about their knowledge of company fraud. In the new standard, this is not only a requirement, but the questions to be asked have been specifically outlined. Questions of financial management include whether:

- They have any knowledge of someone who they may believe is stealing from the company or of any fraudulent accounting entries.
- Anyone has ever asked them to make unusual entries or whether they feel a great deal of pressure to make the numbers.
- Anyone with purchasing authority has conflicts of interests to select a related business or vendor.
- They have observed any coworkers whose behavior has been abnormal.
- They have observed anyone who has access to company assets who may be living beyond their means.
- They understand the risks of fraud in the entity, including any specific fraud risks the entity has identified or account balances or classes of transactions for which a risk of fraud may likely exist.
- Programs and controls the entity has established to mitigate specific fraud risks have been identified and how they expect management to monitor those programs and controls. (Chapter 13 discusses examples of programs and controls an entity may implement to prevent, deter, and detect fraud.)
- Management communicates to employees its views on business practices and ethical behavior.

The auditor also should directly inquire of the audit committee (or at least its chair) about the audit committee's views about the risks of fraud and whether the audit committee has knowledge of any fraud or suspected fraud. An entity's audit committee sometimes assumes an active role in oversight of the entity's assessment of the risks of fraud and the programs and controls the entity has established to mitigate these risks. The auditor should obtain an understanding of how the audit committee exercises oversight activities in that area.

The auditor should also highly consider questioning others outside of financial management (i.e., controller or CFO). Other parties with more of a "ground floor" understanding may be in the best position to detect the fraud. These employees include:

- Employees with varying levels of authority within the entity
- Operating personnel not directly involved in the financial reporting process
- Employees involved in initiating, recording, or processing complex or unusual transactions (for example, a sales transaction with multiple elements or a significant related-party transaction)
- In-house legal counsel

8.6 Increased Testwork

In designing audit tests and procedures, auditors may become too predictable in the types of tests, locations, and accounts that are tested. As a result, the audit teams should consider designing certain audit tests that would be unpredictable and unexpected by the client. Also, audit engagement teams should consider changing the nature and extent of their testing as to test areas, locations, and accounts that might not otherwise be tested because they would ordinarily be considered low risks. Therefore, auditors need to adapt the nature, timing, and extent of the auditing procedures to be performed in order to increase the probability of detecting fraud.

Other specific considerations under SAS 99 include that the auditor needs to presume that revenue recognition is a high-risk area for testing and that management override is possible in any company. Management override would allow, say, a CFO to post a fraudulent accounting entry and override all other decision makers in the organization to get it recorded. The following are examples of modification of the nature, timing, and extent of tests in response to identified risks of material misstatements due to fraud:

- Performing procedures at locations on a surprise or unannounced basis (for example, observing inventory on unexpected dates or at unexpected locations or counting cash on a surprise basis)
- Requesting that inventories be counted at the end of the reporting period or on a date closer to period-end to minimize the risk of manipulation of balances in the period between the date of completion of the count and the end of the reporting period
- Making oral inquiries of major customers and suppliers in addition to sending written confirmations or sending confirmation requests to a specific party within an organization
- Performing substantive analytical procedures using disaggregated data (for example, comparing gross profit or operating margins by location, line of business, or month)
- Reviewing journal entries for unusual activity

One important area for auditing relative to project fraud is management's estimates, as many estimates are made on projects relative to the business case, the current status, and the financial position at any given point in time. Fraudulent financial reporting often is accomplished through intentional misstatement of accounting estimates. As indicated in SAS 57, Auditing Accounting Estimates,[2] "estimates are based on subjective as well as objective factors and there is a potential for bias in the subjective factors, even when management's estimation process involves competent personnel using relevant and reliable data." In addressing an identified risk of material misstatement due to fraud involving accounting estimates, the auditor may want to supplement the audit evidence otherwise obtained by engaging a specialist or developing an independent estimate for comparison to management's estimate. Information gathered about the entity and its environment may help the auditor evaluate the reasonableness of such management estimates and underlying judgments and assumptions. A retrospective review of similar management judgments and assumptions applied in prior periods may also provide insight about the reasonableness of judgments and assumptions supporting management estimates.

8.7 Auditor Communication

Whenever the auditor has determined that there is evidence that fraud may exist, that matter should be brought to the attention of an appropriate level of management. Fraud involving senior management and fraud that causes a material misstatement of the financial statements (whether caused by senior management or other employees) should be reported directly to the audit committee. In addition, the auditor should reach an understanding with the audit committee regarding the nature and extent of communications about misappropriations perpetrated by lower-level employees.

8.8 Summary

Auditing standards, especially SAS 99, Consideration of Fraud in a Financial Statement Audit, provides much-needed procedural steps when completing an audit for project fraud. Appendix B of SAS 99 highlights the key programs and controls an entity should possess. Using these standards, someone looking for project fraud will need to ensure that they utilize professional skepticism when performing their audit procedures, namely brainstorming to detect fraud, inquiring of management, and performing less predictable and more comprehensive tests of financial statement balances.

Questions

8.1   Why do audit standards assist in the prevention and detection of project fraud?

8.2   What current audit standard was issued to reduce organizational fraud?

8.3 What three considerations should be maintained when completing brainstorming sessions on the potential for fraud?

8.4 Are inquiries of management regarding their knowledge of fraud suggested or required as part of new audit standards?

8.5 What additional procedures should be performed on management's estimates to ensure that fraud does not exist?

8.6 SAS 99 (Consideration of Fraud in a Financial Statement Audit[1]), issued in 2002, was part of a broader effort by the CPA profession to reduce the incidences of fraud in financial statements. True or false?

8.7 Other specific considerations under SAS 99 include that the auditor needs to presume that revenue recognition is a high-risk area for testing and that management override is possible in any company. True or false?

8.8 Fraudulent financial reporting often is accomplished through intentional misstatement of accounting estimates. True or false?

References

1. American Institute of Certified Public Accountants, SAS 99, Consideration of Fraud in a Financial Statement Audit, Auditing Standards Board, 2002.
2. American Institute of Certified Public Accountants, SAS 57, Auditing Accounting Estimates, Auditing Standards Board, 1991.

9

Assessing the Organizational and Project Control Environment

9.1 Control Environment Defined

Studies of financial reporting integrity, most notably the Treadway Commission's review,[1] found that the tone set by top management (the corporate environment or culture) is the most important factor contributing to the integrity of the financial reporting process. Stated another way, if the tone is not properly set by management, this will trickle down and infect every part of the organization. The effects will present themselves in financial reporting policies and procedures, in the way investment capital is managed, and in the financial statements themselves. Note that "management" setting the tone may be top management of the company or the top management of the project at hand.

Therefore, the control environment[2] reflects the overall attitude, awareness, and actions of the board of directors, management, owners, and others concerning the importance of control and the emphasis placed on control in the company's policies, procedures, methods, and organizational structure. While a satisfactory control environment does not guarantee the effectiveness of any specific control, it can be a positive factor in assessing the risk of errors and in ensuring that appropriate responses are taken to mitigate any identified risks. Therefore, obtaining an understanding of the control environment is an essential first step

63

in identifying factors that may have a pervasive effect on the risk of errors and fraud. The control environment is comprised of the following pillars, which are more fully defined in this chapter. They are called "pillars" as the environment is the foundation of all resulting entity controls:

- Integrity and ethical values — reducing pressures
- Integrity and ethical values — communicating guidelines
- Commitment to competence
- Board of directors and/or audit committee participation in governance
- Management's philosophy and operating style
- Organizational structure and assignment of authority and responsibility
- Human resource policies and practices

9.2 Pillar #1: Integrity and Ethical Values — Reducing Pressures

The way a company sets and meets its objectives is based on preferences, value judgments, and management styles. Those preferences and value judgments that translate into standards of behavior reflect management's integrity and its commitment to ethical values. Therefore, the effectiveness of a system of internal control cannot rise above the integrity and ethical values of the personnel who create, administer, and monitor it. Integrity and ethical values are essential elements of the control environment, affecting the design, administration, and monitoring of other internal control components.

The environment boils down to management's actions to remove or reduce incentives and temptations that might prompt personnel to engage in dishonest, illegal, or unethical acts. It also includes the communication of the entity's values and behavioral standards to personnel through policy statements and codes of conduct and by the examples the executives set.

As for reducing incentives, financial reporting and project pressures need to be reduced by management. This is easier written than done as investor and management consciousness is more "What have you done for me lately?" than "How will you create long-term lasting value for the company?" More specifically, some of the popular pressures include:

- *Market expectations* — Companies in danger of not meeting analyst expectations.
- *Increase shareholder value* — Companies that may not have an expectation, but want to make themselves more attractive in the marketplace.

- *Make the budget* — Companies are highly budget conscious and sometimes just making the budget is motive enough.
- *Regulatory/contractual* — Meeting debt covenants or other regulatory needs can lead to the wrong reporting decisions.
- *Bonus/profit sharing* — Meeting profit-sharing goals leads to higher personal earnings for employees.
- *Save a job* — Poor financial performance may lead to the closure of a division, product line, or the entire organization.
- *Save my ego* — Executives and management have much at stake when leading organizations and may risk practically anything monetary to save their pride.

The only way to reduce pressures is to implement sound business practices and stick by them. For example, setting achievable performance targets both internally and externally reduces the pressure for improper project and financial reporting.

9.3 Pillar #2: Integrity and Ethical Values — Communicating Guidelines

Many employees do not know what is wrong or, since they have not been specifically told, make improper decisions on their own. Given that practically all frauds are rationalized, employees will then work to find reasons why they are working in the company's best interest. To combat this, a clear communication from management of a company's values and business practices is required. Communication can take the following forms:

- *An established code of conduct* — A code defines all of the ethical business practices of the organization. The code of conduct for employees at all levels, based on the organization's core values, gives clear guidance on what behavior and actions are permitted and which are prohibited. This document is then signed by all employees on a periodic basis, noting they have read and understand the policy.
- *Setting good examples* — The best way to communicate integrity is through example. Management, in difficult situations, not only needs to "do the right thing," but also needs to communicate the right paths taken in meeting business challenges.
- *Flaunting bad examples* — When management finds employees **not** doing the right thing, this too needs to be communicated throughout the

organization. Many professional organizations have programs to make known all members expelled for unethical practices. Companies have similar internal programs using newsletters and such to ensure a deterrent exists for those considering inappropriate activity.

■ *Providing a channel for questions* — Employees should seek additional advice when faced with uncertain ethical decisions and how they should communicate concerns about known or potential wrongdoing affecting the organization. For larger companies, this may be a full-time position as ethics officer or compliance officer. In smaller companies, this will be an additional responsibility held by an existing member of management.

9.4 Pillar #3: Commitment to Competence

Management should specify the competence levels for particular jobs and translate those levels into requisite knowledge and skills. The necessary knowledge and skills may in turn depend on an individual's training and experience. Among the many factors that should be considered by management are the nature and degree of judgment to be applied to a specific job and the extent of supervision that will be provided.

Aside from technical training, ethical training should be considered for all employees or, at a minimum, key employees in a purchasing or financial reporting position. The training should focus on the company's code of conduct, ways to seek advice, and how to communicate potential wrongdoing. Many programs not only focus on the technical aspects of the ethics program, but also provide case study examples for participants to work through and identify the business practice.

9.5 Pillar #4: Board of Directors and/or Audit Committee Participation in Governance and Oversight

Top management can be mistaken for the premier oversight function in the company. However, management is responsible for overseeing the activities carried out by employees, assessing any fraud that may be committed by employees, and implementing new processes as required by other oversight functions. The audit committee, a subset of the board of directors, should evaluate management's identification of fraud risks, implementation of anti-fraud measures, and creation of the appropriate "tone at the top." An entity's audit committee also should encourage senior management (in particular, the CEO) to implement appropriate fraud deterrence and prevention measures to better protect investors, employees, and other stakeholders.

Therefore, while management may be the practical oversight body, the audit committee significantly influences management's decisions and is the appropriate "top of the food chain" for corporate governance. Influencing factors include the board or audit committee's independence from management, experience and stature of its members, extent of its involvement and scrutiny of activities, and the appropriateness of its actions. Another factor is the degree to which difficult questions are raised and pursued with management regarding plans or performance. Interaction of the board or audit committee with internal and external auditors is another factor affecting the control environment.

Through its own activities and supported by an audit committee, the board of directors is responsible for overseeing the accounting and financial reporting policies and procedures. While the specific activities and responsibilities of audit committees vary and need to be modified or tailored to the individual circumstances, the board of directors has a fiduciary responsibility to shareholders and others for reliable financial reports. As a result, the board of directors and the audit committee should be concerned with the company's financial reporting to shareholders and the investing public, and they should monitor the company's accounting policies and the internal and independent audit processes.

9.6 Pillar #5: Management's Philosophy and Operating Style

Management is responsible for directing and controlling operations and for establishing, communicating, and monitoring policies and procedures. The control environment is influenced by the actions and inaction of management, as well as management's approach to risk. In an effective control environment, management's control consciousness and operating style create a positive atmosphere that is conducive to the effective operation of the processes and controls and an environment in which the likelihood of error is reduced.

Control consciousness refers to the importance management attaches to internal controls and thus to the environment in which specific controls function. For the most part, it is an intangible concept, a management attitude that, when communicated, helps to ensure that adequate controls are in place. This intangible manifests itself in the funding that management provides to controls. Does management take an "if it ain't broke" mentality, a "run it loose and bolster back-end process controls" approach, or are they more concerned with preventing mismanagement? The latter requires investment in both time and capital.

9.7 Pillar #6: Organizational Structure and Assignment of Authority and Responsibility

The organizational structure of an entity provides the overall framework for planning, executing, controlling, and monitoring operations. An effective organizational structure provides for the assignment of responsibility, such that all personnel within the company have a clear understanding of their reporting relationships and responsibilities. Further, such relationships should ensure a segregation of duties that will inhibit collusion in fraud, an almost undetectable cloak to the malfeasance. For example, if all check payments are made from an accounts payable department and the associated bank reconciliation is completed by the department supervisor, such a lack of segregation provides a wide opportunity for fraud. Another example may be an internal audit department that does not have a direct line of reporting to a CEO or audit committee, which could lead to it not raising a critical control event to the appropriate level of management.

The appropriateness of an entity's organizational structure depends, in part, on the size and nature of activities. A highly structured organization, with clearly defined reporting lines and controls, may be the best model for a large company. On the other hand, such a structure may impede a small company from meeting its organizational objectives. Either way, the structure should be developed with internal control and segregation of duties in mind.

9.8 Pillar #7: Human Resource Policies and Practices

Human resource policies and practices relate to hiring, orienting, training, evaluating, counseling, promoting, and compensating personnel. These practices send messages to employees regarding expected levels of integrity, ethical behavior, and competence. A company's ability to recruit and retain sufficient competent and responsible personnel is dependent on its human resource policies and practices. In addition, the level of competence and integrity of the personnel involved in a specific process is one of the factors to consider in evaluating the effectiveness of controls over the process.

Research results indicate that wrongdoing occurs less frequently when employees have positive feelings about an entity. Otherwise, employees can feel abused, threatened, or ignored. In a negative workplace environment, there are more opportunities for poor employee morale, which can affect an employee's attitude about committing fraud against an entity. Factors that create a negative work environment and may increase the risk of fraud include:[3]

- Top management that does not seem to care about or reward appropriate behavior
- Negative feedback and lack of recognition for job performance
- Perceived inequities in the organization
- Autocratic rather than participative management
- Fear of delivering "bad news" to supervisors and/or management
- Poor training and promotion opportunities

The entity's human resources department often is instrumental in helping to build a corporate culture and a positive work environment. Mitigating factors that help create a positive work environment and reduce the risk of fraud may include:

- Recognition and reward systems that are in tandem with goals and results
- Equal employment opportunities
- Team-oriented, collaborative decision-making policies
- Professionally administered compensation programs
- Professionally administered training programs and an organizational priority of career development
- Empowering employees to create a positive workplace environment through surveying and suggestion programs

Further, human resource departments can help prevent employment problems before they occur through proactive hiring and promotion procedures, including:

- Conducting background investigations on individuals being considered for employment or for promotion to a position of trust. This could include thoroughly checking a candidate's education, employment history, and personal references.
- Incorporating into regular performance reviews an evaluation of how each individual has contributed to creating an appropriate workplace environment in line with the entity's values and code of conduct.
- Continuous objective evaluation of compliance with the entity's values and code of conduct, with violations addressed immediately.

9.9 Project Environment Defined

Up to this point in the chapter, the content has focused on an organizational control environment starting with the audit committee, extending down through the C-level management, and then further throughout the organizational management layers. While this may appear to *not* have an impact at the project level, the organizational environment acts as the foundation for all of the projects within. It heavily influences project sponsors, project team management, and the team members themselves to act according to the company's bylaws.

With the exception of pillar #4, which is related to the board of directors, all other pillars could relate both at the organizational level and at the project level. Therefore, project sponsorship needs to act ethically, train team members in appropriate business practice, open channels for communication to ensure ethical practices are being followed, and the like. Given this duality, it is suggested that the control environment first be assessed at the entity level and then, with a more narrow focus, applied to the project at hand.

9.10 Control Environment Assessment Questions

Now that the control environment has been defined, critical questions can be asked both from an organizational level and then a project level relative to each environmental pillar:

1. Integrity and ethical values
   - Are the company's code of conduct and other policies regarding acceptable business practice, conflicts of interest, and expected standards of ethical and moral behavior comprehensive and relevant?
   - Do employees fully and clearly understand what behavior is acceptable and unacceptable under the company's code of conduct?
   - Do employees know what to do when they encounter improper behavior?
   - Does top management work to reduce pressures that may lead to mismanagement and fraud?
   - Are examples of good and bad ethical behavior communicated frequently by management to a majority of the workforce?
   - Does management strictly prohibit circumvention of established policies and procedures, except where specific guidance has been provided?

2. Commitment to competence
   - Has management adequately defined the knowledge and skills needed to perform jobs within the entity?
   - Are employees properly trained and capable of performing all jobs within their assigned function?
   - Are employees specifically trained in the company's code of conduct, ways to seek advice, and how to communicate potential wrongdoing?
   - Are employees trained using ethical case studies to help guide them toward more appropriate behavior?
3. Board and audit committee
   - Do directors have sufficient knowledge, industry experience, and time to serve effectively?
   - Does the audit function have a direct reporting relationship with the audit committee?
   - Does the audit committee meet privately with the internal and external auditors to discuss the reasonableness of the financial reporting process, system of internal control, significant comments and recommendations, and management's performance?
   - Does the board constructively challenge management's planned decisions and probe for reasoning on past results?
4. Management's philosophy and operating style
   - Does management accept the appropriate amount of business risk or does it accept a higher than normal risk level?
   - Are objectives established by senior management realistic, achievable, and based on fair assumptions?
   - Does management view accounting treatment for transactions or activities in a balanced manner, neither too aggressively nor too conservatively?
   - Does management appropriately balance the focus on short-term reported results with long-term business objectives and not exert inappropriate pressure to achieve earnings objectives?
   - Is management investing in preventive controls or does it display more of a "run it loose and detect later" approach?
5. Organizational structure and assignment of authority and responsibilities
   - Does the current organizational structure facilitate the flow of information both up and down the entity?
   - Are you aware of any poor segregation of duties?
   - Do managers and process owners in your function have ready access to senior management to address significant issues?

- Does management periodically evaluate the organizational structure relevant to your function in light of changes in the scope, nature, or extent of your operations?
- Are employees expected to work excessive overtime or do more than is expected for their position?
- Are specific limits established for certain types of transactions with delegations clearly communicated and understood by employees?
- Are job descriptions accurate and complete?

6. Human resource policies and practices
   - Do existing personnel policies and procedures facilitate recruiting and developing competent personnel who are able to meet the company's objectives?
   - Do individual performance targets focus on both the long term and short term?
   - Does the company have fair policies in the area of employee relations and compensation (for example, salaries, fringe benefits, performance appraisal, promotions, severance pay) and do these policies compare favorably with those of competitors?
   - Do performance appraisals adequately align to maintaining sound internal controls?
   - Is the morale within the department acceptably positive or are there resonating negative issues within?
   - Does the company use background checks, sensitive positions screening or testing procedures (for example, psychological tests, drug tests, lie detector tests, or a combination of all three), or both where permitted by law?
   - Is management open to "bad" news when it is a fair representation of the issues at hand?
   - Is the management style participative and open to new ideas from employees?
   - Is there a high turnover rate among the project team?

9.11 Summary

To control an entity's activities, two tools are used: rules and principles. Rules are the control activities that need to be followed (i.e., project plans must be kept, business cases must be written before funding, etc.). Principles are the attitudes toward and importance given to control from senior management to project employees. With this premise, this chapter defined the seven pillars of a strong control environment and some tools to assess them within an organization. These pillars are repeated as follows:

- Integrity and ethical values — reducing pressures
- Integrity and ethical values — communicating guidelines
- Commitment to competence
- Board of directors and/or audit committee participation in governance
- Management's philosophy and operating style
- Organizational structure and assignment of authority and responsibility
- Human resource policies and practices

Questions

9.1   What are the seven pillars of the control environment?

9.2   What are three pressures that should be reduced by ethical management?

9.3   Who is the top oversight layer in the entity?

9.4   What is a clear sign that management is serious about controls?

9.5   What are the main tools of assessing a control environment?

9.6   Studies of financial reporting integrity, most notably the Treadway Commission's review,[1] found that the tone set by top management (the corporate environment or culture) is the most important factor contributing to the integrity of the financial reporting process. True or false?

9.7   The way a company sets and meets its objectives is based on preferences, value judgments, and management styles. Those preferences and value judgments that translate into standards of behavior reflect management's integrity and its commitment to ethical values. Therefore, the effectiveness of a system of internal control cannot rise above the integrity and ethical values of the personnel who create, administer, and monitor it. True or false?

9.8   Integrity and ethical values are essential elements of the control environment, affecting the design, administration, and monitoring of other internal control components. True or false?

9.9   An established code of conduct defines all of the ethical business practices of the organization. The code of conduct for employees at all levels, based on the organization's core values, gives clear guidance on what behavior and actions are permitted and which are prohibited. True or false?

9.10 Commitment to competence includes management's consideration of the competence levels for particular jobs and how those levels translate into requisite skills and knowledge. True or false?

References

1. Committee of Sponsoring Organizations, Fraudulent Financial Reporting 1987–1997: An Analysis of U.S. Public Companies, Committee of Sponsoring Organizations, 1999.
2. American Institute of Certified Public Accountants, Internal Control — Integrated Framework, Committee of Sponsoring Organizations, 1992.
3. American Institute of Certified Public Accountants, Consideration of Fraud in a Financial Statement Audit, Auditing Standards Board, 2002.

10

Complete Project
Fraud Risk Assessment

10.1 The Risk Assessment Process

This chapter will apply the information presented in the previous chapters to assess the risk of project fraud and mismanagement. The risk management process is comprised of the following steps:

1. *Identify* — Risks are identified, but not judged as to their scope, magnitude, and/or urgency.
2. *Assess* — Risks are evaluated and prioritized based on their size and urgency.
3. *Respond* — All risks have a corresponding response that ranges from full acceptance of risk to prevention procedures.

To show the importance of a fraud risk assessment process, the Association of Certified Fraud Examiners recently released a Fraud Prevention Check-Up[1] for organizations to assess their level of fraud-fighting processes. The first section of the checkup focuses on the fraud-specific risk assessment process carried out by the organization, the ownership for this process, and the timing for carrying out the assessments. Preferably, the assessments would be completed at periodic intervals, any findings (positive or negative) would be reported to a high level of management, and ownership for any major fraud risks would be given to a senior level of management to ensure that the appropriate resources are applied to the issue at hand.

Note that risk management is normally initiated in the planning stages of a project (after the project has been properly defined) and continues routinely throughout the implementation of the project. However, it is advised to complete a more holistic risk assessment of the corporate environment initially and then the project portfolio environment prior to completing specific project risk assessments. This considers the fact that major frauds usually involve senior members of management who are able to override process-level controls because of their high level of authority.

This holistic assessment could be used by the organization as an opportunity to perform enterprise risk management procedures. Enterprise risk management is an approach toward assessing all risks affecting the organization, including external risks, general internal risks, and associated project risks. While this integrated, companywide approach has been circulating as a business concept for several years, few companies have a solid implementation plan. To assist the momentum of transforming this approach from an idea to an implemented process, COSO (www.coso.org) is working on an Enterprise Risk Management Framework that is expected to be released sometime in 2004. This is the same organization that developed the Internal Control — Integrated Framework document (mentioned in earlier chapters) that has formed the basis of internal control since its release in the early 1990s.

10.2 Risk Assessment: Getting Started

10.2.1 Brainstorm

The first step in the risk assessment process is to identify project risks. This can best be done through brainstorming sessions and preferably with employees independent of the project(s) under review. Brainstorming has become so recognized as an audit tool that it was specifically identified as a requirement for SAS 99,[2] the fraud audit standard enacted in 2002. Brainstorming sessions should allow for open-minded discussion, not be dominated by a few people, and have an understanding that there are no "dumb questions." It is generally helpful to provide every participant in the session with a set of premeeting materials (i.e., list of projects, list of common project fraud risks, etc.) so that everyone can prepare appropriately. Then, in the session, planned questions can be used to start the flow of ideas (Of the various types of fraud, which one is most likely to occur? What fraud type could have the highest dollar effect?). A list of these questions is provided later in this chapter which could form the basis of such a meeting. Finally, it is useful to have a facilitator guide the session, working to best capture the thinking of the group. Many times, these sessions are audiotaped so that later they can be synthesized into meeting notes.

10.2.2 Score and Prioritize Risks

Once all of the risks that have a potential of occurrence in the organization have been identified, the next step is to assess their relative impact and likelihood, defined as follows:

1. *Likelihood* — Can be calculated based on an assessment of:
   - *Threats* — Internal and external events
   - *Vulnerabilities* — Weaknesses within the system
2. *Impact* — The adverse consequences resulting from threats and vulnerabilities, which should be expressed in monetary terms whenever possible

Mathematically, the factors identified in the risk assessment process can be expressed in the following equation: Risk = Impact × Likelihood. The equation should be applied to each fraud type expected within the organization. To ease this process and avoid minutia, it may be useful to set general parameters for impact (i.e., up to $500,000, $500,001 to $1,000,000, and over $1,000,000) and likelihood (10, 50, 75, and 90 percent). After each fraud type is scored, the scores can be prioritized from highest to lowest fraud risk.

10.2.3 Develop Appropriate Risk Responses

Once the top areas for fraud risk are identified, a company looking to reduce fraud in the organization would:

- *Prevent or avoid the risk* — Develop responses that prevent the threat from occurring. For example, controls may be established to eliminate any opportunity for the fraud to occur.
- *Mitigate the risk* — Develop responses that reduce the fraud risk to a more manageable level. For example, audit software reports may be run and reviewed on a periodic basis to monitor fraud threats/vulnerabilities.
- *Transfer the risk* — The risk could be transferred to a third party, such as an insurance carrier.

This chapter will focus on identifying and assessing risks, while Chapters 11 and 12 will focus on precise prevention, mitigation, and detection procedures.

10.3 Assessing Fraud Risks Overview

A common model for fraud risks, ultimately adopted by the Auditing Standards Board in its release of SAS 99, Consideration of Fraud in a Financial Statement Audit,[2] was the fraud triangle (Figure 10.1).

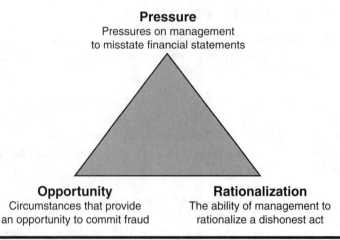

Pressure
Pressures on management
to misstate financial statements

Opportunity   **Rationalization**
Circumstances that provide   The ability of management to
an opportunity to commit fraud   rationalize a dishonest act

Figure 10.1.   Fraud Triangle.

Using the model, the risk of fraud should be assessed for each component of the triangle. The following key questions should be asked for further analysis using a risk assessment process:

■   What pressures are on management to misstate earnings?
■   What opportunities are present to management, either through lax controls or senior management's acceptance of dishonest acts?
■   What factors may allow management to rationalize its actions for the good of the company or its beneficiaries?

More specifically, the following process can be used to assess risks within the fraud triangle:

1. *Consider the general pressures and rationalizations* that management may commit fraud. These pressures may include market or shareholder pressures, personal ego, or an attempt to save one's organizational position. See Chapter 9 for a full discussion of the pressures and rationalizations made by management.

2. *Risk prioritize each fraud type* — One easy way to accomplish this is to take each fraud type as discussed in Chapter 4 and assign a likelihood/ impact to each type of fraud. This assessment will be different for each organization, depending on the industry, control environment, economy, and many other factors specific to that organization.

3. *Complete a more thorough analysis of the opportunities for fraud* —
Either by taking the subset of risks identified in the second step above
or by reviewing all potential fraud risks, the questions in Sections 10.4
to 10.12 of this chapter can be applied to each fraud type. By doing so,
the auditor can assess the levels of opportunity to commit such fraud,
as well as identify key red flags that may signal fraud is occurring within
the project.

4. *Assess the risk of management override* — Because management has the
ability to override controls or to influence others to perpetrate or conceal
fraud, the need for a strong value system and a culture of ethical financial
reporting becomes increasingly important. This helps to create an environment where other employees will decline to participate in committing
a fraud and will use established communication procedures to report any
requests to commit wrongdoing.

SEC rules cite the internal control framework of COSO as being the appropriate basis for internal control evaluations. Yet when it comes to "management override" and financial statement fraud, the 1987 COSO framework
is short on details and does not reflect the results of fraud prevention and
detection research conducted in the past sixteen years. Remember that most
internal controls are useless in preventing financial statement fraud by the CEO
or CFO (the most common kind) since senior executives can easily override
them.[3] The risk of management override is unpredictable and therefore it is
difficult for auditors to design procedures to identify and assess it. Therefore,
the risk of management override of controls should be considered a fraud risk
on every project audit.

10.4 Internal Documents

Per Chapter 4, internal document fraud is defined as fraudulent statements made
by employees that have no direct financial statement impact, such as employee
credentials or other internal/external documents.[4] In order to assess whether the
risks of this fraud are present, focus should be placed in three areas: (1) unsubstantiated business cases including initial project estimates, (2) project progress
from a schedule and cost perspective, and (3) project progress from a quality
perspective.

Below are the opportunity and red flag questions[4] that should be asked in
assessing this potential fraud. It is best that these questions be asked not only
of the project team, but also of the program management office and the end

users of the project to ensure that a complete triangulation of answers is obtained.

1. Overreported and unsubstantiated business case
   - Will the project generate sufficient cash flow to pay project expenses and pay an acceptable rate of return to the organization? In particular, will the net present value (NPV) of these cash flows be positive assuming the acceptable rate of return? (For more information, see Chapter 6.)
   - Are the above estimates based on historical precedence/benchmark in the marketplace?
   - Are the above estimates based on market surveys of price/demand in the marketplace? If so, how extensive were the market surveys of the target market? Further, are there general market trends that can be relied on to assess the forecasted benefits?
   - Was a prototype completed to test the viability of the project's deliverables and assess the true market demand?
   - What competition exists in the marketplace?
     - ☐ Is the industry fragmented among many suppliers or concentrated with a few?
     - ☐ What market share do the top three competitors maintain?
     - ☐ What relationships do they maintain with suppliers that provide a competitive advantage?
     - ☐ How intense is the rivalry among competitors in the marketplace?
     - ☐ Is the business model based more on differentiation (preferred) than price in dealing with competition?
     - ☐ What future competitors are expected and what will their impact be?
   - What competitive advantage/differentiation in the marketplace does the project's deliverables exhibit in this area?
   - If a technology project, where in the life cycle is the technology being utilized (bleeding edge, cutting edge, majority, etc.)?
   - Does the project sponsor have the authority to define project goals, secure resources, and resolve organizational conflicts?
   - Have all of the project sponsors been considered? If so, what is the risk that the project will not be approved by the appropriate sponsors within the participating organizations?
   - Are there any dissenters of the project? What adverse politics affect the successful completion of the project?
   - Have project goals, deliverables, and their associated success metrics been documented and approved by all sponsors?

- Has all legal protection needed for the product/service (e.g., copyright, trademark, etc.) been obtained?
- Has the organization completed a similar project in the past?
- Have we failed in this type of project in the past and, if so, how will we correct for "lessons learned" in the current project?
- Are we reviewing the realization of the business case and do we plan to do so for at least two years subsequent to the project's completion date?

2. Underreported initial estimates of project life cycle costs
    - Are the initial project cost estimates based on historical precedence/ benchmarks in the marketplace?
    - Are the cost estimates in ranges (best, most likely, worst)?
    - Has a contingency estimate (e.g., 15 percent) been entered from a cost perspective?
    - Have maintenance costs for at least one year been estimated as part of the project?

3. Overreported cost and schedule progress
    - Is there a work breakdown structure (WBS) for each major deliverable (in other words, have the key deliverables been documented)?
    - Is there a detailed WBS documenting at least two tiers of deliverables under the top-level WBS deliverables?
    - Has an estimated size of each major deliverable been calculated in cost and work hours?
    - Have the project time values (hours worked and days in duration) been calculated by the project team in a "bottom-up" fashion?
    - Have deadlines been negotiated between the sponsors and the project team (or have they been dictated)?
    - Have the work hours for each task been calculated using the PERT methodology: (1 $*$ Maximum estimate) + (4 $*$ Average estimate) + (1 $*$ Minimum estimate)/6
    - Is the critical path of the project managed on a routine basis?
    - Has communication been established for the entire project including feedback loops for issues and risks affecting the project, as well as routine status reports?
    - Do status reports calculate earned value on the project from a schedule and cost perspective?

4. Overreported quality progress
    - Has a clear vision or "project charter" been developed with the business owners in mind? Has this vision been communicated properly to all members of the project team?

■ For each deliverable, has the following question been answered: "How do we know the deliverable was completed successfully?"
■ For each deliverable, have success metrics or acceptance criteria been defined specifically?
■ Will the ultimate end users be testing the project's deliverables prior to acceptance?
■ If the project is technical in nature, has the appropriate technical experience been acquired as part of the team or on a consulting basis to review the deliverables for quality?
■ Has there been material turnover recently in the project team?
■ Are there backup resources for key tasks (e.g., for knowledge transfer and to act as a contingency if the initial person leaves the organization)?
■ Has a risk management plan been established and carried out for key risks affecting the project?

10.5 Improper Asset Valuations

Per Chapter 4, improper asset valuation fraud is defined as fictitious inflation of asset values or other improper valuations, generally to enhance the appearance of financial statements.[4] Given that this fraud is based mainly on the improper reporting of internal documents (see above), the associated opportunity and red flag questions that should be asked in assessing this potential fraud are the same. In essence, the ramifications of internal document fraud are improper (namely, lower) asset valuations. This concept is more fully defined in Chapter 6.

10.6 Concealed Liabilities and Expenses

Per Chapter 4, concealed liabilities and expenses fraud is defined as financial statement fraud where liabilities or expenses are excluded in the financial statements.[4] Given that this fraud is based mainly on the improper reporting of internal documents (see above), the associated opportunity and red flag questions that should be asked in assessing this potential fraud are the same. In essence, the ramifications of internal document fraud are improper (namely, lower) reporting of liabilities and expenses. Note that there is also a risk that one project in the project portfolio would be assessed more costs than appropriate, which would be siphoned from another project. Such efforts to misstate the project portfolio (making one project a "darling" and another a "dog") should also be assessed.

Given that concealed liabilities may not be reported at all in the project internal documents, a few more questions[4] are added below to assess whether additional expenses are being concealed:

- Have material contract payments been reviewed to ensure they are occurring in the proper period?
- If a long-term project, has a trend analysis been completed over multiple periods to assess whether internal and external costs are complete?
- Have any significant events occurred to the project and/or organization that warrant incurring additional expenses?

10.7 Bribery and Conflicts of Interest

Per Chapter 4, there are four types of improper dealings with external parties that have negative effects on the organization:

1. *Bribery* — The offering, giving, receiving, or soliciting any thing of value to influence an official act.[4]
2. *Illegal gratuities* — Similar to bribery, except that there is not necessarily an intent to influence a particular business decision.[4]
3. *Economic extortion* — The flip side of a bribery scheme where an employee demands a payment to influence a decision.[4]
4. *Conflict of interest* — Employee, manager, or executive has an undisclosed economic or personal interest in a transaction that adversely affects the company.[4]

The following negative impacts will be charged to the organization affected by this fraud:

- Not selecting the best vendor for the task at hand.
- Fraudulent charging of higher prices that go undetected as they are approved by knowingly influenced internal employees.
- Purchasing more inventory, assets, or services than needed. In most cases, any assets associated with these purchases are not used and appropriately written off.
- Vendor scope changes to the project developed, leading to unbudgeted project expenses.
- Fraudulent purchasing of poor quality inventory or services leading to additional purchases or rework, respectively.

Below are the opportunity and red flag questions[4] that should be asked to assess this potential fraud. It is best that these questions be asked not only of the project team, but also of the program management office and the end users of the project to ensure that a complete triangulation of answers is obtained:[4]

- Are materials being ordered at the optimal reorder point? Are they often ordered from the same vendor?
- Is the quality of product received from certain vendors under a normally acceptable range?
- Are the established bidding policies being followed or are rules being broken for certain vendors?
- Are the costs of materials out of line in relation to other marketplace vendors?
- Are certain vendor bids bypassing necessary review procedures?
- Is the buyer providing the contractor information or advice on a preferential basis?
- Is the buyer limiting time for submission of bids so that only those vendors with advance information have adequate time to prepare bids or proposals?
- Is the buyer failing to ensure that a sufficient number of potential competitors are aware of the solicitation by:
  - ☐ Using obscure publications to publish bid solicitations?
  - ☐ Publishing bid solicitations during holiday periods?
  - ☐ Being vague in the solicitations as to the time, place, or other requirements for submitting acceptable bids?
- Are bids being accepted from certain vendors outside of the normal time frame for the solicitation?
- Are bids being accepted from certain vendors that do not possess the requisite skills or products for the project at hand?
- Do bids received from certain vendors contain false statements (concerning contractor qualifications, financial capability, facilities, ownership of equipment and supplies, qualifications of personnel, successful performance of previous jobs, etc.)?
- Are there any known relationships under review between vendors and employees within the organization?

10.8 Expense Reimbursement Schemes

Per Chapter 4, expense reimbursement fraud occurs when a perpetrator (internal or external to the organization) produces false documents that cause the company to issue a check unknowingly.[4] Schemes fall into the following categories:

- *Mischaracterized expenses* — Fraudulent requests for expenses that are personal in nature or would not normally be paid under the company policy.
- *Overstated expenses* — The inappropriate inflating of submitted expenses.
- *Fictitious expenses* — An employee fabricates and submits expenses that were never incurred.
- *Multiple reimbursements* — Submitting the same expense on multiple occasions to defraud the company into paying the expenses twice.

Below are the opportunity and red flag questions[4] that should be asked to assess this potential fraud. It is best that these questions be asked not only of the project team, but also of the program management office and the end users of the project to ensure that a complete triangulation of answers is obtained.

- Are amounts charged for expense reimbursement reviewed and compared to budgeted amounts and are variances followed up on regularly?
- Is the expense register reviewed for material unusual expense reimbursements prior to payment?
- Are expense reimbursements reviewed by the appropriate level of management prior to payment?
- Are expenses over a specified dollar limit or of a certain type approved by a level of management independent of the project team?
- Are expense reports reviewed by accounts payable to ensure that the expenses are properly entered, approved, supported, and of a business nature?
- Are original receipts the only acceptable form of reimbursement document?

10.9 Payroll Schemes

Per Chapter 4, payroll schemes occur when internal or external perpetrators produce false documents (sales order, time cards, and false employee hiring records) that cause the company to issue a check unknowingly.[4] The schemes fall into the following two categories, as they relate to projects:

1. *Ghost employees* — Payments to someone on the payroll who does not exist.

2. *Falsified hours and salary* — Overpayment of wages due to the falsification of hours, wage rates, or other adjustments.

Below are the opportunity and red flag questions that should be asked to
assess this potential fraud. It is best that these questions[4] be asked not only of
the project team, but also of the program management office and the end users
of the project to ensure that a complete triangulation of answers is obtained.

- Are actual payroll amounts reviewed and compared to budgeted amounts
  and are variances analyzed regularly (these amounts include regular, overtime, and bonus payments)?
- Are payroll registers reviewed for material unusual payments prior to actual
  payment?
- Are personnel records maintained independently of payroll and timekeep-
  ing functions?
- Are changes to payroll not made unless the personnel department sends
  approved notification directly to the payroll department (not from the
  project team)?
- Are references and backgrounds checked for new hires?
- Are all wage rates authorized in writing by a designated official, prefer-
  ably independent of the project team?
- Are bonuses, commissions, and overtime approved in advance and re-
  viewed for compliance with company policies?
- Are time clocks used with employee badges to register time in and out?
- Is overtime or hours charged over a specified limit approved by some-
  one independent of the project team?
- Are payroll checks handed to the employee for each pay period by
  someone independent of the project team?

10.10 Billing Schemes

Per Chapter 4, billing schemes occur when a fraudster causes the victim organization to issue a payment by submitting invoices for fictitious goods or services, inflated invoices, or invoices for personal purchases.[4] The schemes fall
into the following three categories, as they relate to projects:

1. *Shell company* — Creates a phony organization on the company's books
   for use in paying fictitious invoices.
2. *Nonaccomplice vendor* — Intentional mishandling of vendor payment in
   order to make fictitious payment to employee.

3. *Personal purchases* — Purchases using company accounts such as a company procurement card.

Below are the opportunity and red flag questions[4] that should be asked to assess this potential fraud. It is best that these questions be asked not only of the project team, but also of the program management office and the end users of the project to ensure that a complete triangulation of answers is obtained.

- Are vendors' invoices, receiving reports, and purchase orders matched before the related liability is recorded? Are invoices checked as to prices, extensions, footings, freight charges, allowances, and credit terms?
- Does a responsible official approve invoices for payment? Are procedures adequate to ensure that merchandise purchased for direct delivery to customers is promptly billed to the customers and recorded as both a receivable and a payable?
- Is receiving (of vendor products) independent from the project team and are these receiving reports sent directly to accounts payable for matching purposes?
- Are invoices "three-way" matched from a purchase order, invoice, and receiving report prior to payment?
- Are system controls in the accounts payable computer system defined to detect and/or prevent duplicate payments to vendors?
- Is the vendor master file checked against the employee master file to identify any potential fraudulent vendors?
- Are vendors added to the master file checked against Dun & Bradstreet databases to ensure that they are a valid business with a valid business address?
- Are actual expenditures compared with budgeted amounts and variances analyzed and explained?
- Are vendor purchases analyzed for abnormal levels on both a monthly and yearly basis?
- Do credit cards have certain "SIC" codes blocked to prevent unauthorized purchases of personal products?
- Are these credit card statements reviewed often for irregularities?

10.11 Inventory and Other Assets Misuse

Per Chapter 4, inventory and other asset misuse is defined as the borrowing or stealing of inventory/assets from an employer by a perpetrator (internal or external to the organization).[4] Below are the opportunity and red flag questions[4] that should be asked to assess this potential fraud. It is best that these questions be asked not only of the project team, but also of the program management office and the end users of the project to ensure that a complete triangulation of answers is obtained.

- Is inventory disappearing from storage?
- Is inventory managed using appropriate documentation of its receipt and movement within the organization?
- Is inventory physically counted on a periodic basis and assessed to the reported inventory on hand?
- Are these counts performed by employees whose functions are independent of the physical custody of inventories and record-keeping functions?
- Is an analytical review of inventory and usage of inventory (with variances followed up) completed on a regular basis?
- Is receiving (of vendor products) independent from the project team and are these receiving reports sent directly to accounts payable for matching purposes?
- Is inventory physically guarded and locked with access limited to authorized personnel only?

10.12 Summary

The purpose of this chapter was to establish the process of assessing risk of project fraud, given the definition of each fraud type, which includes both a general assessment of the overall environment for fraud and then a more detailed assessment of each fraud type. The goal was to assess the three points of the fraud triangle: pressure, opportunity, and rationalization. To assist this process, specific fraud questions were provided for each fraud type. For those frauds that may be likely, Chapters 11 and 12 will define in more detail how to prevent and detect the associated project fraud schemes.

Questions

10.1 What are the three steps in the risk assessment process?

10.2 What are the three points of the fraud triangle?

10.3 What is the last step of the fraud risk assessment process and why is it so critical?

10.4 How are the internal documents, overstated assets, and concealed liability schemes all related?

10.5   What should specifically be considered relative to vendor bids when reviewing for bribery and conflicts of interest?

10.6   Internal document fraud is defined as fraudulent statements made by employees that have no direct financial statement impact, such as employee credentials or other internal/external documents. True or false?

10.7   Improper asset valuation fraud is defined as fictitious inflation of asset values or other improper valuations, generally to enhance the appearance of financial statements. True or false?

10.8   Concealed liabilities and expenses fraud is defined as financial statement fraud where liabilities or expenses are excluded in the financial statements. True or false?

10.9   Bribery is the offering, giving, receiving, or soliciting any thing of value to influence an official act. True or false?

10.10   Economic extortion is the flip side of a bribery scheme where an employee demands a payment to influence a decision. True or false?

References

1. Association of Certified Fraud Examiners, Fraud Prevention Check-Up, Association of Certified Fraud Examiners, 2003.
2. American Institute of Certified Public Accountants, SAS 99, Consideration of Fraud in a Financial Statement Audit, Auditing Standards Board, 2002.
3. Business Crimes Bulletin®, Volume 10, Number 12, Law Journal Newsletters©, January 2004.
4. Wells, Joseph T., *Occupational Fraud and Abuse*, Hyperion Publishing, 2001.

General Responses to Key Project Error and Fraud Risks with Prevention and Detection Procedures

11.1 High-Level Deterrence and Prevention

The risk of fraud can be reduced through a combination of prevention, deterrence, and detection measures. You need all three approaches as fraud involves concealment through falsification of documents or collusion among management, employees, or third parties. Of the three approaches, it is important to place a strong emphasis on fraud prevention, which may reduce opportunities for fraud to take place, and fraud deterrence, which motivates individuals to not commit fraud because of the likelihood of detection and punishment. Moreover, based on numerous studies, prevention and deterrence measures are much less costly than the time and expense required for fraud detection and investigation.

This chapter will focus on the holistic prevention and deterrence measures a company can initiate, while Chapter 12 will focus on the precise antifraud measures for each specific project fraud type (as defined in Chapter 4). The overall antifraud measures an organization can initiate are:

- Code of conduct (Section 11.2)
- Vigilant investigation and follow through (Section 11.3)
- Antifraud training (Section 11.4)
- Whistle-blowing program (Section 11.5)
- Part 1: The power of anonymous employee assessments (Section 11.6)
- Part 2: Establishing an anonymous employee assessment (Section 11.7)
- Complete regular audits (Section 11.8)
- Purchase fidelity insurance (Section 11.9)

11.2 Code of Conduct

Research suggests that the most effective way to implement measures to reduce wrongdoing is to base them on a set of core values that are embraced by the entity. This provides a platform on which a more detailed code of conduct can be constructed, giving more specific guidance about permitted and prohibited behavior, based on applicable laws and the organization's values. Management needs to clearly articulate that all employees will be held accountable to act within the organization's code of conduct.[1] Therefore, a code of conduct should not only be developed, but then signed by the CEO of the organization to allocate the appropriate sponsorship.

Once a code of conduct is written, it must be communicated to employees and preferably explained using training courses. Once employees reasonably understand the code, they should be required to confirm their responsibilities periodically. That not only reinforces the policy, but also deters individuals from committing fraud. Such confirmation may include statements that the individual understands the entity's expectations, has complied with the code of conduct, and is not aware of any violations of the code of conduct other than those the individual lists in his or her response. While people with low integrity may not hesitate to sign a false confirmation, most people will want to avoid making a false statement in writing.

The code of conduct should include the following categories:

- General employee conduct
- Conflicts of interest
- Outside activities, employment, and directorships
- Relationships with clients and suppliers
- Gifts, entertainment, and favors
- Kickbacks and secret commissions
- Organization funds and other assets
- Organization records and communications

- Dealing with outside people and organizations
- Prompt communications
- Privacy and confidentiality

A general code of conduct could be supported through a fraud policy that further stipulates:[1]

1. Definitions of misconduct and dishonesty (see Chapter 4 for a definition of each project fraud type)
2. Organizational policy and responsibilities regarding reporting suspected misconduct
3. Deterrence and detection responsibilities of individuals with supervisory or review responsibility
4. Policy specifying the responsibility and authority related to the investigation of incidents of misconduct and dishonesty
5. General procedures for the follow-up and investigation of reported incidents
6. A statement that questions or otherwise clarifies the fraud policy and its related responsibilities should be addressed to the corporation's chief counsel

11.3 Vigilant Investigation and Follow Through

A prime deterrent is to have a solid incident response program to investigate suspected wrongdoing and the organizational fortitude to take action against organizational wrongdoers. An employee who knows that he or she will not only be investigated but also terminated (or worse, passed on to the local authorities) is more prone to not commit the crime.

As to the incident response program, a plan with accountabilities must be set for the following organizational departments to work together: legal, internal audit, and human resources.

With accountabilities established, associated department members should complete training to ensure that their roles are understood and that a timely response will ensue. A case management system should be deployed to track investigations and help identify patterns. This system could be as simple as an Excel spreadsheet or as advanced as a database tool specifically designed for investigations (i.e., Magnum Case Management by Paisley Consulting [www.paisleyconsulting.com] or CaseMap by CaseSoft [www.casesoft.com]). Once the investigation is completed, regardless if fraud is detected, the internal controls in that suspected area should be closely scrutinized and improved, if needed.

With the incident response program in place and the appropriate parties trained, communication becomes the driving factor separating a good deterrent from a great deterrent. This communication falls into three categories:

1. *Incident program in place* — Just knowing that suspected wrongdoing will be investigated is enough to stop most people from committing project fraud.
2. *Consequences* — For example, a strong statement from management that dishonest actions will not be tolerated and that violators may be terminated and referred to the appropriate authorities clearly establishes consequences and can be a valuable deterrent to wrongdoing.
3. *Let everyone else know* — If wrongdoing occurs and an employee is disciplined, it can be helpful to communicate that fact, on a no-name basis, in an employee newsletter or other regular communication to employees. Seeing that other people have been disciplined for wrongdoing can be an effective deterrent, increasing the perceived likelihood of violators being caught and punished. It also can demonstrate that the entity is committed to an environment of high ethical standards and integrity.

11.4 Antifraud Training

New employees should be trained about the entity's values and its code of conduct at the time of hiring. This training should explicitly cover expectations of all employees regarding (1) their duty to communicate certain matters, (2) a list of the types of matters (including actual or suspected fraud) to be communicated along with specific examples, and (3) information on how to communicate those matters. There also should be an affirmation from senior management regarding employee expectations and communication responsibilities. Such training should include an element of "fraud awareness," the tone of which should be positive but nonetheless stress that fraud can be costly (and detrimental in other ways) to the entity and its employees. Below are links to various fraud-related training:

Case studies on ethical behavior to help employees understand what constitutes fraud (free) — http://www.aicpa.org/antifraud/ business_industry_govt/leading_corporate_governance/ understand_ethic_behavior/homepage.htm

How fraud hurts you and your organization training video series (free) — http://www.aicpa.org/antifraud/training/homepage.htm

Anti-Fraud Resource Center (free) — http://www.aicpa.org/antifraud/ homepage.htm

Association of Certified Fraud Examiners Bookstore — http:// marketplace.cfenet.com/products/products.asp

11.5 Whistle-Blowing Program

Most companies today have a hotline to place anonymous phone calls about fraud and other misconduct such as sexual harassment. Sarbanes-Oxley not only makes it mandatory but also provides civil and criminal remedies to vindicate employees suffering adverse job actions because of their assistance in investigating an employer's perceived violations of securities and other laws (Section 806). Further, Sarbanes-Oxley assigns responsibility to a public company's audit committee for overseeing the internal complaint process relating to charges affecting the integrity of financial reporting.

Therefore, whistle-blowing programs can be effective tools in the detection of fraud. Keep in mind that such programs can be the *best* detector of fraud in an organization. According to the Association of Certified Fraud Examiners' 2002 Report to the Nation,[2] for example, roughly 45 percent of fraud is detected through employee and business partner tips.

11.6 Part One: The Power of Anonymous Employee Assessments

While whistle-blower programs exist (as noted above), a growing concern by companies and their management is the stiff penalties for being found in violation of the new antiretaliation laws in the whistle-blower legislation of Sarbanes-Oxley. Section 806 creates an employee's right to sue a company for any attempt to "discharge, demote, suspend, threaten, harass, or in any other manner discriminate against" him or her for providing information on potential fraud and wrongdoings at a company.

Many companies set up a disclosure process that forces an employee to go "through reporting channels" as the first method of dealing with fraud disclosures. However, that process can prove to be problematic as it has the potential to put both the employee making the report as well as the manager receiving the fraud disclosure at risk. After disclosing a wrongdoing, the employee usually becomes hypersensitized to possible retaliatory measures, and as a result, the manager is now put in the position of having to defend raises, promotions, and other management actions as being appropriate for that particular employee.

To combat these issues when setting up such a program, it is best to keep certain fundamental principles in mind:[2]

- Keep the reporting process completely anonymous and above suspicion of compromise.
- Set up a "neutral group" that can receive, investigate, and report to the audit committee on fraud-related matters.
- Be proactive in the search for fraud throughout the company.

To accomplish the above, web tools have been developed that will send environmental scanning surveys to a statistically valid employee population. These surveys capitalize on the fact that people, not financial statements and computers, commit fraud given that many employees want to share what they know about organizational control issues. Therefore, the tools help tap into the valuable information on fraud detection that often comes from workers, not databases, extending data analysis beyond lifeless financial and transactional data and into the vibrant data stores in employees' and business partners' minds. Not only does this form of analysis broaden the organization's risk and control awareness, but gathering information from a large number of people can also increase the predictability and confidence levels of the assessment.

As Toby Bishop, President of the ACFE, notes,[2] "Yet when it comes to 'management override' and financial statement fraud, the 1987 COSO frame-work is short on details and does not reflect the results of fraud prevention and detection research conducted in the past sixteen years. For example, anecdotal evidence suggests that evaluations currently being conducted do not generally use extensive employee survey techniques that research has found can be effective in uncovering environments conducive to financial statement fraud. If we want to tell the difference between ethics programs that really work and those that are merely a corporate fig leaf, such modern and thorough techniques are vital."

Although such tips are the most common way of detecting fraud, the unfortunate reality is that tips rely on employees feeling compelled enough to come forward — overcoming their fear of retaliation — to contact the company's whistle-blower system. Employees do this knowing that if an investigation ensues, they will need to provide more details and probably their identity. Instead of waiting for the phone to ring, organizations should take a preemptive approach by surveying employees in an anonymous fashion that:

■ *Pushes surveys to employees* — Many websites and advertisers have learned that pushing key content to their audiences is more effective than waiting for them to come and get it. Likewise, people are more likely to respond to an anonymous survey that is sent to them than they are to utilize the internal whistle-blower procedure.

■ *Teaches employees about controls* — Survey questions may educate employees about good internal control structures and practices.

■ *Deters fraud* — Employees may be less likely to commit fraud when they know that a survey system exists. This is especially true when employees know it is completely anonymous.

■ *Reveals trends* — Employee viewpoints of internal control can be analyzed for trends over time, across departments, by location, or by many other criteria.

■ *Complements whistle-blower results* — The results from the analysis could be trended against results of whistle-blower activities to improve the reliability of the whistle-blower procedure and better identify areas for investigation.

■ *Increases level of assurance* — Responses to internal control checklists can be based on questioning both senior management and a representative sample of the organization.

11.7 Part 2: Establishing an Anonymous Employee Assessment

Surveys are therefore superb information-gathering tools when properly designed. Organizations looking to do so should develop and deliver surveys based on a two-step process.[3]

11.7.1 Step 1: Design and Launch the Survey

The first step in survey design is to create a survey development team made up of subject-matter experts from different business functions and with different perspectives. This team will ensure that the survey will be rich in content and have everyone's endorsement. In many cases, it may not be necessary to design a survey from scratch. Many appropriate survey items, including complete surveys, are available through public and private organizations. However, these surveys should be customized to be relevant to the organization. Below are some considerations for the survey design.[3]

■ *Be clear* — Ensure that everyone on the survey development team agrees on the meaning of the survey items. Items that are overly wordy, too complex, or have multiple meanings will not yield accurate information. The following is from an actual internal controls survey: "*My manager encourages us to learn about good internal controls, so we keep doing what we did right and stop doing what we did wrong.*" Even if respondents understand this question, what can be done to improve the situation if the results reveal that the organization has a compliance gap? To avoid this, create a focus group of potential respondents whose job it will be to agree on the meaning of each survey item.

■ *Use proper syntax* — Do not ask questions that use modifiers such as "usually" or "most of the time." These terms will render the results of the question useless because it is not clear how all respondents will interpret them. How frequent is "usually"?

■ *Keep it simple* — Do not include more than one issue in a survey item. When issues are combined, there is no way to determine the degree to which respondents are referring to one issue or the other.

■ *Keep it short* — One question that is always on a survey design frequently asked questions (FAQ) list is "How long should surveys be?" The answer is that shorter surveys work best because they generate higher response rates and allow auditors to survey employees more often. Performing frequent surveys, in turn, will yield useful trend data. It is easier to convince employees to take a monthly twenty-item survey than a monthly hundred-question survey.

■ *Communicate often* — It is important to communicate candidly with employees or potential respondents about the purpose of the survey. The survey should explain what will be done with the results and how improvement efforts that result from the survey will be reported back to employees. Skepticism about surveys is natural, so organizations should create a climate of openness in which management listens to employees' opinions and suggestions and is willing to share successes as well as failures.

■ *Use a web-based platform to launch the survey and disseminate results* — A web-based survey has three advantages: (1) because software and related upgrades are not required, respondents only need a web browser; (2) the survey process can be managed internally or through an outside party; and (3) the survey solution can deliver timely reports. A sample product that can be used in this regard is Compliance Sight (http://www.pcg-sox2002.com/compliancesight.htm), a web-based survey tool with extensive reporting capabilities (see Figures 11.1 and 11.2).

People View

Home

Fraud Assessment

Sarbanes-Oxley Act-2002

Section 3 Of 14

Billing Schemes

	Yes	No
1. Are you aware of any employee setting up a fictitious organization on the Company's books for use in paying phony invoices?	☐	☐
2. Are you aware of any employee intentionally mishandling a vendor payment in	☐	☐

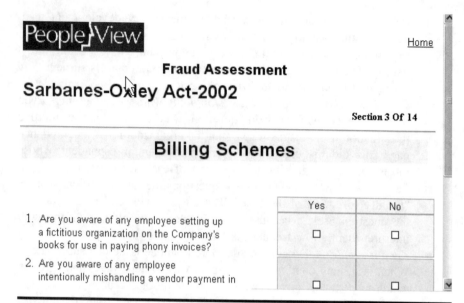

Figure 11.1. Web-Based Survey Questions.

FAVORABILITY INDEX

Result Based on **501** Surveys

Back

BY CATEGORY

Billing Schemes

QUESTIONS	In Compliance	Caution	Non Compliance
1. Are you aware of any employee setting up a fictitious organization on the Company's books for use in paying phony invoices?[Go]	95.4%	0%	4.6%
2. Are you aware of any employee intentionally mishandling a vendor payment in order to make a fictitious payment to himself/herself or another employee?[Go]	95.4%	0%	4.6%
3. Are you aware of any employee making a personal purchase using a Company account such as a procurement or credit card?[Go]	95.4%	0%	4.6%

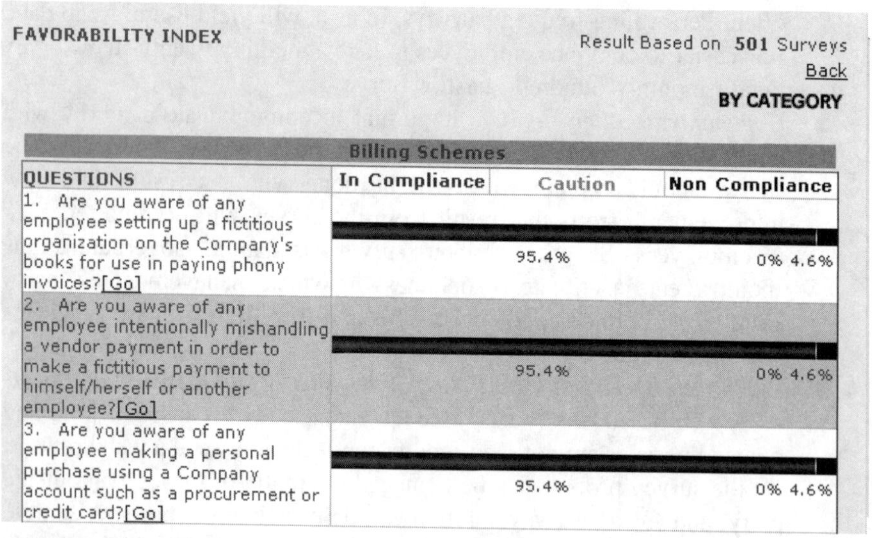

Figure 11.2. Web-Based Favorability Report.

11.7.2 Step 2: Analyze Results Through Several "Lenses"

It is helpful to examine survey data from many perspectives or through many "lenses." Continually ask questions such as "What does this mean?" or "What are the data telling us?" This process could involve an internal dialogue or a focus group that explores survey outcomes in more detail. Below are a few examples of perspectives.

- *Through comparisons* — Look at differences between demographic groups. Are there problems that are unique to some business units or departments? What could be causing these differences? Also, compare and contrast scores between entities and against the organization over-all, using the organization's averages as a baseline. If an entity scores below the organization's average, what is it telling auditors? Is it a management, cultural, training, systems, or business process issue?
- *Through comments* — Employee comments are extremely useful in validating and explaining the survey scores. People are very candid when they have assurances of confidentiality and anonymity. For example, suppose one of the areas being assessed is "conflicts of interest." Low scores may tell auditors there is a problem, but they will not explain the specific nature of that problem. Reviewing comments that are associated with this issue can illuminate those poor scores. Look for a survey application that has a lexical search engine that can quickly find all words or phrases related to a topic. Skimming, stealing, and larceny may all mean the same thing to respondents who are not well versed in fraud terminology. Searching for all three at once may provide quick answers to auditors.
- *Through trending* — Comparing one entity to another entity is useful, but the most important comparisons will be those that are internal to an entity. How well is the entity performing this quarter compared with last quarter? If the entity still needs to improve in an area, is the trend positive or negative? Annual fraud or compliance assessments have little value because they only tell auditors what they should have known months before. When appropriate, monthly or quarterly surveys can reveal how the organization is performing, quickly notify auditors when a problem arises, and show improvement trends.

11.8 Complete Regular Audits

Audits, whether completed by internal or external auditors, can be both a de-tection and a deterrence measure. Auditors can assist in the deterrence of fraud by examining and evaluating the adequacy and the effectiveness of the system of internal control. In carrying out this responsibility, auditors should, for example, determine whether:

- The organizational environment fosters control consciousness.
- Realistic organizational goals and objectives are set.
- Written policies (e.g., code of conduct) exist that describe prohibited activities and the action required whenever violations are discovered.
- Appropriate authorization policies for transactions are established and maintained.
- Policies, practices, procedures, reports, and other mechanisms are developed to monitor activities and safeguard assets, particularly in high-risk areas.
- Communication channels provide management with adequate and reliable information.
- Recommendations need to be made for the establishment or enhancement of cost-effective controls to help deter fraud.

To effectuate the above, auditors may conduct proactive auditing to search for corruption, misappropriation of assets, and financial statement fraud. This may include the use of computer-assisted audit techniques to detect particular types of fraud. Auditors also can employ analytical and other procedures to isolate anomalies and perform detailed reviews of high-risk accounts and transactions to identify potential financial statement fraud.

As to who should complete the audit, a few considerations should be taken into account:

- Independent/external auditors hold a great deal of industry experience and financial statement account analysis understanding.
- Internal auditors usually are more focused on operational issues and understanding how to operate within the culture of the organization.
- Certified fraud examiners can provide extensive knowledge and experience about fraud that may not be available within a corporation. They can provide more objective input into management's evaluation of the risk of fraud (especially fraud involving senior management, such as financial statement fraud) and the development of appropriate antifraud controls that are less vulnerable to management override.

Regardless of who completes the audit, just "knowing someone is watching" is a great deterrent against the occurrence of fraud, even if nothing is ever detected.

11.9 Purchase Fidelity Insurance

When all else fails, there is fidelity insurance. Fidelity insurance covers loss of property due to an employee's dishonesty, as well as a suspicious loss of property that cannot be directly attributed to a particular employee. Coverage usually extends to losses of property due to theft, embezzlement, forgery, and computer crimes. Generally, the policy will cover the loss of property while on the business's premises, as well as while the property is in transit or otherwise temporarily in another location. Because policies differ in these respects, and because employee dishonesty can take many forms, a thorough reading of the proposed policy, in advance, is required to determine the scope of any exclusions.

The risk of loss due to fraud and other forms of dishonesty can never be completely eliminated. Organizations can finance the potential loss either by purchasing fidelity insurance coverage or by self-insuring the risk (absorbing out-of-pocket any losses incurred). It is generally recommended to purchase some fidelity insurance, especially in situations with significant risk or potential loss. In reality, however, many organizations choose the self-insurance default because they either fail to assess the risk and its financial impact or they are simply unfamiliar with fidelity insurance.

11.10 Summary

The purpose of this chapter was to highlight the overarching fraud reduction strategies an organization can take that have impacts in not only the project arena but in every other area in the organization. The key is to prevent fraud before it occurs by having proactive detection techniques (i.e., anonymous tip lines) along with deterrence measures (i.e., regular fraud audits). Such practices are always less costly than an investigation and can effectively stop fraud before it ever starts.

Questions

11.1   What is the definition of fraud prevention and fraud deterrence?
11.2   What are the key categories of a company's code of conduct?
11.3   What are the three types of training that should be considered in any fraud training program?
11.4   To improve on whistle-blowing, what steps should be taken by the organization?

11.5   What type of insurance can be used to insure against fraud?

11.6   The risk of fraud can be reduced through a combination of prevention, deterrence, and detection measures. True or false?

11.7   Sarbanes-Oxley assigns responsibility to a public company's audit committee for overseeing the internal complaint process relating to charges affecting the integrity of financial reporting. True or false?

11.8   Many companies set up a disclosure process that forces an employee to go "through reporting channels" as the first method of dealing with fraud disclosures. However, that process can prove to be problematic as it has the potential for putting both the employee making the report as well as the manager receiving the fraud disclosure at risk. True or false?

References

1. American Institute of Certified Public Accountants, SAS 99, Consideration of Fraud in a Financial Statement Audit, Auditing Standards Board, 2002.
2. Association of Certified Fraud Examiners, 2002 Report to the Nation on Occupational Fraud and Abuse, Association of Certified Fraud Examiners, 2002.
3. Lanza, Richard B., IT Audit, Proactive Control Monitoring, 2003.

Specific Responses to Key Project Fraud Risks with Prevention and Detection Procedures

12.1 Specific Control Activities

As Chapter 11 focused on the general fraud reduction methodologies, this chapter focuses on the specific prevention and detection techniques to combat each fraud scheme within the project fraud subgroup of the Association of Certified Fraud Examiners' (ACFE) classification system (see Chapter 4 for a further discussion of each subgroup).

In essence, this chapter focuses on control activities that are defined by the Committee of Sponsoring Organizations as:[1]

> Control activities are the policies and procedures that help ensure management directives are carried out. They help ensure that necessary actions are taken to address risks to achievement of the entity's objectives. Control activities occur throughout the organization, at all levels and in all functions. They include a range of activities as diverse as approvals, authorizations, verifications, reconciliations, reviews of operating performance, security of assets and segregation of duties.

12.2 A Recap on the Project Fraud Categories

Project fraud, as further defined in Chapter 4, was segregated into the following subgroups. In this chapter, for each of the subgroups below, the specific control activities will be identified to help reduce their occurrence:

1. Fraudulent Statements >> Nonfinancial >> Internal Documents
2. Fraudulent Statements >> Financial >> Asset/Revenue Overstatements >> Improper Asset Valuations
3. Fraudulent Statements >> Financial >> Asset/Revenue Overstatements >> Concealed Liabilities and Expenses
4. Corruption >> Bribery
5. Corruption >> Conflicts of Interest
6. Asset Misappropriation >> Cash >> Fraudulent Disbursements >> Expense Reimbursement Schemes
7. Asset Misappropriation >> Cash >> Fraudulent Disbursements >> Payroll Schemes
8. Asset Misappropriation >> Cash >> Fraudulent Disbursements >> Billing Schemes
9. Asset Misappropriation >> Inventory and Other Assets >> Misuse

12.3 Specific Fraud Prevention: Fraud Types #1, 2, and 3

These three fraud subgroups have been combined as they are interrelated. More specifically, by projects providing overreported benefits in a business case or a project status that is inflated (all internal documents), the company's accounting function may assess the value of a project more so than they should.

To help prevent this fraud, the following control activities are suggested:

- *Business case quality gate analysis* — Business cases should be developed using consistent and specific guidelines. Only through such a unified process can a consistent result ensue. Further, by establishing quality gates and a standard review process using a cross-functional team, business cases can be put to the test prior to acceptance and continuation.
- *Project status audits* — Either using the program management office or an audit function, projects should be detail reviewed with an observation of cost, quality, and schedule progress. Specialists could be

considered for this project to assist in assessing the completion of deliverables, especially their quality. This process can be supplemented with an anonymous reporting system for a health status viewpoint from the project team (see Chapter 11 for anonymous reporting systems).

- *Project accounting audit* — Aside from assessing the status of a project, the actual books and records should be reviewed by a competent accountant to ensure that expenses are recorded in the financial statements completely, accurately, and in a timely manner.

12.4 Specific Fraud Prevention: Fraud Types #4 and 5

Given the high occurrence of project team member outsourcing and need for other material resources, there is an increased opportunity for bribery and conflicts of interest on projects. There are a host of control activities that can be instituted to increase the likelihood of detecting these frauds:

- *Bribery prevention policy*[2] — The prevention of the use of bribery schemes can be difficult. The primary resource for heading off this complex act is a company policy that specifically addresses the problems and illegalities associated with bribery and related offenses. The purpose of the policy is to make the position of the company absolutely clear. The absence of a clear policy leaves an opportunity for a perpetrator to rationalize a bribe or related offense or to claim ignorance to the wrongdoing. Examples of bribery prevention policies are given below:
  - ☐ *Gifts* — No employee or member of his immediate family shall solicit or accept from an actual or prospective customer or supplier any compensation, advance loans (except from established financial institutions on the same basis as other customers), gifts, entertainment, or other favors that are of more than token value or that the employee would not normally be in a position to reciprocate under normal expense account procedures. Under no circumstances should a gift or entertainment be accepted that would influence the employee's judgment. In particular, employees must avoid any interest in or benefit from any supplier that could reasonably cause them to favor that supplier over others.
  - ☐ *Reporting gifts* — An employee who receives, or whose family member receives, an unsolicited gift prohibited by these guidelines should report it to his supervisor and either return it to the person making

the gift or, in the case of a perishable gift, give it to a nonprofit charitable organization.

☐ *Business meetings* — Entertainment and services offered by a supplier or customer may be accepted by an employee when they are associated with a business meeting and the supplier or customer provides them to others as a normal part of its business. Examples of such entertainment and services are transportation to and from the supplier's or customer's place of business, hospitality suites, golf outings, lodging at the supplier's or customer's place of business, and business lunches and dinners for business visitors to the supplier's or customer's location. The services should generally be of the type normally used by the company's employees and allowable under the applicable company's expense account.

■ *Material vendor code of conduct* — Vendors providing material product or services to the company should be asked to sign a statement that they are unaware of any conflicts of interest between them and the company. This could be a part of the standard contract with the vendor. The precise language could be molded from the company's code of conduct statements that generally have specific language associated with conflicts of interest and bribes.

■ *Specific review of material vendors* — Vendors providing material product or services to the company should be specifically reviewed to determine if any conflicts of interest could be identified in the company's history or current employee makeup. For example, a Dun & Bradstreet report could be run on the vendor to review the key owners of the company, which could be cross-related to the company's list of officers; more specifically the project sponsorship. Further, the actual invoices and project deliverables provided by the vendor could be reviewed to determine:

☐ Are materials being ordered at the optimal reorder point? Are they often made from the same vendor?

☐ Is the quality of product received from certain vendors under a normally acceptable range?

☐ Are the established bidding policies being followed or are rules being broken for certain vendors?

☐ Are the costs of materials out of line in relation to other marketplace vendors?

■ *Anonymous reporting and exit interviews*[2] — Exit interviews or other anonymous reporting programs are breeding grounds for information on vendor conflicts of interest and should be reviewed with vigor. Employees are generally the first to observe that a vendor is receiving favorable treatment. Another related question that may be asked of employees is whether any vendor's service (or product) has recently become substandard.

12.5 Specific Fraud Prevention: Fraud Type #6

Expense reports are commonplace on projects as travel, entertainment, and other sundry expenses are incurred daily. The following activities can detect if fraud is occurring or, even better, deter the employee from committing the fraud in the first place:

- *Detailed expense reports submission and review*[2] — Companies should have a process that detailed expense reports be completed and require the following information:
  - ☐ Receipts or other support documentation
  - ☐ Explanation of the expense including specific business purpose
  - ☐ Time period expense occurred
  - ☐ Place of expenditure
  - ☐ Amount

  Further, expense reports should be reviewed (or at least sample tested) to ensure their accuracy, completeness, and proper authorizations prior to payment.

- *Review and analysis of expense accounts* — Generally, expense account review uses one of two methods: historical comparisons or comparisons with budgeted amounts. An historical comparison compares the balance expended this period in relation to the balance spent in prior, similar periods. Budgets are estimates of the money and/or time necessary to complete the task. They are based on past experience with consideration for current and future business conditions. Therefore, when comparing actual and budgeted expenses, determining inordinate expenses or inaccurate budget estimates is important. Likewise, when reviewing for historical trends, an understanding of changes in the company's business is paramount.

12.6 Specific Fraud Prevention: Fraud Type #7

In payroll schemes, the concern is that payments are being made to employees that do not exist on the payroll or are being made in excess of what they should be for the hours worked by the employee. Below are the specific control activities to combat this fraud:[2]

- *Independent payroll distribution* — Ghost-employee schemes can be uncovered by having personnel (other than the payroll department) distribute the payroll checks and by requiring positive identification of the payee.
- *Analysis of payee address or accounts* — If payroll checks are either mailed or deposited automatically, then a list of duplicate addresses or deposit accounts may reveal ghost employees or duplicate payments.
- *Duplicate Social Security numbers* — Because each employee is required to have a Social Security number, a listing of duplicate numbers may reveal ghost employees.
- *Overtime authorization* — Requiring employees to have overtime authorized by a supervisor, having the supervisor be responsible for the time cards, and having the supervisor refer the time cards directly to payroll will aid in reducing overtime abuses.
- *Payroll expense analysis* — The payroll department (or audit function) should scan the time reports and question overtime or high hours charged by employees. Further, an expense analysis by employee could be run (more than likely using a computerized report) to identify high proportionate increases in employee payments.

12.7 Specific Fraud Prevention: Fraud Type #8

Billing schemes occur when a fraudster causes the victim organization to issue a payment by submitting invoices for fictitious goods or services, inflated invoices, or invoices for personal purchases.[2] The following is a list of billing scheme prevention methods that may be helpful in the detection of billing schemes:

- *Independent authorization* — If there is an independent authorization of expenses that is followed by the organization, such practices should detect false billings to the company. This assumes, of course, that the person approving the invoice is not in collusion with the fraudster.
- *Employee to vendor address match* — Vendor addresses, telephone numbers, and/or tax identification numbers can be matched to employee information to determine whether the employee has established themselves as a vendor.
- *Company search* — When establishing the vendor for payment, a Dun & Bradstreet or comparable report should be run to identify any false vendors added to the system for payments.

■ *Abnormal spend* — Vendor purchases should be analyzed for abnormal levels on both a monthly and yearly basis. Any material fraud should be detected in these abnormal patterns.

12.8 Specific Fraud Prevention: Fraud Type #9

Inventory or other project assets are generally used by the project team throughout the project. Therefore, there is a high potential for such assets to be stolen or just misused (i.e., personal use of computer equipment for other company reasons). The following basic control activities should be employed by the organization to reduce this incidence of fraud:

■ *Physical security* — It goes without saying that valuable assets should be secured commensurate to the value of the goods.

■ *Independent counts* — Counts of material dollar assets should be performed by employees whose functions are independent of the physical custody of these assets. This should be performed on a periodic basis and done by surprise (rather than on a consistent schedule).

■ *Asset change review* — An analytical review of inventory or other assets should be performed to determine whether there is a resulting shrink in the asset balances between time frames. Any noticeable change should prompt a control review or, at a minimum, an independent count of the goods.

12.9 Utilizing Technology To Proactively Detect Fraud

Although occupational fraud takes various forms, the results are always the same: The numbers generated by fraud cannot hold up to the unfailing logic of the accounting equation. If executives add false sales and accounts receivable to increase the organization's revenue, profits and cash will be out of kilter. The advancement of technology[3] has systemized this "accounting equation" into computer logic and applied it to company data, according to Joseph Wells, chairman of the ACFE.

The above concept can be applied to the project fraud prevention techniques discussed in this chapter to automate and otherwise allow for 100 percent testing of transactional data underlying the project. This computer logic could take the form of simply matching the human resource file to the accounts payable vendor master file to look for phony vendors established by employees. On the other side of the coin, this logic could be an advanced neural network application focused on detecting money laundering schemes across projects. Regardless of whether it is simple or advanced, data analysis provides many benefits in the prevention and detection of fraud.

To that end, the Institute of Internal Auditors Research Foundation recently released "Proactively Detecting Occupational Fraud Using Computer Audit Reports" (http://www.theiia.org/ecm/iiarf.cfm?doc_id=4248), a free on-line document designed to assist internal auditors, fraud examiners, and management in implementing computer data analysis routines to improve occupational fraud prevention and detection. The full report provides:

- A step-by-step process for implementing audit software from the assessment of risk to the ultimate application of software routines.
- A comprehensive checklist of data analysis reports that are associated with each occupational fraud category based on the ACFE's uniform occupational fraud classification system (including all of the project fraud subgroups).
- A report description and data file(s) needed to effectuate each identified report.

12.10 Summary

The purpose of this chapter was to define the specific fraud prevention techniques to reduce and/or detect project fraud subgroups. In summary, a majority of the controls make good business sense and are not costly additional controls. Some controls, such as specific reviews and audits may cost the organization, but do provide a level of comfort that projects are progressing well and unfettered by fraud — a priceless benefit.

Questions

12.1   What is the definition of control activities?

12.2   What are the three fraud prevention techniques to combat inflated asset fraud?

12.3   How can a fraud payroll scheme be detected?

12.4   Other than independent counts, how can inventory misuse be detected?

12.5   Which association has produced a detailed report on computer techniques to proactively detect fraud?

12.6   Either using the program management office or an audit function, projects should be detail reviewed with an observation of cost, quality, and schedule progress. True or false?

12.7   Given the high occurrence of project team member outsourcing and the need for other material resources, there is an increased opportunity for bribery and conflicts of interest on projects. True or false?

12.8   The prevention of the use of bribery schemes can be difficult. The primary resource for heading off this complex act is a company policy that specifically addresses the problems and illegalities associated with bribery and related offenses. True or false?

12.9   Vendors providing material product or services to the company should be asked to sign a statement that they are unaware of any conflicts of interest between them and the company. True or false?

12.10   Exit interviews or other anonymous reporting programs are breeding grounds for information on vendor conflicts of interest and should be reviewed with vigor. Employees are generally the first to observe if a vendor is receiving favorable treatment. True or false?

References

1. American Institute of Certified Public Accountants, Internal Control — Integrated Framework, Committee of Sponsoring Organizations, 1992.
2. Wells, Joseph T., *Occupational Fraud and Abuse*, Hyperion Publishing, 2001.
3. Lanza, Richard B., IT Audit, Detecting Occupational Fraud Using Computer Audit Reports, 2003.

Utilizing the Audit Function/Program Management Office for Fraud Prevention and Detection While Maximizing Project Investments

13.1 Getting It Done, Establishing Roles

With the deliverables and tasks defined in Chapters 11 and 12 (general and specific fraud reduction measures), all that is left is to identify who is best fit to perform each step. This chapter will focus on defining those roles in general and assigning them to the reduction measures. The roles are as follows:

- Management
- Program management office (PMO) and project management
- Internal audit/external audit
- Fraud examiner

13.2 Management

In this section, management refers to the business owners that sponsor the project and who are the ultimate recipients of the project deliverables. From a project perspective, the business sponsor role is most prevalent. In this case, the business sponsors need to be aware of project fraud and the telltale signs, but unfortunately may not be "close enough to the action" to see whether fraud is actually occurring.

They unfortunately may also be the drivers of fraud as their egos, political capital, etc. may be the main chip on the line when a project is under review. This pressure may lead them to approve a business case that may not hold water or adjust project financials to make a rosier picture, etc. as they would be in the best position to place pressure on the project team to achieve these aims.

13.3 Program Management Office

- Establishes the policies and procedures for project delivery and project management and project fraud
- Supports the search for fraud in the PMO data store
- Implements essential project reporting processes that support project fraud policy management
- Manages the portfolio management for review of overlaps, misalignment, improved cross-functional communication, and review of status, tracking lessons learned, risk management of company initiatives

13.4 Internal Audit/External Audit

Internal audits can play both a detection and a deterrence role.[1] Internal auditors can assist in the deterrence of fraud by their very existence which, if communicated to the project team, will keep "everyone on their toes." Similar to the feeling someone has when driving by a police officer on the road (and appropriately slowing down to the speed limit), the mere presence can have an effect. And, like the police cars that are filled with inflatable dummies, the internal auditor could do nothing more than flip through a few papers once a month in a closed room to have a deterrent effect.

Internal auditors may also conduct proactive auditing to search for corruption, misappropriation of assets, and financial statement fraud. Such auditing is best completed when done by surprise, be it at key milestone dates or in the midst of the completion of a current deliverable. Auditors are known for many traits and one clearly is their ability to sniff out risk in an independent fashion. If they are really good, they not only find the issues, but they also provide the appropriate solutions.

This core competency needs to be maximized through marketing audit services to the owners of projects and/or management. Although a top-down approach may be effective short term in getting access to projects, by marketing directly to the project team and PMO, the auditor creates a longer-term win-win relationship. In other words, executive sponsorship helps, but the reputation and skill of the auditor will "sell" the need to project teams. By helping project teams to respond to risk, they increase the project's chance of success while the auditor receives deep access within the project...more so than if they show up for a "surprise audit." This deeper access will allow for more information, when needed, for senior management.

Similar to internal auditors, external auditors can assist management and the board of directors, including the audit committee, by providing an assessment of the entity's process for identifying, assessing, and responding to the risks of fraud. The board of directors should have an open and candid dialogue with the external auditors regarding management's risk assessment process and the system of internal control. Such a dialogue should include a discussion of the vulnerability of the entity to fraudulent financial reporting and the entity's exposure to misappropriation of assets. While such discussions are not done from a project perspective (mainly at a financial statement level), it is hoped that more of a project focus will filter into such discussions with the governing bodies of organizations.

13.5 Fraud Examiner

Fraud examiners can provide extensive knowledge and experience about fraud that may not be available within a corporation. Most internal auditors (the first line of internal audit defense) may have had some fraud training, but are not expert in the aspects of fraud red flags. Further, once a fraud is identified, they generally lack the skills to complete a full investigation.

Therefore, fraud examiners can provide more objective and comprehensive input into management's evaluation of the risk of fraud (especially fraud involving senior management, such as financial statement fraud) and the development of appropriate antifraud controls that are less vulnerable to management override. Certified fraud examiners also conduct professional examinations using established guidelines to resolve allegations or suspicions of fraud, reporting either to an appropriate level of management or to the audit committee or board of directors, depending on the nature of the issue and the level of personnel involved.

13.6 General Fraud Prevention

With a general understanding of the roles of each party described above, suggested primary and secondary role assignments are applied to the general fraud reduction strategies in Table 13.1 (as discussed further in Chapter 11).

Table 13.1   Role Assignments in Fraud Reduction

General Strategy	Management	PMO	Internal/ External Auditor	Fraud Examiner
Code of Conduct: Clear articulation of the company's set of core values so that they may be confirmed by employees.	P	S	S	S
Vigilant Investigation and Follow Through: Incidence response program and organizational fortitude to take action against wrongdoers in the company.	S	S	S	P
Antifraud Training: (1) Training on an employee's duty to communicate certain matters; (2) a list of the types of matters, including actual or suspected fraud, to be communicated along with specific examples; and (3) information on how to communicate those matters.	S	S	S	P
Whistle-Blowing Program: Hotline to place anonymous phone calls about fraud and other misconduct such as sexual harassment.	P	S	S	S
Anonymous Employee Assessments: Proactive anonymous surveying of employees to assess the perception toward fraud and to identify whether it is occurring in the organization.	S	P	S	S
Complete Regular Audits: Regular reviews tailored depending on the nature of the project mix and suspected wrongdoing to act as a detection and deterrent measure.	S	S	P	S
Purchase Fidelity Insurance: Insurance to protect an organization against loss due to fraud.	P	S	S	S

13.7 Roles for Specific Fraud Risk Responses

With a general understanding of the roles of each party described above, suggested primary and secondary role assignments are applied to the specific fraud reduction strategies in Table 13.2 (as discussed further in Chapter 12).

Table 13.2 Specific Fraud Risk Roles

General Strategy	Management	PMO	Internal/ External Auditor	Fraud Examiner
Project Fraud Types 1, 2, and 3: Internal Documents/Improper Asset Valuations/ Concealed Liabilities and Expenses				
Business Case Quality Gate Analysis: Consistent business case development and review.	S	P	S	S
Project Status Audits: Detailed reviews of project schedule, cost, and quality.	S	P	S	S
Project Accounting Audit: Project books and records are reviewed by a competent accountant to ensure that expenses are recorded in the financial statements completely, accurately, and in a timely manner.	S	S	P	S
Project Fraud Types 4 and 5: Bribery and Conflicts of Interest Project Fraud Risk Assessment				
Bribery Prevention Policy: Policy statement confirmed by employees clearly articulating the company's position toward bribery.	P	S	S	S
Material Vendor Code of Conduct: Vendor confirmation of no conflicts of interest with the company.	P	S	S	S
Specific Review of Material Vendors: Independent review of material dollar vendors to assess the existence of conflicts of interest.	S	S	P	S
Anonymous Reporting and Exit Interviews: Utilize anonymous reporting channels or exit interviews with employees dealing with vendors to identify any vendor conflicts of interest.	S	S	S	P

Table 13.2   Specific Fraud Risk Roles (continued)

General Strategy	Management	PMO	Internal/ External Auditor	Fraud Examiner
Project Fraud Type 6: Expense Reimbursement Schemes				
Detailed Expense Reports Submission and Review: Requiring detailed information be provided with all expense reports.	P	S	S	S
Review and Analysis of Expense Accounts: Independent review of expense report documentation for errors and irregularities.	S	S	P	S
Project Fraud Type 7: Payroll Schemes				
Independent Payroll Distribution: Distribution of payroll checks by person(s) independent of the line management.	S	P	S	S
Analysis of Payee Address or Accounts: Review of employee addresses for duplication and irregularities.	S	S	P	S
Duplicate Social Security Numbers: Identification of possible ghost employees through the symptom of duplicate Social Security numbers.	S	S	P	S
Overtime Authorization: Ensure management independently approves all employee overtime.	P	S	S	S
Payroll Expense Analysis: Independent analysis of regular and overtime payroll payments.	S	S	P	S
Project Fraud Type 8: Billing Schemes				
Independent Authorization: Ensure management independently approves all invoices.	P	S	S	S
Employee to Vendor Address Match: Match vendor to employee addresses to identify phony vendor accounts.	S	S	P	S
Company Search: Review of vendor list to independent databases to identify phony vendors.	P	S	S	S
Abnormal Spend: Assess total and trajectory of spending to vendors for potential irregularities.	S	S	P	S

Table 13.2   Specific Fraud Risk Roles (continued)

General Strategy	Management	PMO	Internal/ External Auditor	Fraud Examiner
Project Fraud Type 9: Inventory and Other Assets Misuse				
Physical Security: Ensure physical security for all assets.	P	S	S	S
Independent Counts: Perform an independent physical count on a periodic basis to assess changes in assets.	S	S	P	S
Asset Change Review: Review of asset shrink for irregularities.	S	S	P	S

13.8 Summary

This chapter focused on establishing the roles for project reduction strategies both at a more general level and then, through a matrix, to each specific employee group within the organization. This matrix could be used as a responsibility assignment matrix when developing a project plan for fighting project fraud. Note that roles and company positions are two different paradigms as an auditor and fraud examiner may be one person in the company or may be in completely separate departments.

Questions

13.1   Who unfortunately may be in the best position to start the project fraud ball rolling?

13.2   Who has the most extensive knowledge about fraud prevention and detection?

13.3   What role keeps "everyone on their toes"?

13.4   Who has primary responsibility for a company's whistle-blowing program?

13.5   Who has primary responsibility for independent payroll check distributions?

13.6   A general strategy for general fraud management is to create a code of conduct that clearly articulates the company's set of core values so that they may be confirmed by employees. True or false?

13.7   From a project perspective, the business sponsor role is not the most prevalent. In this case, the business sponsors do not need to be aware of project fraud or the telltale signs because they unfortunately may not be "close enough to the action" to see whether fraud is actually occurring. True or false?

13.8 Although a top-down approach may be effective short term in getting access to projects, by marketing directly to the project team and PMO, the auditor creates a longer term win-win relationship. True or false?

Reference

1. American Institute of Certified Public Accountants, SAS 99, Consideration of Fraud in a Financial Statement Audit, Auditing Standards Board, 2002.

Part 4:
Enabling the PMO
and Audit Function
to Support Corporate
and Financial
Reporting Governance

14

Defining the PMO/ Internal Audit Value Proposition for Project Fraud Prevention and Detection

14.1 Size of Projects in the Global Economy[1]

In the United States, organizations spend more than $2.3 trillion each year on projects of all sorts, according to a Project Management Institute (PMI) study. The Standish Group reports that U.S. organizations spend $275 billion annually on application software projects alone. These IT projects are loaded with risks that often lead to failure. According to a Standish Group survey, only 16 percent of technology projects are completed on time and on budget and 31 percent are cancelled altogether. Moreover, cost overruns average 189 percent of original estimates.

These alarming trends tell only half the story. Many times, customer service and employee morale and productivity suffer when projects do not produce finished products on time or when these products are delivered with minimal functionality and bugs due to poor testing. Failed projects also increase the chance of litigation between companies when they involve outside developers.

14.2 General Fraud Statistics

Of all of the studies done on fraud, the Association of Certified Fraud Examiners most probably has the best given their focus in the area and the extensiveness of their research. The Report to the Nation — 2002[2] was based on 663 occupational fraud cases that were reported by the certified fraud examiners who investigated them. In total, the cases in this study caused over $7 billion in losses.

The report focused on five areas: the cost of occupational fraud and abuse, the methodologies, the victims, the perpetrators, and the legal outcomes of fraud cases. The report presented the following conclusions:

- Certified fraud examiners estimate that 6 percent of revenues would be lost in 2002 as a result of occupational fraud and abuse. Applied to the U.S. Gross Domestic Product, this translates to losses of approximately $600 billion, or about $4,500 per employee.
- Over half of the frauds in this study caused losses of at least $100,000 and nearly one in six caused losses in excess of $1 million.
- Over 80 percent of occupational frauds involve asset misappropriations. Cash is the targeted asset 90 percent of the time.
- Corruption schemes account for 13 percent of all occupational frauds and they cause over $500,000 in losses, on average.
- Fraudulent statements are the most costly form of occupational fraud with median losses of $4.25 million per scheme.
- The average scheme in this study lasted 18 months before it was detected.
- The typical perpetrator is a first-time offender. Only 7 percent of occupational fraudsters in this study were known to have prior convictions for fraud-related offenses.
- Small businesses are the most vulnerable to occupational fraud and abuse. The average scheme in a small business causes $127,500 in losses. The average scheme in the largest companies costs $97,000.

It is most likely an impossible task to calculate the cost fraud imposes on the American economy because not all fraud is detected or reported. There is also no organization charged with accumulating data on fraud offenses and relatively few studies have been done on the subject. Given these limitations, the Report to the Nation - 2002 makes one of the best attempts to provide some insight into the magnitude of this economic issue.

14.3 What Is a PMO?

In most organizations today, the PMO is typically defined as the project management office. However PMO can define a program management office as well. There are many different labels that can be applied to what a standard

PMO should do. Our observation is this...however your organization labels your PMO-type entity, you will want to become good friends with the people who work in this group. They have your best interests in mind. PMOs are normally established to add business value to some area of the business. If you are not utilizing the PMO in your business today, you are leaving a great deal of personal value at the curb. Throughout the remainder of this book, the PMO function is considered a key component to managing for project fraud prevention and detection. In the area of project delivery, there is simply no other entity within an organization that can bring the necessary understanding and skills required in project management to facilitate successful achievement of organizational fiscal year project investment objectives.

PMOs can be anywhere in an organization where project management value is essential. Most often, PMOs are established within IT departments. Sometimes PMOs are created for the business side of the organization. Today, PMOs are rising up within corporate internal auditing departments to manage their work. This is very interesting because internal auditors are normally trained in project management. Let us assume that this is true. The next question becomes: Just how does the internal auditing PMO add value to the business? Our observation is that PMOs can be anywhere in any skill-set discipline. The PMO concept is generic in nature and value. PMOs today are found in government, healthcare, transportation, insurance, financial services, military, nonprofits, etc. Internally within the corporate organizational structure, we see PMOs in marketing, finance, human resources, IT, engineering, and plant floors. We also see enterprise PMOs that support the entire business for those businesses that understand the value proposition of project management — growing business prosperity.

14.4 Defining the PMO Value to the Business

Today, many businesses apply their PMO resources to perform many of the following actions:

1. Audit project delivery
2. Support project teams
3. Mentor project resources
4. Project performance oversight
5. Standardize development work processes to manage business risk

All of these approaches are important, but place more responsibility on the PMO than is really necessary. To determine what the correct approach (project charter) is for a PMO, let us examine first what the organizational segment (typically the enterprise) seeks to achieve in the time interval (normally the fiscal year). Given the fiscal year as a baseline, the project charter for the PMO can be determined in such a manner that helps to grow the organization it serves. If your PMO does not do this today, believe us in that the PMO is leaving large amounts of value at the table to the organization and PMO credibility each time it interacts within the organization.

14.5 Defining the PMO Value Model

The PMO project charter should contain a section on preventing and detecting project fraud and how the PMO expects to achieve this service value. Project fraud within the organization is unmeasured and unmanaged in almost every business today. Billions of business investment dollars are wasted in project investments that fail every year, particularly in IT due to someone committing project fraud or not attempting to prevent it. Retrieve the Standish Group "Chaos" Report and note that a large percentage of projects fail each year. Why? Were the root cause failures of project failure a result of project fraud? How do you know? Preventing and detecting project fraud through the PMO can seem very scary to the PMO team. They may feel like they are working in Jurassic Park given that projects are failing all around them. Actually, managing for project fraud does not have to be that difficult. Let us take a look at a typical project management community within a typical business that has 500 or more IT personnel working to support current business operations while they deliver new projects worth $30 million in the fiscal year in project investment funding. Applying today's standard workplace culture where everyone is in fear of being outsourced for someone offshore, the current workforce is highly motivated to protect their jobs. Most projects in this typical scenario have executive funding owners, a project sponsor, and a project team with a project manager and three to ten team members. If the PMO attempts to manage for project fraud detection and prevention directly with each project team and related stakeholder(s), it will exhaust its available resources and not be able to perform other vital PMO services. If the PMO applies an "outsourced" approach by self-involving the project teams in project fraud prevention and detection processes, the PMO will have to help only those teams that have problems, thus minimizing resource utilization. Additionally the PMO should seek to establish a service level agreement (SLA) with the organization's internal audit department to perform project reviews as required. Involving the internal audit department removes the PMO from being perceived as the "project police" and helps the PMO sell itself as the "best friend" of the project team. After all, don't PMOs want to be happy and successful? This is the key premise in the value provided to the organization by the PMO and in particular when attempting to manage for project fraud prevention and detection. Applying the "outsourced" approach, by requiring simple project management processes of all project teams, such as individual status reports (project schedules that have work time-labor actuals posted to the project schedule with the project critical path automatically updated every day), will subtly cause the project teams to shift their personal attention to the day-to-day project schedule to determine if they are safe themselves. If they are not, they will take action. They may even report it to the project manager. As you can see, this approach raises visibility in project delivery among the team members and this visibility improves each person's ability to recognize good and bad project work influences and to act on these when they occur. If everyone feels safe in the project team, then the project's chance for delivery success improves dramatically and incrementally since people will work with less caution if they feel less at risk. Do your project teams feel safe today? These methods mentioned above are a basic tenet to preventing and detecting project fraud. The PMO must own the processes behind it.

14.6 Defining the Service Level Agreement with Internal Auditing

In defining and executing the SLA with the internal audit department, the PMO value model becomes stronger in value to the business as well as to the value model of the internal audit department. Essentially the PMO and internal audit become joined at the hip, inseparable forever. Below are several key value points that the internal audit department should be willing to perform for the benefit of the PMO:

1. Project audits of the top ten project investments for the fiscal year at a minimum. If possible, project audits should be performed on the top 40 percent of all funded projects being worked in the fiscal year in order of strategic importance. Auditing the top 40 percent of the project portfolio lets the workforce know they may come under scrutiny sooner or later and that they are expected to be ready when this occurs to demonstrate that they are complying with project fraud prevention and detections processes within the project team.
2. Project audits of each corporate objective that the organization expects to achieve during the fiscal year. Internal audit will use project delivery data that are typically turned in every monthly reporting cycle to the PMO by project teams by examining extracted data from centralized and/

or various PMO data stores to validate organizational expectations regarding current project progress.

3. Whenever there is a need to change project managers in a project, internal audit should conduct a project audit that baselines the project progress to date and the change. That establishes accountabilities for results that occurred in the project life cycle. Any future impact of problems from the previous project manager on the project itself should not impact the new leader. Failure to accomplish this task can increase the opportunity for project fraud to have more impact on the project and on the corporate objective that the project was created to help achieve.

4. In the PMO monthly report to corporate governance, internal audit should have a section that expresses its summarized findings and recommendations for project fraud risk (positive and negative) for the reporting period along with a 30/60/90 day outlook in the project investment risk.

5. Other value points in the SLA involving internal auditing from PMO support include:

- Provide internal audit with a monthly project portfolio report that reflects tactical progress of the projects listed in the portfolio compared to what was expected to be achieved by this calendar date with an assessment of options for possible improvement.
- Provide internal audit with a monthly resource portfolio report that reflects tactical progress and future estimates of resource utilization listed within the resource portfolio compared to what was expected with an assessment of possible options for improvement.
- Provide internal audit with a monthly corporate objective portfolio report that reflects tactical progress and future estimates of positive or negative risk to the achievement of each specific corporate objective with an assessment of possible options for improvement.
- Provide internal audit with a monthly asset portfolio report that reflects tactical progress and future estimates of positive or negative risk to the achievement of each supported asset with an assessment of possible options for improvement.
- Provide internal audit with direct system access to the PMO data repository of all project artifacts.
- Train internal auditors on the PMI Project Management Body of Knowledge (PMBOK®) to improve their cognitive skills in project fraud detection.
- Provide project management process standards to project teams that demonstrate Sarbanes-Oxley compliance to all relative requirements of the law so as to improve the internal auditing level of effort to conduct project audits.

14.7   Why Should the PMO Care?

Given the Sarbanes-Oxley legislation and the penalties for failure to comply, many CEOs are implementing polices in their businesses that require people down the line from the CEO, who have had their hands in the money, to sign statements certifying that the financials they have reported are accurate. The project management community has long been a black hole to business where current project financials are typically thirty days or older. This means that thirty days of project fraud could be going undetected before the next cycle is processed. This problem is a large opportunity for the PMO to add value for itself and for the business by enacting the methods described above. Most importantly is that when the PMO accomplishes this value, the result is often improvement in workplace culture because they feel they have been protected (from each other and other work place predators). This sense of safety is real and can be incremented over time where everyone aggressively protects their own space from project fraud while increasing their work pace.

Stating this in another fashion, raising a strong emphasis on project fraud prevention and detection, through the PMO to project teams it supports, the opportunity to commit project fraud is more controlled. As a result of this stronger control, work behavior is more urgent in delivery with project teams because slow delivery becomes more apparent to those awaiting the output of another team member's work. This improved visibility was created by the strong emphasis given to the project fraud compliance requirement by the PMO onto all project teams. Thus, intentional slow work delivery is another, but yet most frequent, type of project fraud in project teams.

As project teams improve their delivery ability and their compliance ability to Sarbanes-Oxley at their level, positive and negative changes occur that had not been planned for. The overall management of these changes (value) for the benefit of the organization serviced by the PMO is why the PMO should care. The PMO management of these changes assists the business in achieving the business objectives for the year sooner or much later if misapplied or missed completely. In summary, these actions by the PMO can lead to true business transformation that has positive impact to the bottom line of the organization.

14.8   Summary

Understanding the value of the PMO to the management of project fraud prevention and detection is the critical step in regaining control of business objectives. The Sarbanes-Oxley legislation will reach all businesses if not directly, then indirectly. In much the same manner of impact that Y2K and Total Quality

Management (TQM) had on the business world, we predict the same for fraud management. Our opinion is that fraud management carried to the project delivery levels of business will become more important than any initiative ever undertaken to improve business performance. This opinion is simply based on the observation that many businesses today do not manage for project fraud and are leaving critical project investments flapping in the breeze to fend for themselves. No wonder project investments by business are considered the riskiest business investments a business can make. Your customers and suppliers may choose NOT to do business with your firm if you do not have a fraud management policy internalized within your business. Can you really afford this?

Everyone in the organization should come to appreciate the positive impact that Sarbanes-Oxley can have on how people work with each other to achieve improved project delivery results. If your organization can grip the concept that project fraud is a basic tenet of business that must be prevented, what is your business doing about this? How do you know if project fraud is NOT occurring in your business today? Ask yourself if you are aware of any deployed fraud policies in your organization. If you are not, then guess what is most likely occurring?

You may have surmised by now that managing for fraud at the project level is essential. Consider that the optimal benefit of fraud policy compliance by a business can lead to true business objective achievement earlier or at least on time and on budget. Paraphrased, Sarbanes-Oxley can lead your business into achieving true business transformation. The following chapters will examine this supposition in tactical and strategic detail.

Questions

14.1 PMO is defined as:
   a. Project management overhead
   b. Project management opportunity
   c. Project management office
   d. Prime minister office
14.2 Sarbanes-Oxley can be a positive influence in business transformation. True or false?
14.3 The PMO should work in collaboration with internal auditing to:
   a. Manage project delays
   b. Prevent and detect project fraud
   c. Assess project management policies
   d. Perform portfolio management

14.4   PMOs are only for supply-side business units. True or false?

14.5   Project fraud prevention and detection in project delivery is best managed by the PMO. True or false?

14.5   In establishing a service level agreement between the PMO and internal auditing, the PMO should seek assistance from internal auditing to NOT perform which service:

    a.   Project audits

    b.   Project manager change audit

    c.   Executive performance auditing

    d.   Corporate objectives portfolio auditing

14.7   PMOs should seek to work directly with each project team to manage for project fraud. True or false?

14.8   The PMO can help improve the internal auditors' cognizance of project fraud by training them in the concepts of the Project Management Body of Knowledge from the Project Management Institute. True or false?

14.9   The PMO can help internal auditing assess project fraud risk by providing:

    a.   Project portfolio reporting

    b.   Resource portfolio reporting

    c.   Corporate objectives portfolio reporting

    d.   Project team member resumes

14.10   The PMO data store is a valuable tool for internal auditors and fraud examiners. True or false?

References

1. Lanza, Richard B., IT Audit, Technology Projects: The Riskiest Parts of the Business, 2002.

2. Association of Certified Fraud Examiners, Report to the Nation — 2002, Association of Certified Fraud Examiners, 2002.

15

Utilizing a PMO Data Store That Supports Project Fraud Prevention and Detection

The PMO is often the only department in the organization that collects project-related tactical data from all projects for the fiscal year and past fiscal years. These data are often in the form of project schedules, project status reports, project work papers, project meeting minutes, and other related project artifacts. In our travels among many businesses, we have witnessed many instances where sensitive project data are not maintained at the master copy level anywhere in the organization except for the hard drive or briefcase of the project team member. As project artifacts are created, remember that the work involved to create these artifacts was funded by the business. The business owns these artifacts and it is the due diligence of every person in the business that a master copy of any artifact (intellectual property) be stored in a secure location, hopefully in the PMO centralized enterprise project management (EPM) tool and related systems.

15.1 What Is the PMO Data Store?

The PMO data store is typically a single repository database of project-oriented information regarding project progress and related artifacts such as work products and project deliverables. There are many PMO data store products in the marketplace today that can support the organizational PMO and project management community. These products are more well known as EPM tools. Many of these products provide feature-rich automated support that reduces and/or eliminates manual effort to relate project items with other project artifacts into meaningful value. Some of these products include the following vendors:

1. Systemcorp's PM Office Enterprise
2. Primavera's TeamPlay
3. Artemis
4. Niku
5. Microsoft Project and Server
6. Oracle
7. Kintana

To gain a better understanding of which product might fit your needs best, obtain a copy of Gartner Group's Magic Quadrant report that assesses how these products best meet customer requirements. Great care should be exercised if you choose to purchase one of these products for your business because many of these type of products are NOT end-to-end in features that best support project management practice within an organization. This might include risk management or time entry, for example. Others are more extensive in areas such as client training. The organization's PMO is best suited in assessing and recommending a selection in these types of products if the organization decides to buy versus building a similar system. Further information regarding the assessment and selection of EPM tools can be found in the PMO book written by Gerald Kendall and Steve Rollins.[1]

15.2 Elements of a PMO Data Store and Project Fraud Impact

Basic PMO data stores are comprised of basic artifacts produced by project teams during the life cycle of those projects. These basic artifacts include the following:

1. *Project status report* — The project status report is a basic tenet of project management. The message to be conveyed by this artifact to the PMO and key stakeholders is: What is the progress health of the project relative to expectations of the business? Reporting news to management and other key stakeholders about progress of the project is why this artifact is so important. However, in situations where the project

is under duress, the necessary information can be stated in a manner that limits negative implication. Stating that a project is on schedule and/or on budget when it is not is, in essence, project fraud. The project manager owns the responsibility for ensuring that the project status report accurately reflects the progress of the project. Project status reports that do not reflect time and cost increase the opportunity for project fraud to develop and flourish. Furthermore, this lack of information can inhibit the measurement of a corporate objective achievement that the underreported project is supposed to be primarily linked to.

2. *Project schedule* — A critical element to any PMO data store is the project schedule. A project schedule will indicate start and end dates and where the project currently is in progress. Vital to the value of the project schedule is the critical path of the schedule or, in other terms, the longest route in time to complete the project. Any project schedule that does not reflect critical path is creating opportunity for project fraud. To enable critical pathing within a project schedule, team member time-labor actuals must be posted against the planned time that was estimated for each team member. The presence of a critical path in a project schedule should indicate to an internal auditor whether the project is progressing as expected. The absence of a project critical path will indicate that project progress assessment is more of a subjective opinion than it is fact. Additionally, team members' work management may be out of alignment since they may not be able to determine how their work and pace impact the successful progress delivery of the project.

3. *Project charter* — Normally, the project charter is developed and approved early in the life cycle of the project, most often in the initiating phase. It is at this time that all key stakeholders are on board with the mission of the project and the identified expectations. Normally, the project charter is drafted by the project manager and submitted for approval to the project sponsor and/or the funding project owner (customer). Project charters that are not approved, but the project has progressed beyond the planning phase,[2] should be of critical concern to the PMO, internal auditors, and fraud examiners. The project charter becomes the basis for which other constructed project artifacts such as project scope, project risk, project management plan, associative work products and deliverables, and change management items may impact the project charter and other project artifacts. In the scenario of an unapproved project charter with project work progressing into the "executing phase," great concern should exist for project fraud.

4. *Project scope statement* — The project scope statement details specifically what requirements are to be fulfilled and what requirements are considered to be out of scope for this project. It is important for project auditors to review the project scope statement in any project audit for change control updates against all historical change requests within the project. Every occurrence of change request update against the project scope statement should be approved by signature by the project sponsor, if not the project funding customer.

5. *Project management plan* — The project management plan is derived in part from the project scope statement and the project charter. This artifact narrates the expected delivery path of work identifying key deliverables and work products. The project management plan must be updated to reflect project change requests that are approved. Updated project management plans should be approved by the project sponsor. The project schedule critical path must also be updated to reflect approved change requests.

6. *Project risk plan* — The project risk plan identifies potential positive and/or negative project risk and identified mitigation plans to reduce, eliminate, or acquire that risk. Project audits should review project scope, project schedule, project charter, and project management plan for appropriate updates to those artifacts. Otherwise, the consequences may cause the project to under- or overstate the reported progress expectations of the project. This particular artifact is of high importance to business transformation as it is here that project delivery acceleration opportunity and/or delivery threat is initially perceived.

7. *Work products* — Work products are those artifacts that are created during the course of project delivery including time sheets, test scripts, one-time project tools created to construct a project deliverable, etc.

8. *Deliverables* — Creating project deliverables is what constitutes the value of the project to the funding customer. These artifacts should be well defined in the project management plan and clearly stated in the project schedule. Completion approval by the project sponsor should be contained within the project deliverable if at all possible.

9. *Meeting minutes* — Meeting minutes are a telling indicator to the overall health of project progress. Inadequate meeting minutes are a strong indicator that further audit action is required. Reviewing these documents for outcome validation — if these meetings achieved what they intended — provide perspective on project health and the risk of project fraud.

10. *Change management items* — Often during the course of the project life cycle, unplanned events occur. These unplanned events may result

in change requests to the project mission. When this occurs, project documentation that manages the project such as the project scope statement, project management plan, project risk statement, etc., must be updated to reflect any impacts. The consequences of failing to do so may result in key stakeholder comprehension of the updated information leading unintentionally to misrepresentation of tactical project information.

15.3 Developing PMO Data Store Processes That Help Detect and/or Prevent Project Fraud

Assuming that a PMO data store has been established in your organization, project fraud detection processes should be designed and implemented that scan the project artifacts stored. These detection processes should seek items that are outside of expected compliance for the project fraud policy. Several key processes to consider for deployment through PMO against the PMO data store include:

1. Project related
   - Project progress in time
   - Project progress in cost
   - Approved project artifacts relative to progress
   - Team member work estimates versus actuals
   - Improvement in progress from previously identified high-risk projects
   - Project issue resolution
2. Project portfolio related
   - Projects that are over- or underspent by more than 20 percent and past the planning phase
   - Projects without sponsors
   - Interproject relationships where the predecessor project is delayed or accelerating
   - Project delivery forecasts in opportunity and threat for the next 30/60/90 days
   - Identification of the most critical project in the project portfolio to the corporate objectives for the fiscal year
3. Corporate objective portfolio related
   - Changes in aggregated planned/actual spending for one or more specific corporate objectives

- Changes in what is the most critical project objective for a specific corporate objective
- Changes in expected achievement date for any corporate objective
- Unlinked projects to any corporate objective (this should never occur)

4. Asset portfolio related
   - Changes in schedule achievement for any supported asset improvement
   - Changes in costs in asset improvement
   - Project changes that impact the top ten corporate assets

5. Resource portfolio related
   - That resources are performing their work in the correct strategic order as defined by the project portfolio
   - That resources are not overallocated beyond corporate expectations
   - That resources are not underallocated beyond corporate expectations
   - That resources are working on approved projects only

6. Person related
   - Process that collects all individual work papers for further review (includes time sheets and completed work artifacts)
   - Process that assesses a person's plan versus actual ratio of assigned work with a project or any collection of projects
   - Process to assess person's time sheets against project schedules they contributed work to

7. PMO related
   - Process to publish in cyclical fashion (monthly) the "plan of record" that reflects overall assessment of portfolio progress against business expectations from data within the PMO data store
   - In collaboration with internal auditing and under special cover, should publish a cyclical project fraud assessment that compares the current portfolio environment with project fraud policy

15.4 How to Manage Lack of Compliance by Project Teams or Team Member

Whenever a situation of significance is uncovered that is out of compliance with project fraud policy, the information should be turned over to the internal auditing department for handling. It is important that the PMO not attempt to manage this itself as this will cast the PMO in the light as an "enforcer" and will damage its perception to the workforce as a friend. This concept is critical to the stability of any PMO. A PMO may choose to send in a project mentor to help the project team or team member, but this should always be in a positive manner with positive results.

15.5 Using the PMO Data Store to Raise Visibility and to Improve Delivery Speed Leading to Business Transformation

It is important to note that an implemented project fraud management policy designed to prevent and detect project fraud may actually be the lever that frees your project management community from their constant caution regarding personal risk.

Since the PMO may already be publishing a monthly plan of record, organizational portfolio information is already available. A high-value meeting event that the PMO should conduct is the cyclical (often monthly) portfolio management meeting that all portfolio-related project managers are required to attend. In this process, each project manager will have previously filed his or her most recent project status report within the PMO data store several days prior. This meeting should follow two to three days later whereby each project manager is asked to state the following about their project status in less than two minutes per project manager:

1. What is the project health?
2. What has been accomplished since last report?
3. What are your progress plans for this reporting period?
4. What delivery hurdles do you need help with?
5. What acceleration opportunities do you perceive?
6. Where do you see other value to the organization portfolio regarding opportunity and threat?

The result of this meeting will reaffirm project progress that is interdependent in impact with other projects represented in this meeting. The end result will motivate those interdependencies to choose other progress options potentially for their project in order to optimize their resources and time. As this information is reported, it becomes "owned" by the reporting project manager and understood by all other project managers thereby sharing accountability with the participants. In this manner, the information is raised in visibility in a real-time manner thereby reducing project fraud opportunity through improved cross-collaboration. Now everyone knows!

In deploying the meeting process, it is imperative that no more than two minutes are utilized by the project managers to make their report since more time will lengthen the meeting. The PMO is only seeking to raise visibility to overall portfolio progress as a means to foster business achievement goals.

In most organization portfolios, interdependent relationships can be observed that identify pending project delivery car-wrecks waiting to occur for specific projects and/or a chain of projects as detailed by the portfolio information. When this information is made available to an audience such as this, and in this fashion, each project manager will be keenly interested in this information as it relates to his or her project. When a project manager does determine a level of risk requiring action, he or she will most often raise that awareness in this meeting. Often, these observations are incurred from project schedule changes managed by other project managers, not by the PMO. In this manner, the PMO raises visibility to project delivery opportunity or threat to all portfolio-related projects depending on the circumstance of the event in question. Because of this new and improved visibility to project positive and negative risk, the PMO has reduced opportunity for project delivery mismanagement and associative project fraud to develop or begin since more people are aware of possible impact to them. In addition to this process benefit, the motivation of the offending project manager to not impact their peer(s) is another mechanism to prevent project fraud. In this manner, the PMO can maintain its image of being the project manager's best friend in helping them to be successful in project delivery.

Deploying this process is very cost effective to lessening the time and cost to implement project fraud prevention and detection processes. Given that the PMO should be performing many of these processes already only furthers the value proposition of the PMO to the business and the value of the project management promise — to grow business prosperity.

15.6 Summary

The PMO data store is a critical tool in the battle to manage project fraud prevention and detection. Choosing an EPM tool that best suites the needs of the business is not the essence of this chapter, but rather what should be expected in the utilization of such a strategic tool to combat project fraud. The value proposition of the PMO data store can be a key catalyst to achieving corporate objectives in the fiscal year in the most optimal manner. Great care in selecting a product should be exercised, as these software tools are very extensive and very good. The key issue for any organization to consider in tool selection is how it will fit in the organization's processes. Will your organization have to improve (more money) current processes and resource skills to receive the expected value?

Our approach to managing project fraud prevention and detection is behavior driven. We recommend that the PMO should always wear the "white hat." Let the internal auditors wear the "black hat." The PMO image of being the "best friend" to the project management community in your organization is a critical aspect behind the successful delivery of projects and toward the achievement of corporate objectives that are project delivery sensitive.

Questions

15.1   A PMO data store collects:
  a. Project status reports
  b. Project schedules
  c. Project scope statement
  d. Team member personal information

15.2   The project schedule critical path requires planned and actual labor in order to calculate progress. True or false?

15.3   The PMO should be direct and supervisory in its approach with the project management community. True or false?

15.4   In portfolio meetings facilitated by the PMO with project managers, which is NOT required?
  a. What is the project health?
  b. What has been accomplished since the last report?
  c. What acceleration opportunities do you perceive?
  d. What people are not performing?

15.5   In portfolio review meetings, improving the understanding of potential acceleration and threat from project interdependencies is the goal. This information helps reduce the opportunity for project fraud. True or false?

15.6   Work products are those artifacts that are created during the course of project delivery. True or false?

15.7   Whenever a situation of significance is uncovered that is out of compliance with project fraud policy, the information should be turned over to the internal auditing department for handling. True or false?

15.8   A project charter that is not approved when the project has progressed beyond the planning phase[2] should be of critical concern to the PMO. True or false?

15.9   The absence of a project critical path will indicate that project progress assessment is more subjective opinion than fact. True or false?

15.10   The PMO data store is typically a single repository database of project-oriented information regarding project progress and related artifacts such as work products and project deliverables. True or false?

References

1. Kendall, Gerald and Rollins, Steve, *Advanced Project Portfolio Management and the PMO: Multiplying ROI at Warp Speed*, J. Ross Publishing, Boca Raton, FL, 2003.
2. See Project Management Institute, Project Management Body of Knowledge (PMBOK®) for further insight into the Phases of the Project Life Cycle.

Implementing Project Management Policies Through the PMO That Support Fraud Detection and Prevention

16.1 Defining Policy Requirements

The purpose of the project fraud management policy addresses how the business will manage for project fraud prevention and detection across the business where project work is being performed. All organizational units and employees are expected to comply with this policy. The organization project management office (PMO) will manage the application of this policy onto all project teams. Internal audit will assess policy compliance on a prescribed basis in collaboration with organizational management and the PMO. This policy provides guidelines for project teamwork delivery in project fraud prevention and detection. This policy identifies actions required by business workforce members to minimize project fraud opportunities and to control work issues that might lead to project fraud.

16.2 Applying the Project Management Body of Knowledge (PMBOK®) to Project Fraud Policy

The rigor and discipline of the project fraud management policy is in parallel to the Project Management Institute's Project Management Body of Knowledge (PMBOK®), the generally accepted accounting principles (GAAP), and the Sarbanes-Oxley legislation, in particular Section 404. It is because of this close interelement relationship and the already present rigor and discipline within each of these three elements that enables the innate value that is expected to result from the implemented project fraud management policy. The PMBOK® Areas of Knowledge create the generic perimeter of function around project work. This perimeter includes:

1. Project integration
2. Project time management
3. Project human resource management
4. Project quality management
5. Project scope management
6. Project procurement management
7. Project risk management
8. Project cost management
9. Project communications management
10. Project professional responsibility management

This framework represents the standard aspects of any project work. Not all projects use all aspects of this framework all the time, but the potential for this to occur is ever present. Applying the PMBOK® framework to the project fraud management policy can be enabled in several easy steps:

1. All project schedules must utilize critical path scheduling techniques in their project schedules.
2. All project schedules must contain the five life cycle phases in the project schedule framework:
   - Initiating phase
   - Planning phase
   - Controlling and monitoring phase
   - Executing phase
   - Closing phase
3. All project teams are to conduct project status meetings twice a month, minimally.

4. All reported project labor is to be posted to the project schedule within two weeks of occurrence.
5. All project teams are to perform a project audit in collaboration with internal auditing at least once during the project life cycle and on conclusion of the project.
6. Each strategically identified project is to develop the following documents for project sponsor approval:
   - Project charter
   - Project scope statement
   - Project management plan
   - Project schedule
   - Project risk plan
   - Project communications plan
   - Project staffing plan

16.3 Desired Results/Objectives

1. Business staff members will have a clear understanding of the business requirement to minimize and control perceived project fraud events.
2. Business staff members will understand what action they need to take to report project fraud.
3. Those in charge of executing the project fraud management policy will understand their responsibilities and actions to implement this policy.
4. The customer public will have confidence in the business integrity and in the products and services that the business delivers.
5. This policy will minimize the potential for business value to be compromised in the event that project fraud does occur.
6. The implementation of this policy will enable project teams to improve their visibility to work acceleration opportunities and threats that enables a greater rate of work delivery for the benefit of the business.
7. The implementation of this policy will enable more value toward business transformation resulting from change management in the business.
8. All project investments will be mapped in alignment with corporate objectives that will raise visibility for improved business navigational decision making and project fraud detection.
9. The PMO is responsible for the application of this rigor and discipline across the business regarding project delivery work.
10. Internal auditing will oversee the functional compliance to Section 404 of the Federal Legislation — Sarbanes-Oxley.

16.4   Who Owns the Policy?

The PMO will oversee policy compliance in the project delivery space for the organization. Internal auditing will recommend approval for the developed policy based on federal law requirements and how the policy enables compliance with the federal requirements and with how the policy supports the business needs.

16.5   PMO Role and Responsibilities

The PMO role in managing for project fraud is to enable project support processes that will actively prevent and detect project fraud directly within intra- or interproject team relationships within the organization. These processes include:

1. Portfolio management
   - Corporate objectives portfolio
   - Project investment portfolio
   - Resource portfolio
   - Asset portfolio
2. PMO data store access
3. One hundred percent data integrity with the PMO data store
4. Project delivery mentoring
5. Whistle-blowing help desk (integrated into PMO help desk)
6. Service level agreements with internal auditing and strategic planning departments
7. Project management standard methods and templates
8. Essential project governance facilitation support at various levels of the organization
9. Project fraud management training
10. Project management training

16.6   Internal Auditing Role and Responsibilities

The internal auditing role in managing for project fraud is to support project audits and approved overall project fraud management policy implementation and change management to that policy. In addition, the role is to ensure that the business is meeting federal compliance expectations in part with this policy applied to intra- or interproject team relationships within the organization.

In the execution of the project audit, auditors are to examine project records that are required by this policy and for the presence of policy expectations within the work outputs of the audited project. This includes the following items minimally:

1. Project charter
2. Project scope statement and actions
3. Project management plan and actions
4. Project risk plan and action
5. Project change management plan and actions
6. Project communications plan and actions
7. Project staffing plan and actions
8. Project schedule iterations
9. Utilization of critical path techniques
10. One hundred percent resource labor reported within policy guidelines within the project
11. Project sponsor approvals at the appropriate points

16.7 Summary

This chapter conveyed the necessary steps and information to construct and implement a basic project fraud management policy that will enable project fraud prevention and detection for the organization. The essential output from the policy implementation is to increase workforce awareness of project fraud significantly and understanding of how important prevention and detection of project fraud is to the interests of the company. A project fraud management policy template is presented as Appendix 3 and is also available for download at www.jrosspub.com.

Questions

16.1   The purpose of the project fraud management policy addresses how the business will manage for project fraud prevention and detection across the business where project work is being performed. True or false?

16.2   This policy identifies actions required by business workforce members to minimize project fraud opportunities and to control work issues that might lead to project fraud. True or false?

16.3   The rigor and discipline of the project fraud management policy are in parallel to the Project Management Institute's Project Management Body of Knowledge (PMBOK®), the generally accepted accounting principles (GAAP), and the Sarbanes-Oxley legislation, in particular Section 404. True or false?

16.4 All project schedules must utilize critical path scheduling techniques according to this policy. True or false?

16.5 The PMO will oversee policy compliance in the project delivery space for the organization. True or false?

16.6 The PMO role in managing for project fraud is to enable project support processes that will actively prevent and detect project fraud directly within intra- or interproject team relationships within the organization. True or false?

16.7 The internal auditing role in managing for project fraud is to support project audits and approved overall project fraud management policy implementation and change management to that policy. True or false?

17

Creating a Safety Net for the Project Teams

17.1 The Common Bond Between Project Managers and Astronauts

Like most space missions, the project manager's job is fraught with job danger. Fail on project delivery and your job may be eliminated. Why is it then that businesses most everywhere fail to protect their project investments? Do they not like their project managers? The business decision to fund a specific project investment is at the expense of other potential options to spend that money. Does the management team not want to grow their business? When a spaceship hits a space rock during its flight, where is the backup that keeps the spaceship on course? Conversely, where is the safety net for a failing project to help it get back on course when an unplanned event occurs? Normally, any space debris will cause severe damage if it collides with a spaceship. This could be life threatening. The astronauts will do anything and everything in their power to avert losing their life, even if it means violating policy. Our space agency, NASA, has invested billions in taxpayer monies to make space travel as safe as they can. What has business delivered to provide a safety net for project managers and their projects? In most cases, in most businesses, projects are expected to make it on their own! How motivated do you think project managers and their teams will be to do everything possible to stay employed when their project is failing? Will these actions violate the expectations of Sarbanes-Oxley? Will you, the executive, be held accountable for some tactical project event beyond your control that was fraudulent? When project managers violate

Sarbanes-Oxley compliance expectations, everyone in direct line of how the project money is spent is at risk because of those actions. Project investment has become the riskiest part of business a business can be involved in given the high number of project failures everywhere. There must be a better way! There is.

17.2 Impact of Project Fraud on Project Failure

In a traditional sense, project failure is often related to unfulfilled requirement delivery or unavailable resources, or not enough time or something to this extent. But if we choose to investigate further why projects do fail, the true root cause often begins with misrepresentation and misunderstanding from that misrepresentation that leads to the wrong project action being applied. Like a rock skipping across a lake on a calm summer day, there is a ripple effect that reduces the reaction time to take corrective project action and every subsequent and related corrective action that was necessary when correction must occur. This misrepresentation may be intentional or unintentional, it truly matters only in a court of law. The effect of this misrepresentation on you and the project is already realized and it can be bad news. We must be better at preventing this misrepresentation, intentional or otherwise.

17.3 Defining the Safety Net for Project Delivery Success

In order to prevent and detect project fraud while the business supports the safety of active project teams in their quest for delivery success, there must be a central agency that can interpret potential acceleration and threats to the project mix and to specific project investments. This agency is the program/project management office (PMO). The cyclical information flow of tactical progress information that is provided by active projects must be a closed loop through the PMO that provides the PMO the ability to assess the health of project delivery throughout the organization it serves. This assessment will enable the PMO to make recommendations on course changes to the organization portfolios relative to changing business conditions and while understanding consequences of those recommendations. In Figure 17.1, we can see how the PMO supports the achievement of corporate objectives by constantly assessing project investment progress performance against what the business said it wanted to achieve. The PMO produces the monthly plan of record report for

Figure 17.1.   The PMO Safety Net.

corporate governance and key stakeholder consideration. This report reflects the progress of all project investments compared to corporate governance expectations. The effect of this communication causes raised visibility to project investment progress within corporate governance expectations and downward within each represented business unit in corporate governance. From this information, corporate governance is then enabled to make tactical project investment decisions that are strategic in nature. As these corporate governance decisions unfold, the PMO may be directed to become involved to help failing projects get back on course. The resulting improved visibility provided by the PMO reduces the opportunity for project fraud to develop or continue. Important to note is that not all project fraud will be detected, but if the people who seek to commit project fraud know that everyone is watching, their willingness to risk detection will be significantly lessened and thus prevented. The monthly plan of record reporting process utilized through the PMO is the keystone to essential project governance from a reporting perspective and to this deterrence. Without this aggregation and interpretation for all sponsored project investment progress, the organization will not have a holistic perspective that is fresh and measured against current business expectations from a tactical perspective as compared to overall business expectations.

In Figure 17.1, various components of the business provide support for the project investment safety net. These are:

1. Corporate governance
2. Business units
3. Project teams (not pictured)
4. PMO
5. Internal auditing (not pictured)

17.4 Corporate Governance Role

Typically, membership is comprised of business units that have project investments at risk. These business units would delegate a person, usually the business unit leader, to work with their peers in corporate governance toward a consensus that best supports the business. The main accountability of corporate governance is to ensure that project investments are in strategically force-ranked order by project investment based on what is important to the business. By aligning project investments in this manner, the order of work does not become an issue initially, if at all.

17.5 Business Unit Role

Each business unit that has accountability to support achievement of one or more of the business objectives is asked to sit on the corporate governance board. As the corporate governance board meets each cycle (monthly), each business unit is seen as accountable for each project investment that is listed in the project and corporate objectives portfolios that they funded or "own." This means that the "business side" of the business will be accountable for overall project investment achievement, not necessarily the "supply side" (unless they own it). This further implies that each corporate governance board member will communicate with their peers on the corporate governance board during the intervals between each board meeting. When business unit project investments value changes in either a positive or negative direction, it is the responsibility of the owning business unit to make recommendations to corporate governance on what the most appropriate action should be taken by corporate governance that would ensure that the most optimal investments are aligned in value to business strategic expectations. Corporate governance action may take the form of increasing the force ranking of a particular investment, lowering the force ranking, or possibly canceling the project investment alto-gether for the good of the business.

17.6 Project Team Role

Each strategic project investment is expected to report progress cyclically against the expected plan to a higher authority in order to maintain visibility of progress. In each reporting period, the project manager organizes the project status report with input from project team members, project schedule, and other related information. If the project has interdependencies with other projects, the project manager may seek awareness from those teams to further determine project health status. As we know, when you live in the forest, it is sometimes difficult to see the trees. This is why portfolio management is so vital to project teams.

17.7 PMO Role

In each reporting cycle, the PMO collects, analyzes, and makes assessments of overall portfolio health for corporate objectives, resources, projects, and assets as a result of project investment reported status for the period. This assessment is published as a matter of record and as such is known as the monthly plan of record. This document is distributed to key stakeholders for appropriate action. It is important that this publication not be regulated to electronic copy only because the information is normally less than thirty days old. This is very important to those managing the business. These people do not necessarily sit around in front of a computer all day long. They will use a published document like this if it is available.

17.8 Project Prioritization Roles

Prioritizing project investments for the first time can make the owner of that task feel like they are in Jurassic Park, politically speaking. There are man-eating creatures everywhere and you are the bait. If you are a supply-side business unit leader (CIO) that normally determines project selection for the enterprise, you understand this very well. Often the supply-side executive lead-ing this effort cannot win and really cannot say "no" if his or her political standing is weak. Otherwise the raptors will get them! But there is a way to manage this for the safety and benefit of all interested parties. Assuming port-folio management is not in place, the task at hand is to establish the order of work that best supports the business from an IT perspective. It is incredible that the CIO might be doing this today in many companies. Why? CIOs only know IT, technology, etc. CIOs do not know very much about business cases except for what they read. But CIOs are shot at (and sometimes fatally hit) if they should fail to support project delivery adequately for a particular raptor that led to failure or missed opportunity! If this is you, consider the following proven approach. Most of the raptors that are chasing you originate from the business side of the business. If they will not come together (corporate governance) and force rank project investments according to strategic value to the business, then will they live by your priority decisions in a similar manner? You should ask them to. They have a choice. Your way or theirs. When dysfunction reigns supreme, the supply-side executive will always be first to try to force rank project investments because of the pressure. Count on it. What follows will be similar to what was occurring before. The executive is chased around the island until he or she is eaten or changes the order only to be chased by some other meat eater. Most CIOs run. What should happen is to state, "If you don't like it, you figure it out. I asked you to form a governance group to do this, but it was refused. You can't have your cake and eat it too. Make a choice. My method or yours." We guarantee you that this approach will force a governance group to form, much to your relief, that will take over the prioritization process. The dinosaurs are caged! So what just happened? Looking back at Figure 17.1, the enterprise strategy is now driving business decisions for project selection on throughput optimization, not supply-side delivery strategy. Consider the implications for project fraud. When the safety net is finally established, the PMO becomes highly valued by everyone. Have you heard of firms where business decisions that increase shareholder/stakeholder value are subordinated to technical architecture policy in IT? In those businesses, does the business side know what that means to them? How some companies continue to exist in spite of themselves is interesting.

17.9 Portfolio Management Role

The portfolio management role provides the measurement of current organization progress against the business expectations for the measured period. In this manner, progress is assessed against the corporate objectives portfolio, project investment portfolio, resource portfolio, and asset portfolio for satisfactory performance. Standardizing what is satisfactory progress is the same as "meeting expectations" for portfolio achievement. Understanding the next level of execution and above or next level below satisfactory in a uniform manner is essential to project investment governance and reporting. This understanding across the workforce strengthens the fiber of the safety net and worker buy-in to business-alignment expectations.

17.10 Project Fraud Management Policy Role

Policy provides the language, framework, and processes to manage project fraud for prevention and detection across the applicable organization. This includes corporate governance vertically to the project team member and horizontally from business unit to business unit. The policy should stipulate policy management, purpose, who is governed, desired results and objectives, definitions, dissemination, responsibilities, and procedures. In most businesses with a PMO, this should be the PMO since the PMO is expected to produce the monthly plan of record based on portfolio management results that implicitly comply with fraud policies.

17.11 Portfolio Review Meetings Role

Every month (or more often), someone from the PMO meets with the project managers from each of the respective portfolios (functional or type) to review the reporting period results as related to the audience. Normally these meetings are conducted subsequent to the last corporate governance meeting. The expected meeting outcomes are to raise visibility to delivery opportunity and/or threat to any entity in the specific portfolio under review in order to minimize waste and to improve good flow of throughput ahead of portfolio achievement expectations. Additionally, project investments, corporate objectives, assets, or resources are considered for their performance health (red, yellow, green) and what that might mean directly or indirectly to those project managers who participate in the specific portfolio. This improved visibility will strengthen cross-collaboration within each represented project investment team that will influence their sense of urgency regarding their project investment responsibilities. This is a dynamic benefit of these meetings that improves the strength of the portfolio safety net for those project teams. The face of project fraud changes all the time!

17.12 Project Audit Role

The job should belong to internal auditing and not the PMO for reasons already mentioned in this book. Project audits should normally occur within time and progress of each project investment's life cycle. In other words, every three to six months, maybe at the conclusion of key life cycle phases. The job of the project auditor is to assess compliance and project actions toward business decisions made by the project team or other members of the workforce that have had influence on the project expenditures and progress. Because internal auditors are expected to understand fraud policies in general and because they are skilled in auditing, their utilization is key to the successful management of any project fraud management policy. These folks keep the safety net together in a tactical manner.

17.13 Enterprise Project Management Tools Role

The EPM tool is tool of choice for project information mining by those performing project audits. Normally, the project management standard is to store all project-related master copies of work in the PMO data store for the EPM tool to be applied in a uniform manner. EPM tools in some businesses allow for labor reporting by the workforce and mechanically integrate with downstream human resources and accounting systems. Input entry into the PMO data store made easier by the EPM tool is a cost benefit to the business and an enabler to prevent and detect project fraud. Safety net strength for project delivery teams is dependent on how well the PMO data store is managed and the volume of data that is guaranteed to have 100 percent data integrity.

17.14 Timing Impact

Cyclical reporting periods should be at least bi-weekly on all status reporting within all applicable portfolios. The plan of record produced by the PMO should be monthly. In the beginning, these cycles can be more frequent, but level off within three to four months.

The plan of record should be communicated to the portfolio teams before the report is provided to the supply-side leadership for their action in the beginning. After the initial period is over, the plan of record should be presented to the portfolio teams after the monthly corporate governance meeting.

17.15 Summary

As your firm begins the march to control fraud, gaping holes in support for project investment development management may be prevalent. Is there a PMO in place to support project teams? Are projects well aligned to corporate objectives and so on? We (You) must have better methods and policies to ensure their safety so fraud is prevented. If the people who work in the project development life cycle do not feel safe because others before them have perished (figuratively), why would they continue to want to go over the cliff? Complying with Sarbanes-Oxley Section 404, that requires better internal controls (translated safety net installation), can be accomplished in a much cheaper and much more efficient manner in the project delivery space. We must leverage the people and their behavior about how they do their work and how they work with each other, to how the business raises visibility for project delivery acceleration opportunities and or project delivery threats. Give the project teams quality information and a sense of support and business transformation will result. Ignore these improvements and your firm will continue down the same old path of misery and failure, plus your firm's ability to comply with Sarbanes-Oxley will be much less effective. Section 404 compliance requirements should be seen as the catalyst to improve efforts toward achieving business transformation.

Questions

17.1   The cyclical information flow of tactical progress information that is provided by active projects must be a closed loop. True or false?

17.2   The main accountability of corporate governance is to ensure that project investments are in strategically force-ranked order by project investment based on what is important to the business. True or false?

17.3   When business unit project investments value changes in either a positive or negative direction, it is the responsibility of the owning business unit to make recommendations to corporate governance on what their most appropriate action should be that would assure that the most optimal investments are aligned in value to business strategic expectations. True or false?

17.4   Each strategic project investment is expected to report progress cyclically against the expected plan to a higher authority in order to maintain visibility of progress. True or false?

17.5   The portfolio management role provides the measurement of current organization progress against the business expectations for the measured period. True or false?

17.6   The job of the project auditor is to assess compliance and project actions toward business decisions made by the project team or other members of the workforce that have had influence on the project expenditures and progress. True or false?

17.7   Cyclical reporting periods should be at least bi-weekly on all status reporting within all applicable portfolios. True or false?

17.8   The monthly plan of record is produced by the business units. True or false?

18

Connecting Project Investments with Corporate Objectives to Improve Project Fraud Control

18.1 Throughput Optimization Versus Cost Optimization

18.1.1 Cost Optimization

In most businesses today, projects are allocated funds to spend when applied to the project life cycle for results delivery. In many cases, these project funds are allocated by project task as defined in the project schedule. The allocated project task-level funds are calculated based on the estimate level approved by the project manager and possibly by the project sponsor. In the execution of project task-level work, the allocated funds are drawn from the project allocation to cover the project costs associated to the resource(s) assigned to perform the project task. Project team members performing the project task-level work most often know and understand the estimate assigned to the specific project task level of effort. They know innately that they are within task-level cost tolerance if they do not exceed the estimate in time for the project task. Since these same project team members know that time equals money, they do not worry about overspending the work effort if they are under the high level of the task work effort estimate. They feel safe in reporting labor up to the estimate. Again, this is accepted behavior in most project delivery work. Important to note is that there may have been an opportunity to complete the project task sooner than planned, thus saving the business the expense. This would mean that the project team members would have to continue their work pace and sense of urgency onto the next assignment in their work queue. As the business performs the oversight of this travesty, possibly finance or someone from management, the opportunity that may have been present to deliver sooner will go unnoticed if every second or cent of the project task money was used since a 100-percent-expensed project task cost allocation is considered within expectation for good work effort. This is, in part, a portion of the rule behind cost optimization in project costing and project estimating. In an entirely different scenario, project team members are asked to complete methodology templates to 100 percent accuracy not knowing that only 80 percent is sufficient. The extra 20 percent additional effort extends the cost of the project work they are performing, but as long as the work is completed within estimate or cost expectations, then this is acceptable. That additional 20 percent effort could be the difference between the project completing on time and on budget versus being late and/or over budget. Cost optimizing places more demand on the project manager to manage project task work completion. Sometimes this is just too much to ask for. Projects managed in a cost-optimizing manner will spend up to 40 percent or more than is necessary in completing the work, but may still look good by completing work within the planned time frame. The cost-optimizing approach limits the value of project management to the business and can hide project fraud under what is considered reasonable work expectations. By limiting the value of project management, the business is limiting how much it could prosper. Is this really what business wants?

18.1.2 Throughput Optimization

The idea behind throughput optimization is based on completing the most amount of work within a prescribed criteria set such as time, scope, or resources. In a business setting, completing the most work possible in a fiscal year scenario may mean more profitability. If more projects are completed in a fiscal year than were planned, for instance, what would the difference mean to the business management team — possibly a competitive business advantage within the industry, more profits, maybe just staying in business. Project teams that use the throughput-optimization approach will seek to deliver completed project work ahead of time and under budget. On time and on budget would be the worst-case expectation of a project team in this mode. Essentially, they expect to be early in delivery. They expect to be under budget in delivery. When projects deliver early, they create opportunities for other interdependent projects to progress sooner than expected. This is also true for achieving specific corporate objectives. Projects mapped specifically to a specific corporate objective can cause early achievement of a specific corporate objective by simply completing early. In another example, 80 percent completion of a project methodology template is perceived as efficient if that work is deemed sufficient to move ahead. The saved 20 percent cost and effort can then be applied to subsequent efforts in the project possibly earlier than expected, impacting subsequent project work to be early in completion and so forth.

18.1.3 Impact on Project Fraud

As noted earlier, completing project work within the estimated effort may actually hide passive project fraud. In this context, passive project fraud is defined as meeting expectations, but misrepresenting what was possible. In passive project fraud, injury is caused by losing the opportunity for better achievement because the opportunity was not presented for action...intentionally. Passive project fraud is a significant detriment to business prosperity. It is difficult to measure, but can be present in the work culture if the sense of urgency in project delivery and work teams is passive. Passive project fraud is often a by-product of the cost-optimization model where spending fiscal work allocations is more valued than work progress that could be achieved earlier than planned since people performing work will relax more in their efforts when the pressure to deliver becomes less. A great method to combat passive project fraud is to shorten the task work intervals to enable consistent effort by the people performing the work.

In throughput optimization, completing work within the full estimated effort is the absolute worst-case scenario. In the throughput-optimization model, passivity is perceived as lag among the project team members. Project team members seek to eliminate lag as a means to improve safety time to complete project work down-line in the project life cycle. Passive project fraud typically does not exist in project teams since they are motivated to complete work at speed. Their sense of urgency is driven by time. The more time saved is more value to the project team. Because the emphasis is on delivery speed, project fraud is found more in the work product and deliverable completion areas.

18.2 Who Owns It?

The responsibility for business alignment (project investments to corporate objectives) rests with corporate governance. In this accountability, the expectation is that the members of the corporate governance board together own the strategic and tactical accountability to accomplish the fiscal year work plan for the business. Determining how to accomplish the approved corporate objectives for the fiscal year is the challenge. This challenge is resolved through the identification of project investments that are funded to achieve specific corporate objectives. In some cases, the project investments provide benefit to more than one specific corporate objective. However, a standard rule must be that each project investment is assigned primarily to a specific corporate objective and no more than one as this will confuse tactical efforts to deliver the project, further enabling opportunity for project fraud to occur. Each specific project investment is owned, funded by a specific business unit represented in the corporate governance board. As project investments are identified and mapped to specific corporate objectives, the corporate governance board member that owns the most approved (by corporate governance) project investments per corporate objective should become accountable for the overall achievement of that particular corporate objective for the fiscal year. In this manner, all approved project investments assigned to support a specific corporate objective are linked at the participating role level through the alignment of project investments to a specific corporate objective. This linkage is critical to setting baseline expectations for project investment delivery and defining what is satisfactory performance relative to the achievement of the specific corporate objective. Can you see how a cost-optimization model would negatively constrain this effort versus the throughput-optimization effect? Can you also see how much easier it will be to define project fraud instances against the approved work plan for each specific corporate objective and their related project investments? In this approach, everyone from the top of the organization to the very lowest level are linked strategically and tactically to achieve specific corporate objectives. The pressure to perform is focused on working together to improve delivery speed. This way of life, this new attitude, thus reduces the opportunity for project fraud to occur since project fraud will cause misrepresentation and this will be noticed by everyone who is watching progress toward the goal of supporting corporate objective achievement. If project fraud does occur, the project management office (PMO) may be the first to recognize this.

18.3 PMO Role

The role of the PMO is to help the organization achieve its organizational objectives. This support is directed and provided through results determined by the monthly plan of record process, which gives a monthly assessment of project investment development progress compared to the expected results originally stated in the fiscal year strategic plan. The comparison process is performed using portfolio management techniques that assess project progress performance year-to-date against what was expected. This process is also performed for assets, resources, and corporate objectives. The PMO is the only organizational entity that can provide this analysis since it typically contains experts in project management and would normally own the project fraud management policy for project delivery.

In supporting corporate governance, the PMO normally attends each corporate governance meeting to be available to answer questions about project investment performance and to take action items to support corporate governance decisions. This also includes answering questions that may arise regarding Sarbanes-Oxley certification to the government for various project investments. As business processes mature in Sarbanes-Oxley management, the PMO may eventually be required to sign internal certification documents that substantiate Section 404 code compliance from a project management and delivery perspective.

18.4 Portfolio Management Defined

The PMO owns the management of the business project investment portfolio. Internal to this process is the oversight to project investment achievement to projects, corporate objectives, assets, and resources. In each of these four portfolio types, the value provided is insight into the progression of the mix. Questions can be asked, such as: "Are the project investments progressing in the delivery order as was planned?" "Does the portfolio have extra money available to move around to other project investments that makes throughput more optimal?" "Which items in the portfolio should be stopped?" "Do we have extra money available to start more work this fiscal year than was planned?"

As every project investment has an owner, so does every asset, resource, and corporate objective.

When portfolio management is applied to business alignment, project fraud does not have a chance to impact the business since any anomaly will be detected by the portfolio in a throughput-optimization model. This critical benefit should be compelling to justify any PMO and to ensure that the PMO performs portfolio management. The PMO is the corset to business alignment and to project fraud management.

18.5   Defining the Need for Enterprise Project Management Tools

In the past, enterprise project management (EPM) tools have provided standard features that helped project teams apply the rigor and discipline of project management to their work. Now EPM tools provide portfolio management processes that can be aimed at certain areas of the business to improve business alignment and project fraud management. EPM tools are single-repository software packages that can be the most important software tools outside of payroll that a business can own. More information on EPM tools and their impact can be found in subsequent chapters.

18.6   Defining the Corporate Governance Charter

The purpose of corporate governance essentially is to achieve planned corporate objectives within the allotted time. Membership into this board should come from the leadership of each line of business within the corporation. Membership responsibility is to own accountability of project investment achievement that supports the achievement of corporate objectives. Each specific corporate objective is to be managed for the corporate governance board by a specific board member strategically and tactically. The time period for measurement is the corporate fiscal year. Project investments identified as strategic to achieving the corporate objectives fall within the purview of the corporate governance board. Each project investment is to be assessed for importance in value to the corporate strategic corporate objectives and force ranked in a correlated manner in a process supported by the corporate PMO. The underlying purpose of the corporate governance board is to complete as many strategic project investments as possible within the fiscal year (throughput optimization). Given that most corporate strategic fiscal year work plans contain contingency in their project investments, as much as 30 percent or more of total planned costs for each project investment, the opportunity to do more in the fiscal year is available if project investments can be completed in a more timely manner.

18.6.1   Board Meetings

The corporate governance board is to meet monthly or more as required. Each monthly meeting is to review corporate objectives portfolio progress and determine board actions from these results. Each board meeting must approve the current corporate objective portfolio and the related project investments strategic force rankings. In each board meeting, the corporate objectives portfolio is to be reviewed for potential realignment of corporate monies to other project investments that are deemed more strategic to the business. The governance board should always be seeking to find new monies from the existing strategic fiscal year work plan and supporting budget to begin new work. Conversely, project investments no longer deemed strategic in nature to the business should be considered for stoppage or other action thereby saving unsunk project investment funds for other ventures.

The strength of the corporate governance charter will influence the strength of the business alignment and make Section 404 compliance much easier to achieve. A weak corporate governance charter will weaken business alignment and place more management burden on tactical management efforts to manage for project fraud.

18.7 Enabling Corporate Alignment

Key to the alignment of project investments to corporate objectives is a standard project investment prioritization model that can be applied in a universal manner across the enterprise to all project investments. It is a basic tenet of business management to understand the work levels in a business unit such as a department. This includes gaining the knowledge of what work is more important than other work, which work should be completed first, etc. In almost every instance, this work can be separated into what is strategic in nature versus what is operational only to the owning organization (department, business unit). A common difficulty for most businesses is how to cause all organizations within the enterprise to prioritize their strategic work in the same manner universally to enable corporate alignment. Operational work within an organization's department is considered out of scope, strategically, in establishing corporate alignment. Thus the corporate need for a uniform method to order project investments value to corporate gain in a strategic correlated manner is key to establishing corporate alignment. This task should fall within strategic planning and/or the PMO departments.

Essentially, the process development should be short lived in development. Under the leadership of the assigned corporate governance board delegate, a cross-functional team is to be brought together representing each business unit from the company. The purpose of this team will be to develop a project investment prioritization model that enables project investment teams to assess the value of their project to the corporate objectives of the business. This model will measure scalable perceived value of the project investment per corporate objective as determined by the project manager and/or project sponsor given their best knowledge. Input to this model will be brought forth by members of the cross-functional team in how their organizations are currently performing this same task within their organizations. The outcome from the cross-functional team will be a proposed model and process that collects project investment value information related to each corporate objective. When this model and process is approved by corporate governance, and as the approved model and process is deployed across the enterprise, each participating project manager will submit their project investment prioritization assessment to the PMO for inclusion into the corporate objectives portfolio. Most project managers and/or project sponsors are very tactical in knowledge of the corporate objective mission and their assessment will be heavily skewed in this manner. The members of the corporate governance board are very strategic in knowledge of the corporate objectives mission and their utilization of the tactical assessment from the project managers as portrayed in the corporate objectives portfolio will provide a clear picture illustrating differences in opinion between the two groups. The corporate governance board will caucus on what the strategic order (force ranking) of project investments should be overall to the business. Each corporate objective owner from the corporate governance board will then caucus with other board members to determine the strategic order of each project investment linked to their corporate objective. Subsequent monthly corporate governance meetings will reaffirm the strategic order and related changes. Project investment project managers will update their assessment to the PMO of the prioritization value as the business climate changes during life cycle development.

18.8 Reducing Project Fraud Opportunity Through Alignment to Improve Business Transformation

Project delivery brings about change in the business. Hopefully, all changes are for the good of the business. We all know from experience that there are changes that impact the business in a negative manner. If the business can achieve business alignment through corporate governance, the management of change will be made easier because when change does occur, it will be more visible because of the business alignment. Whenever business change is thrust on the workforce, current processes are often impacted through their process interaction with the specific change item. In the practice of project delivery, the PMO will be monitoring for this change and potential impact to limit any negative consequence to business expectations. We should be mindful that project delivery induces change in business methods. This change is the same as value when considering what the business expected in results from the project investment. Deploying the new project investment value to the business is made more likely through the PMO portfolio management processes to the workforce and corporate governance. Through the portfolio process review of new project investment delivered value, opportunities to achieve business transformation begin to emerge tactically. This emergence is made visible by the PMO to the business and in this manner protects the business environment from project fraud risk during the maturation of new value process adoption by the workforce. The maturation process increases over time at a speed that is determined by the degree of visibility to the new value through the incremental cross-collaboration that will occur as more workers and business units become aware. This maturation growth further reduces the opportunity for project fraud to start and/or continue.

18.9 Roadmap to Corporate Alignment

In Figure 18.1, a basic model is illustrated to establish and support corporate governance through the PMO that enables corporate project fraud management policy. It is in this manner that the framework for essential project investment governance and reporting is determined for the organization. The PMO is a critical component of achieving this goal since the PMO is truly the recognized subject matter expert in project delivery for the business and owner of the project fraud management policy for the organization.

18.10 Summary

Obviously, business internal alignment is critical to the war on project fraud and Sarbanes-Oxley Section 404 compliance. Is your business aligned? How do you know? Consider the following questions about your organization and your work:

1. Do you know who is accountable at the executive level for each corporate objective? If you answer "the CEO," is this really appropriate for the business? What do you need the CEO direct reports for?
2. Can you identify the corporate objectives for the fiscal year? If not, why? Should you know this?

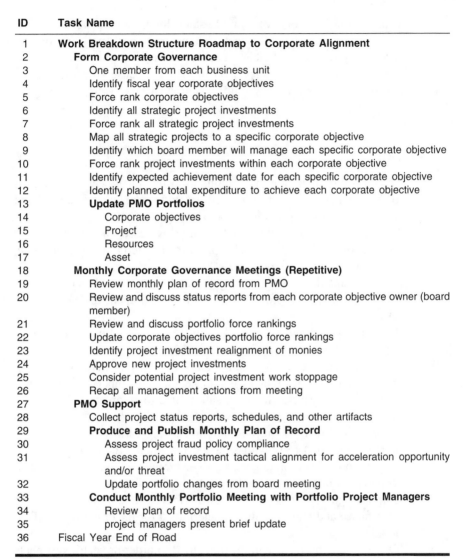

ID	Task Name
1	**Work Breakdown Structure Roadmap to Corporate Alignment**
2	**Form Corporate Governance**
3	One member from each business unit
4	Identify fiscal year corporate objectives
5	Force rank corporate objectives
6	Identify all strategic project investments
7	Force rank all strategic project investments
8	Map all strategic projects to a specific corporate objective
9	Identify which board member will manage each specific corporate objective
10	Force rank project investments within each corporate objective
11	Identify expected achievement date for each specific corporate objective
12	Identify planned total expenditure to achieve each corporate objective
13	**Update PMO Portfolios**
14	Corporate objectives
15	Project
16	Resources
17	Asset
18	**Monthly Corporate Governance Meetings (Repetitive)**
19	Review monthly plan of record from PMO
20	Review and discuss status reports from each corporate objective owner (board member)
21	Review and discuss portfolio force rankings
22	Update corporate objectives portfolio force rankings
23	Identify project investment realignment of monies
24	Approve new project investments
25	Consider potential project investment work stoppage
26	Recap all management actions from meeting
27	**PMO Support**
28	Collect project status reports, schedules, and other artifacts
29	**Produce and Publish Monthly Plan of Record**
30	Assess project fraud policy compliance
31	Assess project investment tactical alignment for acceleration opportunity and/or threat
32	Update portfolio changes from board meeting
33	**Conduct Monthly Portfolio Meeting with Portfolio Project Managers**
34	Review plan of record
35	project managers present brief update
36	Fiscal Year End of Road

Figure 18.1. WBS Roadmap to Corporate Alignment.

3. Can you identify the top ten strategic project investments in the business? If not, how would you recognize project fraud if it occurred for any one of them?

4. Do you know what corporate objective your work is linked to? If not, how do you know if your work is aligned or not?

This chapter basically reviews how to establish corporate governance that aligns project investments toward business transformation. Achieving overall business prosperity requires efficiency and proactivity on everyone's part. If you do not subscribe to this concept, you most likely cause your own job to lose value and this is your choice. Wouldn't you rather grow your value in your job?

Questions

18.1   The cost-optimizing approach limits the value of project management to the business and can hide project fraud under what is considered reasonable work expectations. True or false?

18.2   The idea behind throughput optimization is based on completing the most amount of work within a prescribed criteria set such as time, scope, or resources. True or false?

18.3   Project teams that use the throughput-optimization approach will seek to deliver completed project work on time and under budget. True or false?

18.4   Passive project fraud is defined as meeting expectations, but misrepresenting what was possible. True or false?

18.5   In the throughput-optimization model, passivity is perceived as lag among the project team members. Project team members seek to eliminate lag as a means to improve safety time to complete project work down-line in the project life cycle. True or false?

18.6   The responsibility for business alignment (project investments to corporate objectives) rests with strategic planning. True or false?

18.7   The purpose of corporate governance essentially is to achieve planned corporate objectives within the allotted time. True or false?

18.8   Corporate governance is the framework for essential project investment governance and reporting that is determined for the organization. True or false?

18.9   The corporate need for a uniform method to order project investments value to corporate gain in a strategic correlated manner is key to establishing corporate alignment. True or false?

18.10   A common difficulty for most businesses is how to cause all organizations within the enterprise to prioritize their strategic work in the same manner universally to enable corporate alignment. True or false?

19

Defining
Where to Start

As a CEO, CFO, COO, you may be in your office and faced with the daunting task of signing your name to official corporate correspondence. What makes this so frightening is that you may be unknowingly falsifying information to the government that states you are certifying the corporate fiscal statement that details of the corporate quarterly fiscal report are true and accurate. In fact, you know that because of the rapid pace of change in your business this past year, you are not sure anyone knows the correct answer. Your team, at best, can only make a calculated guess that may have more significant errors in this required assessment prepared for the government than the government allows.

In realizing the consequences of certifying this report to the government, you worry about what you are doing. Are placing your career, your job, your family, at risk every three months? You bet you are and more. You fear that you are risking personal financial penalty and jail time when in fact you may have nothing to do with the errors in the report. This is the best your team can do given the information at hand.

What can YOU do about this? As one of the executive leaders in your business, you have the opportunity to initiate improvement in fiscal controls to lessen risk for the corporate entity that you serve, as well as you and others who are subjected to this same standard and penalty. Knowing what the business must do to control project fraud should be the goal.

19.1 Getting Started

Gaining total control over project fraud requires the ability to recognize project fraud at all levels of the workforce. In addition, the organization must be able to evaluate work results compared to what the organization expected and must establish an environment that consistently reduces the opportunity for project fraud as a means to improve project fraud prevention. A key construct to project fraud control is improving visibility to work results at all levels.

19.2 How Do We Train Our Workforce to Manage Project Fraud?

Project management delivery success has been improving in recent years in companies that have project management as a practice. It use to be that five out of six IT projects failed every year due to some type of project failure. Given these odds, why would anyone want to work on project teams? Now with the current economic pressure to minimize project resources (costs), the pressure is even more intense. Project fraud management should be perceived as an improvement to the culture behind the project delivery environment. As these polices are implemented, these new rules will add more protection to the blind sides of the project team from those people who might be inclined to take advantage of the project. Project teams should welcome this news with open arms in most businesses if the message is communicated well. This embracement will help facilitate the project team training necessary to support project fraud management policies.

Project teams should be trained on how to manage to a project schedule using critical path/critical chain techniques. A four-hour awareness class will do initially for all project team members. Subsequent project status meetings should include this scheduling technique as part of the review process so that all project team members are kept informed as to current progress of the project.

Project sponsors should be trained in a uniform manner to manage for project fraud. If your business is not training project sponsors for this type of support, opportunity to catch the project fraud early in the process will be lost. Project sponsors will not consider project fraud management as part of their job.

Corporate governance committees should be communicated to and trained on organization project fraud management policies as well using operational data to help them navigate difficult project decisions.

19.3 What Policies Should Be Implemented to Manage and Communicate on Project Fraud Effectively?

Our objective in managing for project fraud is to prevent and detect project fraud while reducing project delivery costs. While this may seem improbable, consider that the information listed below is what you should be accomplishing today, but for some reason this is not happening. Furthermore, the cost associated with performing these policies are really a one-time event primarily for the creation and implementation of the project fraud policies. In a mature state, these new policies and processes will become second nature with no apparent direct cost other than through the PMO and/or internal auditing when performing project fraud functions.

To achieve this objective, policies are required to establish necessary guidelines for:

1. Necessary project information
2. Resource role accountabilities
3. How to conduct project audit events
4. Organization governance support
5. Service level agreements between internal auditing, strategic planning, and the PMO
6. How to report project fraud
7. How to manage for project fraud

This is a start for most likely policies to be implemented. There may be others that you will need for your business. The bottom line of these policies should yield the following benefits:

1. Reduced rework resulting in 6 percent of budget or more
2. Reduced investment in projects that do not meet return on investment guidelines.
3. Improved corporate governance to leading, managing, and navigating fiscal year tactical work plans
4. Improved workforce work satisfaction
5. Improved project delivery success

19.4 The Value Proposition of the PMO in Detecting and Preventing Project Fraud

The PMO can be a very effective soldier in the war against project fraud. Through effective portfolio management techniques, service level agreements with internal auditing, strategic planning, and direct support to the corporate governance team, a PMO can significantly reduce project fraud while helping the business become more viable by making progress data more visible to the workforce.

19.5 Defining Portfolio Management

Portfolio management is defined as the measurement of achievement of a group of related projects, objectives, assets, or resources for a period of time that encompasses a fiscal year, for the purpose of optimizing the organization's support to complete these related efforts successfully. Further information can be obtained from the book *Advanced Project Portfolio Management and the PMO: Multiplying ROI at Warp Speed.*[1] This book details the necessary steps and value to be gained in establishing a PMO that will help your business prosper.

Types of portfolios in organizations to be considered:

1. Projects
2. Corporate objectives
3. Assets
4. Resources

19.6 Defining Corporate Governance

In establishing corporate or organizational governance, the following five questions are important to answer:

1. Is the business strategically aligned with the approved strategic fiscal year work plan? Are we working the plan in the order we expected?
2. Are our project investments delivery risks managed well? Do we have executive leadership on point strategically and tactically for each corporate objective that we seek to achieve this fiscal year?
3. Do we have project fraud management policies in place that prevent and detect project fraud and is our workforce aware? How do we educate our workforce to recognize project fraud? How do we best implement a project fraud management policy?
4. Does our workforce primarily perform the daily work according to their personal needs or do they perform the daily work according to what the business expects them to do?
5. Is there a safety net in place to protect our project investments from fraud? Are we communicating sufficiently to raise project fraud awareness internally?

Each fiscal year, when the business implements its strategic plan for that business cycle, the business knows what it wants to be. It must know that it knows when an objective will or will not be achieved, relative to all of the project investments primarily supporting it, so that senior management can make appropriate management decisions to optimize the business work plan. The following initial action steps will help you consider options to regain executive control over your organization.

19.7 Initial Action Steps To Regain Executive Control

1. Is the business strategically aligned with the approved strategic fiscal year work plan? Are we working the plan in the order we expected?
   - Objective: All projects are mapped one for one with each corporate objective.
     - ☐ Step 1: Form an organizational governance committee to own the aggregate of the organization portfolio of projects.
     - ☐ Step 2: All strategic project investments are mapped one for one with a primary corporate objective.
     - ☐ Step 3: All project teams are reporting project progress using critical path techniques in their schedules.
     - ☐ Step 4: PMO produces a cyclical progress report detailing project investment progress compared to governance expectations.
2. Are all of our project investments delivery risks managed well? Do we have executive leadership on point strategically and tactically for each corporate objective that we seek to achieve this fiscal year?
   - Objective: Corporate objective achievement accountability — Assign one of your direct reports to manage each corporate objective strategically and tactically over the fiscal year.
     - ☐ Step 1: One senior executive is assigned to each organization objective to be accountable for strategic and tactical achievement of that objective.
     - ☐ Step 2: All project investments within each organization objective are tracked and ranked in a force-ranked order.
     - ☐ Step 3: All project investment predecessor and successor relationships are identified within the portfolio of projects for each organization objective.
     - ☐ Step 4: Organization objective most critical project is always known. Project investment opportunities and threats are always known for each organization objective project portfolio.
3. Do we have project fraud management policies in place that prevent and detect project fraud and is our workforce aware? How do we educate our

workforce to recognize project fraud? How do we best implement a project fraud management policy?

- Objective: Reduce project fraud opportunities by raising visibility.
  - ☐ Step 1: PMO publishes monthly progress report of strategic project investments.
  - ☐ Step 2: Organization governance committee meets regularly to review project investment portfolio progress.
  - ☐ Step 3: Top ten strategic project investments progress are consistently posted in common areas.
  - ☐ Step 4: Workforce has been trained in project fraud management policies.
  - ☐ Step 5: Train the workforce to be aware of the fiscal year corporate objectives and how their work relates.
  - ☐ Step 6: Project teams are employing critical path/critical chain scheduling techniques in their project schedules.
4. Does our workforce primarily perform their daily work according to their personal needs or do they perform the daily work according to what the business expects them to do?
   - Objective: Improve the sense of urgency for project delivery completion.
     - ☐ Step 1: Implement critical path scheduling in all project teams to raise awareness for "what's next."
     - ☐ Step 2: Conduct regular project progress status meetings.
     - ☐ Step 3: Perform project audits on a predetermined basis such as every three months and/or at the end of each project phase.
5. Is there a safety net in place to protect your project investments from project fraud? Are we communicating sufficiently to raise project fraud awareness internally?
   - Objective: Establish or amend the charter for the organization PMO to manage project fraud prevention and detection.
     - ☐ Step 1: Implement portfolio management techniques.
     - ☐ Step 2: Establish service level agreements between the PMO, internal auditing, and strategic planning to support project fraud management.
     - ☐ Step 3: Implement organization governance committees to support the work in alignment with objectives and project teams.

19.8 Summary

Project fraud is all around us. As we traveled all around the United States for the last several years, we have asked corporate America what they thought about project fraud. Does it exist in their business? How do they know? What are they doing about it? Aren't they worried? They answer: "Project fraud does exist, we just don't know what it looks like most of the time until it is too late." "We can't control what we can't see or recognize."

Given the Sarbanes-Oxley legislation as the cause, the effect will eventually become larger on corporate America and the world more than is realized today. More so than Y2K ever was. Why? Because companies will not do business with your company if your company cannot demonstrate that project fraud is under control. Remember when Total Quality Management swept through corporate America? Many Fortune 1000 firms refused to do business with others unless they had a viable quality program in place. The same will happen with project fraud management. It will not matter if your firm is publicly traded or not. Corporate project fraud management programs will be expected by your partners, your customers, and your workers. We hope this does not sound glum!

It may seem overly expensive to implement part or all of these suggestions. The fact is, your business may actually operate much easier and cheaper on a day-to-day business by reducing and/or eliminating regular costs for work processes that acted as defensive project fraud mechanism for various project works.

Managing for project fraud prevention and detection makes great business sense. What exactly is your firm doing about it? Does the senior team have their personal action plans in place to compensate for federal penalties and/or jail time should they be found guilty of fraud? We wish you well!

Questions

19.1 Improved project delivery success is a top benefit for managing project fraud detection and prevention. True or false?

19.2 Strategically aligning business with the approved strategic fiscal year work plan is not essential to the PMO. True or false?

19.3 Gaining total control over project fraud requires the ability to recognize project fraud at all levels of the workforce. True or false?

Reference

1. Kendall, Gerald and Rollins, Steve, *Advanced Project Portfolio Management and the PMO: Multiplying ROI at Warp Speed,* J. Ross Publishing, Boca Raton, FL, 2003.

20

Searching for Project
Fraud within the
Project Investment

20.1 Recognizing Project Fraud

Fraud is defined by Webster's Dictionary as "deceit; trickery; cheating." A person who intentionally deceives or is not what they pretend to be is a fraud. Thus, anyone that is a part of a project team, directly or indirectly, that deceives, tricks, or cheats in the project work they do, is committing project fraud technically speaking.

Accounting/finance departments in most businesses are performing an adequate job in auditing and improving financial reporting except for those areas of the business where fiscal management can be manipulated to support personal career management, personal reward, or other personal interests that are not in the corporation's best interests or are not what the business paid for. Auditing project investments for project fraud requires detailed understanding of project management concepts and related types of project fraud. Project investment auditors can acquire project management concepts and improve their skills by becoming certified as a Project Management Professional (PMP) by the Project Management Institute. A number of businesses have asked their PMO to conduct project investment audits because they have project management expertise to recognize problems and any related fraud. Our recommendation is that great care should be exercised in asking the PMO to perform this function as the PMO will be perceived as an enforcer of management rather than as help to project teams struggling for delivery success. We believe that an enforcement PMO image is detrimental to the business and to the project investments the business expects to achieve because project teams will not trust the PMO for help.

20.2 Examples of Project Fraud

1. *Project sponsor mismanagement* — Project sponsors that lead the project team knowingly in a direction that they know is not what the business has requested.
2. *Overestimation of work level of effort at the project and/or task level* — Project members who overstate work estimates for personal benefit.
3. *Intentional suppression of project progress reporting information* — Not reporting correct project status, even when the information is negative, is misrepresentation.
4. *Internal business partner unwillingness to assume accountability for project success or failure for the project they funded* — This example is tricky; however, the lack of ownership creates opportunity for project fraud to develop.
5. *Business case justification misrepresentation* — Have you seen any business cases that were overstated because it helped make the case for project activation?
6. *Internal business-side partners that compete with other business-unit peers for project delivery support not in alignment with the fiscal year work plan of strategic projects* — CIOs are often targets of business-side project owners to deliver their projects when they have not been approved to do so.
7. *Worker sense of urgency that is personal-need driven versus business-focused driven* — Workforce members who work on what they want to do when they want to do it.
8. *Worker vendettas that prevent project delivery progress* — Enough said!
9. *Including customer requirements into an existing project when the new requirements were not approved* — Project teams have enough to do.
10. *Adding unplanned project vendor workers to the project team without approval to do so* — This costs the business money it did not expect to spend.

These types of fraud appear most often in the project delivery sphere and represent the tip of the iceberg on types of project fraud that eat away at corporate fiduciary accountability and personal risk.

20.3 How Do We Prevent and Detect Project Fraud in Project Investments?

Several methods exist that will help the business prevent project fraud as soon as they are implemented.

1. Project fraud requires the opportunity to actually become realized. *Reducing the opportunity* for project fraud will reduce project fraud. Opportunity for project fraud can come from anywhere. Rigor and discipline from the practice of project management when applied in a uniform manner will aid the prevention effort.

2. *Raise the visibility* of project progress to all workforce members involved. Team members should be aware of the project's critical path schedule and who is currently on the "hot seat." Best method is to use project status meetings and individual status reports.

3. *Enlist the PMO* to design, develop, and implement project fraud management policies that will improve project fraud prevention and detection when implemented. Internal auditing or strategic planning are not the best solution since those require seasoned understanding of the principles of project management and how that rigor and discipline is applied in the business. A best method approach includes the establishment of service level agreements with internal auditing and strategic planning regarding their roles in project fraud management.

4. *Reduce multitasking and work pressure on the project workers.* When the time left to complete the work is less than the work left to complete, pressure to succeed increases. Desperate people do desperate things. When desperate actions are taken, the project results normally suffer. If the project manager can raise the visibility of the project's critical path along with obtaining assistance from the PMO, this may help everyone relax.

20.4 Project Delivery Environmental Contributors That Enable Project Fraud Opportunities

A number of basic project environmental enablers can lead to an attitude that does not manage for project fraud.

1. A business environment that accepts project delivery success as "close" to expected delivery date and budgeted cost

2. Project sponsors that have not been trained in a standard business model for leading project investments

3. Missing entity to support and facilitate tactical progress of all project investments, such as the PMO

4. Poor visibility to down-range project delivery hurdles, inter- or intraproject

5. Poor executive sponsorship to promote project fraud control management in the organization

6. Lack of awareness by the workforce for the current year fiscal objectives — what the business expects to achieve for this fiscal year

7. Inappropriate force ranking of project investments in alignment with the corporate objectives for the fiscal year

8. Inefficient support for the workforce for project management rigor and discipline

9. Business model that embraces cost optimization compared to throughput optimization

10. PMO as an enforcer for project delivery policy compliance

20.5 Examining Project Teams

In most companies, this activity falls to internal auditing, strategic planning, or to the PMO. Internal auditing or strategic planning are good choices to start with if a PMO does not exist. However, neither internal auditing nor strategic planning normally possess sufficient project management principles expertise to perform this role over the long term. Adding project fraud management to the charter of the PMO does not mean that the PMO must take on a "police" role. In fact, great care must be given to how this new service is communicated to the workforce. In many companies today, the PMO is emerging as a "help desk" to help project teams overcome unplanned hurdles in project delivery. If these project teams begin to believe that "what they say may be used against them in a court of law" do you think they will ever visit the PMO again for help? The PMO should be collaborating with internal auditing for internal auditing to perform the project fraud audits so that the PMO can maintain its helpful role with the project teams.

In addition, the PMO should assist in ensuring that:

■ All strategic projects are linked to a primary corporate objective.

■ All project teams are educated about current project fraud policies.

■ Uniform project fraud detection and prevention procedures are implemented.

- All project sponsors are trained in the project fraud management policy.
- An ethical tone is set from the top.
- All reported fraud tips are taken seriously and each of them is investigated.
- A project fraud management policy is implemented.

Whoever performs project audits should consider the following project fraud checkpoints:

- Does the project apply critical path scheduling for the project?
- How was work estimation for the top project tasks performed?
- Are all project resources working project work in the correct priority order?
- Are project requirements well defined and approved?

In addition, project auditors should consider the checklist in Figure 20.1. Every section of this checklist should achieve a 70 percent rating to be considered satisfactory in their current performance. A rating of "Above Expectations"

Project Team: _____   **Date:** _____
Completed By: _____   **E-mail:** _____

Legend   Exceeds Expectations = 30; Meets Expectations = 20; Below Expectations = 10

Process   Select the most appropriate legend value from above for each assessed checkpoint below. Sum the Total Achieved Score and divide into Total Possible Score for Final Percentage Grade. Internal auditing and/or PMO determine legend expectations.

Project is considered a "high" project fraud risk if "Final Percentage Grade" is less than 70 percent.

Checklist categories are considered "high" risk if category score is below 70 percent.

Business Case Justification
Problem Opportunity
Gap Assessment Completed   _____
High Level Benefit Analysis   _____
Customer Needs Assessed   _____
Strategic Alignment Determined   _____
Project Priorities   _____
Project Interdependencies   _____
Market Impact-High Level   _____
Risk/Impact of No Action   _____

Figure 20.1. Project Fraud Checklist.

Alternative Options to Project   _____
Score   _____

Project Charter
Project Demographics   _____
Problem/Opportunity Statement   _____
Project Objective   _____
Magnitude   _____
Deliverables   _____
Level of Authority   _____
Change Management Plan   _____
Financial Resources   _____
Expected Activities   _____
Project Interdependencies   _____
Project Intradependencies   _____
Value/Priority   _____
Assumptions   _____
Risks   _____
Constraints   _____
Sponsor Approval   _____
Score   _____

Project Infrastructure
Assumptions List   _____
Responsibility Matrix   _____
Task Description Worksheet   _____
Task Estimating Worksheet   _____
Work Breakdown Structure List   _____
Project Scope Change Log   _____
Score   _____

Work Breakdown Structure Review
All tasks to accomplish the project are identified   _____
WBS is structured as information will be used   _____
Levels of detail allow for realistic estimating   _____
Levels of detail allow assignment to single organizational control unit   _____
Level of detail is limited to level of control   _____
The result of each lowest level is a deliverable   _____
An action verb initiates each WBS description   _____
Score   _____

Estimate Review
Review the definition of the project   _____
Review the ground rules, constraints, and assumptions   _____
Focus on the sources of the data   _____
Determine whether the estimating methodology is acceptable   _____
Review the resources to be used and the activity costs   _____
Compare estimate against best practices industry standards   _____
Analyze activity and resource cost drivers   _____
Ensure that estimate incorporates risk   _____
Score   _____

Figure 20.1.   Project Fraud Checklist (continued).

Project Scheduling
Master Schedule developed in detail? _____
Project Sponsor and Customer agree on Master Schedule? _____
Master Schedule achievable? _____
Agreement among all functional organizations for the execution of the
defined project tasks? _____
Project Network Schedule been developed that includes all project tasks? _____
Critical Path identified? _____
Does the Critical Path satisfy the Master Schedule with sufficient
contingency for surprises? _____
Are all team members committed to the planned approach to project
execution? _____
Have detailed schedules been developed for the individual tasks of the
project? _____
Are the performing organizations signed up and committed to executing
these tasks as described? _____
Have project risks been evaluated at all levels with appropriate risk
management actions incorporated into the planning for project execution? _____
Score _____

Project Risk Management Model
Risk Identification _____
Risk Quantification _____
Risk Response Development _____
Risk Response Control _____
Score _____

Management Evaluation
Are the project goals and objectives realistic? _____
Is the resource allocation plan realistic? _____
Is the project budget reasonable? _____
Is the project schedule feasible? _____
Is the project organization structure sound? _____
Are the control systems adequate? _____
Are project management tools being applied to the project on a regular
basis? _____
Is the risk management plan being followed and updated? _____
Are management reserves adequate? _____
Score _____

Organizational Evaluation
Does the project organization contribute to the project goals and objectives? _____
Does the project manager exercise adequate authority? _____
Do the project team members know their roles within the project matrix? _____
Does the customer (internal or external) understand the project organization? _____
Is there adequate communication within the project matrix? _____
Is the project team kept abreast of ongoing developments within the project? _____
Do documented project status meeting minutes exist? _____
Score _____

Figure 20.1.   Project Fraud Checklist (continued).

Project Control
Where is the project relative to the schedule?   _____
Where is the project relative to cost?   _____
Where is the project with respect to meeting specifications?   _____
Where is the project with respect to overall objectives and goals?   _____
Where are the WBS elements with respect to the project schedule?   _____
Where are the WBS elements with respect to costs?   _____
Where are the WBS elements with respect to meeting technical
requirements?   _____
Where are the WBS elements with respect to project goals and objectives?   _____
Project areas execution expectations?   _____
What concerns are developing within the project?   _____
What risks and opportunities are evolving from the project?   _____
Is the project still in line with organizational objectives?   _____
Is the client/customer satisfied?   _____
Is the project team satisfied?   _____
Have outside sources examined project progress?   _____
Is the project team functioning well?   _____
Is the project still a strategic fit for the organization?   _____
Does the project remain profitable?   _____
Are there any potential showstoppers on the project horizon?   _____
Score   _____

Total Score
Final Grade (Total Achieved Score/Total Possible Score as a %)   _____

Figure 20.1. Project Fraud Checklist (continued).

might be 80 percent while "Excellent" might be 90 percent or better. If one section of this checklist fails the 70 percent rule, then the entire checklist has failed. The rules that your organization applies in the utilization of this checklist for project audits may be more stringent. Remember, the more management burden placed on the project member, the more will be taken away from their time to produce. There must be a happy medium and this is the challenge today.

20.6 Summary

Our intent in this chapter was to provide awareness for basic, low-cost processes that any organization can implement to manage for project fraud. In order to manage for project fraud, it will be important to plan for the potential types of project fraud that might appear in your business. As this knowledge is completed, a project fraud checklist should be constructed that project teams can use as a self-check for project fraud compliance.

The PMO should work in unison with internal auditing and strategic planning to map out a tactical approach to project fraud prevention and detection that includes teaching the project team members how to do the same in their project team.

Questions

20.1   Project investment auditors can acquire project management concepts and improve their skills by becoming certified as a Project Management Professional (PMP) by the Project Management Institute. True or false?

20.2   A type of project fraud is project sponsors leading the project team knowingly in a direction that they know is not what the business has requested. True or false?

20.3   Reducing the opportunity for project fraud will reduce project fraud. True or false?

20.4   All project sponsors should be trained in project fraud management policy. True or false?

20.5   The PMO should be collaborating with internal auditing for internal auditing to perform project fraud audits so that the PMO can maintain its helpful role with the project teams. True or false?

20.6   A business environment that accepts project delivery success as "close" to the expected delivery date and budgeted cost creates project fraud opportunity. True or false?

20.7   The level of detail in the work breakdown structure allows for realistic estimating in the Business Case Justification section of the Project Fraud Checklist. True or false?

20.8   Worker vendettas that prevent project delivery progress are another type of project fraud. True or false?

Essential Project Reporting Processes That Support Project Fraud Prevention and Detection

21.1 Defining the Objective

As we have stated in earlier chapters, every strategic project investment should be mapped to a specific corporate objective. In this manner, business alignment becomes more established and the safety net for project delivery is created and strengthened as the alignment model becomes more and more developed. Imperative to this alignment is the project tactical detail that identifies progress according to the project schedule. Managing the project schedule in a critical path manner provides ongoing assessment to interested parties about how they should react to project delivery progress. Most of the time, everyone wants to know if the project will deliver on time and/or on budget. In other scenarios, project team members may want to know when they will receive work product output from project tasks they may be waiting on. In general though, people really want to know ONLY what will impact them. When people limit their need for awareness in project delivery, they are in essence limiting how much energy or time they will spend considering information. They do not care about anything else. People who seek to commit project fraud look for these types of opportunities where no one is watching. You can prevent this by becoming more observant about project delivery risk, good and bad. You can also help prevent and detect project fraud by making the results of your work more visible. This does not really cost you any more, but it could save your work, your project, your department, etc.

21.2   Roles and Responsibilities

21.2.1 Corporate Governance

The job of corporate governance requires business alignment knowledge of how the business is performing against strategic expectations. The outcome of each corporate governance meeting must reaffirm the business alignment of project investments to corporate objectives, thereby establishing the framework for measuring project investment delivery for satisfactory performance. Each month when the business alignment is reaffirmed by corporate governance, the process mechanisms that provide the business alignment perspective (portfolio management) are updated to reflect the new force-ranking, corporate governance decisions for strategic project investments. Reporting tactical data of project investment and related corporate objective progress that is organized in an aggregated manner provides a clear perspective for management choices at the corporate governance level to increase business throughput. This process should be provided by the PMO through the monthly plan of record.

21.2.2 Corporate Objective Executive Owner

The goal of the corporate objective executive is to achieve fulfillment of the corporate objective in a timely manner that is within the planned end date and planned costs for the fiscal year. Essential reporting processes to this role are specific to the corporate objectives portfolio from the monthly plan of record. The corporate objectives portfolio is derived from the reporting period project investment schedules and status reports often contained within the PMO data store. In the role as the corporate governance executive for the corporate objective, this person will seek to understand how the objective is progressing as compared to the other corporate objectives in the portfolio. Normally, the corporate objectives are force ranked against each other by corporate governance based on strategic value. Sometimes during the course of the fiscal year, this force-ranked order may change because the business climate has changed within the business, outside the business, or both. The executive is watching other corporate objective executives in how they are progressing knowing full well they are doing the same with him or her. This is necessary because opportunities and/or threats may emerge that may impact the effectiveness of their role. This high visibility is part of the innate check and balance process to project investment fraud prevention and detection. When these executives are competing for the same scarce resources from within the business, project fraud does not have a chance to occur as a result of the scrutiny being brought forward from overall corporate governance of corporate objective progress.

21.2.3 Business Unit Management

Business unit management is more dependent on tactical information that is related to project investment progress. Essential to this role is the portfolio reporting from the monthly plan of record that is intrabusiness-unit reflective for projects, assets, and resources. The business unit leader will also be interested in how the business unit is performing relative to business unit support for the corporate objective portfolio. The PMO data store is a valuable real-time asset to participating business units if they can get at it through an EPM tool. The business unit primal need is for ad hoc data support as business situations dictate. If they cannot see the pitch, they cannot hit it!

21.2.4 PMO

Since the PMO supports every aspect of business alignment through the PMO data store and the EPM tool, the essential reporting requirements of those PMO customers are managed and facilitated by the PMO. Since the PMO will normally own the definition and standard management of these reporting processes, the PMO itself becomes essential.

The most critical reporting process of the PMO is the monthly plan of record. The contents of this report define project investment delivery risk (positive and negative) in relationship to corporate objective achievement. Essential project governance reporting for the PMO includes timely project status reports and project schedules that are "critical pathed" and stored in the PMO data store through EPM tool access. The monthly plan of record is the essential visibility that is raised to the next level of awareness for various segments of the workforce. If this document is published on a monthly cycle, the reported data provided will never be more than one month old.

21.2.5 Project Team

Essential to the project team are status reports and schedules. Both of the documents are cyclically provided to the PMO. Project schedules must always illustrate the remaining critical path of the project as forecasted by the reporting period. Anything less will render the value of the project schedule to business alignment useless as the project schedule will be considered unsubstantiated.

21.2.6 Project Team Member

Essential to the team member is the project schedule and individual status reports. Generally speaking, individual status reports should be weekly, but never more than bi-weekly. Project status meetings for development projects should be weekly and maybe daily if the demand to crash (shorten) the project schedule is high. The team member must be kept informed daily from others within the team about work progress that has a direct/indirect impact on their work. In most project teams, gaining that information is left to the team member. This is not sufficient. The project manager should ensure that team members are communicating individual work progress to other team members, thus enabling higher cross-collaboration as a means to improve progress rate while avoiding unnecessary delays.

21.2.7 Internal Auditor/Fraud Examiner

Essential to the internal auditors' and fraud examiners' project examinations are the work papers produced by the project team. This artifact collection (project control book) will portray the life cycle progress of the project team. Inspection of these papers (project status reports, project schedules, etc.) will reveal if the project team worked the project according to policies and approved authorizations.

In the PMO data store, the project work papers normally will be organized in a similar fashion for easy access by authorized users.

21.3 Essential Data Elements in Project Governance Reporting

The following data elements are necessary to perform minimal project fraud prevention and detection analysis:

1. Date of project report
2. Project name
3. Project description
4. Project owner

5. Project sponsor
6. Project manager
7. Project budget (dollars or hours)
8. Project actuals (dollars or hours)
9. Business unit project supports
10. Project plan start date
11. Project plan end date
12. Project actual start date
13. Project actual end date
14. Project supported corporate objective
15. Project supported asset
16. Project level predecessors
17. Project level successors
18. Project delivery interval (days, length of critical path)
19. Project task resource assignments
20. Project task description
21. Project task plan start date
22. Project task plan end date
23. Project task actual start date
24. Project task actual end date
25. Project task resource plan allocation
26. Project task resource actual allocation
27. Project milestone plan achievement date
28. Project milestone actual achievement date
29. Current critical path interval
30. Project manager project health assessment (red, yellow, green)

The following data elements are necessary to perform minimal project fraud prevention and detection analysis at the PMO level. The value of these data elements are constructed each reporting cycle by the PMO from collected project reporting information.

1. Strategic project investments that have current or predicted future health of red or yellow
2. Corporate objectives that have current or predicted future health of red or yellow
3. Strategic assets that have current or predicted future health of red or yellow
4. Resources (excluding project managers) that have current or predicted future health of red or yellow

5. Business units that own strategic project investments as an owner or supplier that have current or predicted future health of red or yellow
6. Project managers who have current or predicted future health of red or yellow for their project investments
7. Project investments that expect to achieve early delivery
8. Corporate objectives that expect early achievement from project delivery
9. Strategic assets that expect early improvement achievement from project delivery
10. Resources that are coming available early for more project delivery work
11. Baseline total of corporate objectives fiscal year spending
12. Expected total of corporate objectives fiscal year spending at completion
13. Available project monies for potential reallocation
14. Baseline total project investments expected to be completed in fiscal year
15. Forecasted total project investments expected to be completed in fiscal year

21.4 The Value Proposition of Status Meetings

Status meetings are often unproductive because they not organized very well, particularly in establishing participation expectations for meeting outcomes prior to the meeting. Most every status meeting collects and provides information. When the project information flow is linked in a manner that connects worker to worker versus supervisor to subordinate, the power of personal relationships can be leveraged to influence people to behave in the direction that is expected within the project even when they had initially resisted the same request earlier from someone in authority.

Project status meetings normally review project schedule status against the critical path that is dynamically changing every time a project task is completed on the critical path, or when time passes without expected progress to cause the critical path to change by the addition of other previously unrelated project tasks, etc. In these types of discussions, visibility to other people's work is the value gained by the project team members. This visibility is very often missing even in status meetings because meeting participants are not reporting THEIR status to peers. In the course of daily work, much can happen that was supposed to or was unplanned but had a significant impact on some of the project work. These unexpected events must be communicated even if the event was expected. Confirmation of work completion is an event. Communicating this event as a change in project value has value because someone else must now take that output and use it to further the project effort. Forcing people to communicate progress to others in their work group can be very difficult at times. It can be more difficult to accomplish when the communication is expected to occur without supervision on a one-to-one basis. When a project manager asks for specific team member status, they may receive information from the team member that the team member thinks the project manager wants to hear, but in reality is not the truth. This is misrepresentation and in project delivery is one of simplest forms of project fraud. To combat this problem, the project manager should consider organizing the project status meeting and reporting process in the following manner:

> Let us assume that the project team meets every two weeks to review project progress. The project team is expected to enter their work effort into the project schedule tool each week by 10 AM the following Monday. At the same time, the team member is to post his or her personal status report to the project in the PMO data store using their access through the EPM tool by the following Monday at 10 AM. Everyone in the project team has access to the project schedule and to the individual status reports. The project manager had previously organized project status meetings for every other Wednesday at 2 PM for one hour during the project life cycle. In the project status meeting, each team member is expected to update the team on his or her work status in a brief manner not to exceed two minutes (each). The brief update is because the individual status reports were just posted two days ago and everyone can read those if they need to. Each team member is expected to state the latest information on work progress relative to: what they accomplished in the reporting period, what they expect to accomplish in the next reporting period, what needs they had, what issues or risks they were managing, what potential acceleration and/or threats there might be associated with their work, and where they felt project opportunities and/or threats to the project might exist from their position in the project schedule. During the team member presentation, other team members might be following along with the current project schedule and making notes about impact to them. As each person completes the brief update, the next team member steps in and gives their update. This continues until every team member has updated the team. Next, the project manager will ask for any questions, issues, opportunities, or threats from the team based on what they just heard

and witnessed. In the beginning of this style of project status meeting, each team member learns to be prepared to state clearly any information that does not impact other team members, their peers. This motivation is the result of the more personal relationship team members have with each other because they often work closely together. In the course of day-to-day work activities, the wrath of a teammate is often perceived as worse than the wrath of the supervisor. The preparatory work the team member must perform to satisfy peers is often thought of as more than what would be done for the supervisor. This extra effort may not have taken any more time to perform. The key difference is that the passion associated with helping the peer teammate be successful is much more than the passion the reporting team member would place into the report effort for a supervisor. We define this as horizontal management, where team members on a project team are leveraged against each other in a positive manner to cause project delivery to accelerate and to raise project delivery visibility enough to improve project fraud prevention and detection intrateam for direct safety of the project team. Thus the value proposition of project status meetings is significant if these meetings are conducted in the proper manner. As this is accomplished, the project team should expect project meeting outcomes to improve intraproject trust and support among the team members incrementally. The quality of completed project work also improves from the improved visibility as well. Everyone benefits, even the corporate objective that the project is supporting. This improved trust does not cost the business. The improvement gains are innate to the process of raising visibility of progress intrateam. There are many other benefits to this approach that are too numerous to list here. Contact us if you would like to discuss how to clean up your dysfunctional project team and improve project delivery speed and/or project fraud prevention and detection for the direct benefit of the project team.

21.5 Summary

Essential project reporting is a basic tenet of business. The professions of project management, internal auditing, and fraud examination require it as a basic standard in work completion. The critical factor for project reporting value to project fraud management is as a catalyst to human behavior, as is expected in a team member role in any work group setting. How a person is managed and in what tone can be the difference between project success and failure. Essential project reporting must leverage human behavior if businesses are to optimize their success in project delivery.

Questions

21.1   The outcome of each corporate governance meeting must reaffirm the business alignment of project investments to corporate objectives, thereby establishing the framework for measuring project investment delivery for satisfactory performance. True or false?

21.2   The goal of the corporate objective executive is to achieve fulfillment of the corporate objective in a timely manner that is within the planned end date and planned costs for the fiscal year. True or false?

21.3   Business unit management is more dependent on tactical information that is related to project investment progress. Essential to this role is the portfolio reporting from the monthly plan of record that is intrabusiness unit reflective for projects, assets, and resources. True or false?

21.4   Since the PMO will normally own the definition and standard management of these essential reporting processes, the PMO itself becomes essential to the business and to project fraud management. True or false?

21.5   Project schedules must always illustrate the remaining critical path of the project as forecasted by the reporting period. Anything less will render the value of the project schedule to business alignment useless as the project schedule will be considered unsubstantiated. True or false?

21.6   The project manager should ensure that team members are communicating individual work progress to other team members, thus enabling higher cross-collaboration as a means to improve the progress rate while avoiding unnecessary delays. True or false?

21.7   Essential to the internal auditors' and fraud examiners' project examinations are the work papers produced by the project team. This artifact collection (project control book) will portray the life cycle progress of the project team. Inspection of these papers (project status reports, project schedules, etc.) will reveal if the project team worked the project according to policies and approved authorizations. True or false?

21.8   When a project manager asks for specific team member status, the project manager may receive from the team member information that the team member thinks the project manager wants to hear but in reality is not the truth. This is misrepresentation and in project delivery is one of simplest forms of project fraud. True or false?

21.9   "Horizontal management" is where team members on a project team are leveraged against each other in a positive manner to cause project delivery to accelerate and to raise project delivery visibility enough to improve project fraud prevention and detection intrateam for direct safety of the project team. True or false?

21.10   Essential project reporting is a basic tenet of business. True or false?

Training the Organization to Manage Project Fraud Prevention and Detection

22.1 Determining the Type of Training Required

Every person in the organization will come into contact with fraud from time to time. The questions is: How will they react? Will they recognize fraud if it is near them? Fraud is something everyone must be on guard for at all times, in their job and in their personal life. Awareness and knowledge does not cost once the knowledge is acquired, it only helps to improve the benefit of outcomes produced by people who know how to manage fraud prevention and detection. Benefits from this acquired knowledge are lifelong. Therefore, existing training programs within your organization should be reviewed to possibly include fraud management policies in the skills training as a direct benefit to achieving business results and beyond.

22.2 Training Courses and Expected Outcomes

Training the workforce to acquire project fraud prevention and detection skills should consider focusing workforce training in project management, business analysis, and fraud management concepts. The following courses and expected training outcomes are recommended to enable the integration of these skill areas for improved fraud management in all areas of project delivery.

22.3 Project Management Skills Area

- **General project management training expected outcomes**
  1. *Project management philosophy* — Learn what project management is about and understand the mindset necessary to achieve project goals.
  2. *Project management as a strategic initiative* — Identify the importance of project management in meeting your company's business goals.
  3. *The language* — Project management has a language of its own that is simple to understand. Learn the meaning of WBS, CPM, Gantt chart, project budget, and more.
  4. *What project team members do* — Identify the role each project team member plays, including project manager, sponsor, stakeholder, and customer.
  5. *How can you help?* — Discover how this initiative impacts you and what contributions will be necessary to make project management a success at your company.
- **IT project management training expected outcomes**
  1. *Project management philosophy* — Understand the mindset necessary to achieve project goals.
  2. *IT life cycles* — Understand how IT projects are managed in alignment with this cornerstone philosophy.
  3. *The Project Management Body of Knowledge (PMBOK®)* — Review the core base of knowledge developed by the Project Management Institute.
  4. *Benefits of a project office* — How many organizations are achieving better project results through the infrastructure of a PMO?
  5. *Elements of program success* — Understand program versus project versus process management and what factors most influence the success and failure of IT projects.
  6. *Project goal alignment* — Ensure, through effective scope planning, that a project's goals are in sync with both business and IT objectives.
  7. *Project quality* — Learn how quality can be applied throughout the project life cycle to enhance productivity and participation.

8. *The human aspect of managing projects* — Understand the role of a project leader and behaviors critical for success. Build a foundation for managing people issues and inherent cross-functionality on your IT project.

9. *Definition of project requirements* — Requirements definition and agreement is the most critical aspect of IT project management. Learn to capture, prioritize, and deliver mutually agreed requirements and objectives.

10. *Project management and the human dynamic* — Understand and manage the classic business versus IT human resource challenges inherent in technical projects.

11. *Project execution planning (PEP)* — Discover the most important components of these key documents and how together they form a roadmap for project completion.

12. *Project time estimating and scheduling* — Build realistic schedules that include resource and cost estimation against clearly defined deliverables.

13. *Project control and reporting* — Refine the planning and validating process, integrating change management, and understanding variances, earned value, and testing.

14. *Project change management* — Create effective, real-life change strategies to manage project budgets and scope effectively.

15. *Project close out* — Utilize punch list concepts to close out against all project requirements.

■ **Engineering project management training expected outcomes**

1. *Project management process and critical deliverables* — Work through a deliverable-based engineering/project management methodology that can be easily scaled across varying project requirements.

2. *Developing the scope of services* — Develop initial and detailed scope of services, turning the scope into tangible deliverables using the work breakdown structure and other scope development tools.

3. *The project's execution plan* — Develop a realistic and rigorous execution plan, with targeted and specific subsidiary management elements to keep the client and our own internal resources on track and within scope, schedule, and budget.

4. *Project time estimating and scheduling for engineering* — Examine different accepted methods (and levels) of scheduling and estimating to coincide with varying project requirements, complexities, and sizes.

5. *Project control and reporting* — Utilize the execution plan as a baseline, examine the standard tools and strategies to build in con-

trol and affect accurate project status and change control without spending the "war debt."

6. *Project close out* — Utilize the principles from close-out plan portion of the PEP, examine the best practices available to complete the scope of work, receive client sign-off, facilitate client satisfaction, close out the project against the documented project requirements, conduct lessons learned, and positively effect "follow-on work."

■ **Project planning training expected outcomes**

1. *Management realities in project organizations* — Identify the inherent, realistic, and underlying success factors for managing projects in organizations.

2. *Understanding the complexities of multiple projects management* — Uncover and understand the high-risk areas and usually overlooked linkage topics involved in multiple project and program management.

3. *Project risk: the probability factor* — Build an understanding of random occurrence, risk identification, risk quantification, and mitigation planning.

4. *Realistic project monitoring and proactive control* — Apply the current state-of-the-art variance determination techniques and the ability to inject urgency with real-time results.

5. *Outsourcing as a solution* — Design a metric-driven checklist and the accompanying risk assessment of the realistic capabilities for the project organization and project team. Where do we draw the line?

6. *Advanced scheduling techniques* — Utilize advanced task dependencies to crash and shorten the critical path. Determine the feasibility of path compression with bottleneck analysis and trade-off analysis.

■ **Project performance monitoring and controlling training expected outcomes**

1. *Introduction to the process improvement life cycle* — Develop an understanding of the importance of process improvement and how to balance people, project management processes, and technology. Define those who are responsible for process improvement.

2. *Overview of the project management maturity model* — Learn about several industry models including the SEI Capability Maturity Model, a Project Management Maturity Model, as well as the PMBOK® knowledge areas and maturity profile.

3. *Assessing and reporting maturity level* — How to design and report against the maturity of the organization. Understand and define the process maturity baseline and identify gaps against it.

4. *Metrics to identify improvement opportunities* — Prioritize and rank improvement opportunities.

5. *Tools to investigate and prioritize improvement opportunities* — A look at standard tools that can be used to assist in this effort including problem-solving models, brainstorming, fishbone, force field, and more.

6. *Commissioning improvement initiatives* — Understand the characteristics of an improvement program versus an improvement initiative. How to define scope, monitor, control and finally, close the initiative.

7. *Implementation challenges* — Consider perceived value, cultural fit, and sponsorship among other potential issues.

■ **Project infrastructure training expected outcomes**

1. *PMO standard overview* — An overview of a project management operating standard and what it can do.

2. *Roles of project team members* — Define team roles and selection criteria.

3. *Project initiation* — Create a procedure for defining ideas, separating projects from processes, and deciding which projects will be approved.

4. *Effective planning* — Understand the mechanics of a project plan and budget in order to gain approval for progression to the next step.

5. *Scheduling and monitoring work* — Define how the project should be launched, assigned, and scheduled and what measures should be taken to monitor and control it.

6. *Implementation and project close* — An important and overlooked step. Review how to put deliverables into production and the benefits and procedures necessary to build and organize project documentation.

■ **Project leadership/team effectiveness training expected outcomes**

1. *Identify your personality profile* — Utilize the personality tools to learn about and assess the project teams you work in.

2. *The dynamics of project teams* — Create a roadmap for successful communications that can reach across projects and cross-functional boundaries.

3. *Build professional behaviors* — To allow for team-based discussions that lead to consensus in a timely fashion.

4. *Resource alignment* — Position yourself and other members of the team to achieve success by utilizing the right person for the job.

5. *Meeting management basics* — Complete more productive meetings in less time by driving accountability and standards into the process.

6. *Develop ground rules* — Build a framework on which your team will function and implement their newly learned skills.

- **Customer relationships training expected outcomes**
  1. *A cognitive and operational model for negotiation* — Identify and understand the critical success factors necessary to achieve high-yield negotiations consistently.
  2. *Goal value analysis* — Determine objectives from varied sources to set the tone for a comprehensive and goal-oriented plan. Build in room for changing and varied circumstances.
  3. *A model for power and resistance* — Identify and utilize these two dynamics to access information necessary to achieve win-win results.
  4. *An insightful model for sender-receiver success* — Examine the inherent pitfalls to exacting and rigorous communication and maintain leadership through directed and consistent communication methods.
  5. *Develop a conflict management style* — Learn how to interact with conflict and mitigate anger, reactivity, and frustration, thus transforming conflict into an opportunity for problem solving and coalition building.

22.4 Business Analysis Skills Area

- **Fundamental overview training expected outcomes**
  1. *The business analyst role* — Learn about project and process definition and define the role with respect to requirement definition and management. Also, define a formal business analysis strategy.
  2. *The business analyst and requirements* — Basic elements of the requirements gathering process and documentation of requirements.
  3. *The business analyst and modeling techniques* — Business modeling is the "as is" part of the overall model. Use case diagrams and scenarios for process and data modeling.
  4. *The business analyst and testing* — Create the testing strategy document. Understand the importance of testing in the overall project and create test case templates.
  5. *The business analyst and object-oriented analysis* — Understand the basic principles and impact of object-oriented analysis.
  6. *The business analyst and financial analysis* — Basic financial analysis and the application of the analysis to management decisions.

- **Gathering and documenting user requirements training expected outcomes**
  1. *The requirements management process* — Understand requirements and the project life cycle.
  2. *Factors influencing requirements* — Symptoms and causes of requirements problems.
  3. *Stakeholders* — Identify stakeholders, determine risks, and plan appropriate action.
  4. *Identifying requirements* — Requirement types; functional, non-functional, and global and identify their interaction with risk.
  5. *Generating requirements* — Identify the steps required and select a method. Understand traceability and types.
  6. *Requirements and change management* — The reason for requirements change and how to manage it.
  7. *Getting from requirements to development and beyond* — Learn important techniques to move the project from requirements to development and through its life cycle while not losing track of the project's scope.
- **Managing requirements training expected outcomes**
  1. *The project management and requirements management life cycles* — Steps in the requirements management process. Fixed and evolving requirements.
  2. *An assessment of stakeholders* — Identification and categorization. Create a communication plan. Understand risk factors.
  3. *Requirements factors influencing project problems* — Understand the common requirements issues that lead to project challenges.
  4. *Multiple views* — How to reconcile multiple views. A consideration of legal and market risks in the relationship management process.
  5. *Critical success factors* — Understanding traceability and global requirements mapping
  6. *Requirements definition* — Identify multiple views and global requirements. A review of documentation standards.
  7. *Evaluation and approval* — Select tools and techniques. Requirement/prototype review.
  8. *Change management* — Evaluate policy for project needs and establish business criteria for change control.
  9. *Validation of project outcomes* — Understand acceptance criteria and project test results.

22.5 Fraud Management Skills Area

- **Managing fraud prevention and detection in the business expected training outcomes**
  1. General awareness on topic for one-hour seminar to general workforce.
- **Project governance and reporting: Preventing and detecting project fraud training expected outcomes**
  1. Identify the value proposition of project governance.
  2. Review of Sarbanes-Oxley expectations.
  3. Review of business expectations today and what they should be regarding project fraud.
  4. Review of information flow for project delivery susceptibility to project fraud.
  5. Establish project fraud management policy baseline expectations for prevention and detection.
  6. Prevention techniques.
  7. Detection techniques.
  8. Policy development.
  9. Business case development.
  10. Work within the organization PMO to improve cross-collaboration.
  11. Define the PMO role.
  12. Portfolio management.
  13. Corporate governance oversight to project fraud.
  14. How project fraud policy can transform the business into competitive gain.
  15. Value audit form and the organizational fire drill.
  16. Create the roadmap to implement project fraud processes.
  17. Create project team roadmap (MS Project).
  18. Create project fraud business case (MS Word).
  19. Apply templates and various supplied metrics to project level exercises.
- **Applying project management metrics to manage project fraud prevention and detection training expected outcomes**
  1. Metrics methodology.
  2. Project fraud policy axioms.
  3. Project fraud and PMO relationship.
  4. Portfolio management.
  5. Importance of project schedules.
  6. Project fraud prevention metrics.
  7. Project fraud detection metrics.

8. Project fraud prevention scenarios.
9. Project fraud detection scenarios.
10. Assessing and reducing project fraud risk.
11. Project fraud metrics implementation roadmap.
12. Project fraud metrics business case generation.

22.6 Summary

Depending on the nature of a person's job, the extent of fraud management knowledge should be uniform across the business organization. In some cases, only essential training is required. In others, extensive training that integrates current job skill requirements along with fraud management is necessary. The bottom line for the business should focus on ensuring that visibility has been raised sufficiently across the organization regarding the potential for internal and external fraud. In many companies today, much of this training is already in place, but without the understanding of its importance and relationship to fraud management compliance.

Training has long been a building block to any organization hoping to grow. Through education of the workforce for fraud management compliance, businesses should prosper. Workers should eventually feel more at ease each day fraud management polices are in place.

23

Using Enterprise Project Management Tools for Project Fraud Detection

23.1 Defining Enterprise Project Management

In the perfect world, a perfect business would projectize all work performed for any fiscal year of the business. In this perfect model, all work would be measured for success regarding time, cost, and value to the requesting customer. In this manner, all work would be projectized following a prescribed methodology for project delivery success as defined by business management. Since all work is limited within the business or the enterprise, project management would be throughout the business and thus the application of the project management practice, rigor, and discipline would be enterprised. This is the concept behind enterprise project management (EPM), simple as it may be.

In today's business world, the presence of a perfect business that projectizes all work is indeed rare. Understanding that the value of project management to business is to help the business grow, it becomes an interesting question as to why project management is not utilized more to do just this!

23.2 Purpose of EPM Tools

EPM tools consolidate information flow produced by projects. In addition, this type of software is sometimes designed to interface with business systems such as time entry, accounting systems such as labor distribution, general ledger, human resource systems, and many more. EPM tools can enable faster information flow from the originating source, such as a project team member entering his or her labor for the week which within five minutes can be ready for accounting treatment in the business general ledger, to restating the business corporate objectives portfolio progress based on a completed milestone of a significant strategic project that has six other projects waiting for that milestone to be completed so that those six projects can accelerate their work.

EPM tools are basically a single-repository systemic group of software processes that collect original data (i.e., project schedules, project artifacts, time-entry data, expenses, etc.) in such a manner that visibility to the impact on a project can be immediate. This immediate result is what typically separates EPM tools from more traditional accounting systems. In many cases, the data age within accounting systems is weekly and/or monthly before it is processed and provided to management for analysis. If the timing of project data results is important to your business, your business should consider a hard look at a business case to implement an EPM tool.

23.3 Determining EPM Tools for the Overall Benefit of the Enterprise

Knowledge is everything in business. Identifying EPM tools for the business should consider how the business values project alignment. Project alignment is the relationship of a project in support of a particular corporate objective, asset, or resource. Fiscal efficiencies can be gained for the business if projects are aligned effectively. Another consideration would be end-to-end full feature support for project management rigor and discipline as defined contextually by the Project Management Institute's Project Management Body of Knowledge (PMBOK®). The exclusion of a key feature in an EPM tool can render the data from an EPM tool ineffective and limit impact visibility. Key features in EPM tools provide effective support for the following project management areas of knowledge:

1. Project integration
2. Scope management
3. Time management
4. Cost management
5. Human resources management
6. Procurement management
7. Quality management

8. Risk management
9. Communications management

Can you imagine implementing an EPM tool that does not contain support for risk management? Microsoft Project, until recently with the 2003 version, did not have a risk management feature within its software. Microsoft managed this with an add-on from their strategic partner Risk+. Imagine your PMO trying to determine portfolio risk with the EPM tool and the risk feature does not work within the software. In the case of Microsoft and Risk+ software, we can imagine both firms blaming the other for causing the problem with the feature functionality. This is the potential risk any PMO would face when they have EPM tools implemented. Why would anyone want to be in that situation? To be fair to Microsoft Project, Microsoft remedied this problem with their 2003 version that is fast becoming a favorite among PMOs everywhere.

23.4 Implementing EPM Tools

Great care must be undertaken when implementing an EPM tool across the enterprise. The issue is not so much the software itself, but the people who will be asked to utilize the EPM tool when it is operationalized. Often the workforce will resist EPM tools because the software is too complex for their current work and to learn how to apply the EPM tool in their current work might place them behind their planned schedule. Keep in mind that loading project data into EPM tools takes time. There is a cost in EPM tool utilization. Expect project teams to spend 15 percent or more of the project manager's time in tool usage. Expect project team members to spend 8 percent or more of their weekly work time doing the same — that is 3.2 hours per person each week entering time, updating their portion of the project schedule, and interacting with project work products and deliverables stored in the repository of the EPM tool. Other basic factors to consider include:

1. User training
2. EPM tool rollout
3. Project team work conversion
4. Portfolio management setup
5. System connectivity with enterprise systems (time entry, general ledger, human resources)
6. Data integrity protection
7. Corporate governance support

23.5 Training the Workforce on EPM Tools Utilization: What They Must Learn

User training in utilizing the EPM tool must teach basic concepts in project management in association with specific features provided by the software. Users should learn how to establish project schedules, manage issues and risks, create and store status reports, manage project artifacts, and save support documentation. In addition, users should learn how to critical path a project. Learning to crash or manage the schedule with the software is critical knowledge for any project team member who is expected to support project delivery at the best possible speed.

Training in best practice methods with the EPM tool should teach people how to find work acceleration opportunities and/or work delivery threats within their assigned project teams. Imagine the value to be gained by the business with all EPM tool users always on the watch for opportunities to deliver quicker or work threats they want to avoid. An EPM tool can make this essential behavior innate in regular users. Again referencing Microsoft Project 2002, this EPM tool (not to be confused with end-to-end EPM tools) provided users with an overview of work relative to a perceived level of risk associated with time and cost after they had logged into the system. This was a great step forward in the EPM tool space. Today, competitors of Microsoft Project are taking this feature further. Soon, EPM tool users will not have to wander aimlessly through the data store of the EPM tool searching for impact. Users will be able to see all threats and opportunities that might be related to their work when they log into the EPM tool. Teaching users to think this way should be a major objective in any EPM tool training. As the user EPM tool training is conducted, users should become indoctrinated in how the project fraud management policy is manifested by the EPM tool. Teaching the EPM tool users about how the EPM tool is managed for project fraud prevention and detection is mission critical to successful organizational achievement of the project management fraud policies. Teaching project team members how to uncover future work opportunities that lead to business prosperity for the business when completed is the essence of project management value. This last point is made clearer by considering the following example:

> Suppose today is Monday. As a valued project team member, you notice that a key project milestone for which you are accountable is coming due in two weeks. Further inspection through the EPM tool indicates to you that this milestone is critical to delivery progress of six other interdependent projects in the business project portfolio.

If this milestone can be achieved earlier than planned, these other projects could accelerate in progress correspondingly. You further learn that these six other projects use 100 allocated project resources that are fully dedicated. If you can complete this milestone by Friday of this week by working three extra hours, you would be responsible for helping your project team and the six other projects gain one week in project schedule progress opportunity per resource. How motivated would you be to help? As you calculate the potential value, you determine that 4000 person hours could be gained (one week per resource) by these six projects at an expected $100/hour labor rate per resource (very normal) for a total budget impact of up to $400,000 to the business.

If you could help make this potential become real, would you? Teaching project team members to mine for these types of opportunities is very valuable to them and to the business. If you found project team members who had this skill and project knowledge as depicted in the example and found that they chose not to act, not inform anyone, do nothing, is that fraudulent? Maybe.

23.6 How Project Teams Should Use EPM Tools

In a perfect world, there is not a single project that should not be organized by the five phases of the PMBOK® life cycle: initiating, planning, controlling and monitoring, executing, and closing. This framework is the accepted standard throughout the world and allows for easy management of project managing, tracking, and reporting. That said, the project manager will personally develop or oversee the project schedule construction until the project schedule is approved (baselined). Project schedule approval requires that the project's critical path be determined within the project schedule. The baseline project schedule establishes the project expectations for delivery achievement. This visibility to the project team defines satisfactory performance for the project. In user training of the EPM tool, project team members must be trained how to interpret the project schedule critical path for work acceleration opportunity and/or work delivery threat relative to their work assignment expectations and related progress, including how they might learn to help others in the project. Teaching project team members how to gain this awareness increases project team member visibility to project events that they can affect. People who want to commit project fraud will be aware of this and will either stop their efforts or attempt other means. Demonstrating project fraud scenarios within the EPM tool during

EPM tool training is a tremendous method in performing this knowledge transfer. These scenarios might include:

1. Overestimating work
2. Underreporting work status (avoiding bad news)
3. Working project work not related to the project's critical path
4. Reporting work completion for the full estimate when the work was actually completed in less time (Parkinson's Law, work expands to meet the estimate)
5. Vendor sabotage, delaying work intentionally
6. Project expense handling
7. Project/vendor misrepresentation
8. Purchase order control
9. Project sponsor mismanagement
10. Unauthorized project requirement work

23.7 How Internal Auditors and Fraud Examiners Should Use EPM Tools

The EPM tool (aka PMO data store) is a wealth of tactical project information. All project work products, deliverables, and other related artifacts should be stored as master copy within the repository of the EPM tool. Internal auditors and fraud examiners can data-mine this repository with help from the PMO to extract trending data and/or specific project-related artifacts.

In many businesses, project team resources are often multitasked with other project assignments usually unrelated, but often competing for their time. Determining how project work is completed and the manner in which that was expected by the business should be a roadmap to detect project fraud. Project fraud inspectors should seek to retrieve the following artifacts or information from the EPM tool repository:

1. Project schedule and related cyclical updates
2. Project team member time sheets
3. Critical path work completion analysis
4. Abnormal lag time between connected work tasks
5. Project charter
6. Project scope statement
7. Project management plan
8. Project sponsor approvals

9. Project customer approvals
10. Project status meeting minutes
11. Project change requests
12. Project portfolio force ranking
13. Project expense records
14. Assessment of completed project work quality and related work effort estimates and actuals

Much of this information can be collected through mechanized processes pre-established through the PMO that when executed will identify project areas to further inspect. Internal auditors and fraud examiners should seek out the PMO for data availability and support for any project-related investigation.

23.8 The Value Proposition of EPM Tools to the PMO to Prevent and Detect Project Fraud

Aggregating project data into a single common data repository can be a tremendous corporate asset of fiscal year opportunity and threat risk to the business. The Association of Certified Fraud Examiners has estimated that an average of 6 percent of business fiscal year project spending is lost to fraud. How much is your business spending this fiscal year on project investments? Finding 6 percent or more of fraud instances in project delivery may be the compelling business reason that justifies the purchase and operation of an effective EPM tool in your business. A 6 percent or more return on investment (ROI) against a $100 million fiscal year project portfolio is an excellent value considering that most EPM tool purchases cost less than $1 million per 750 seat licenses. Consider these other ROI value points to determine if an EPM tool makes sense for your business:

- Assuming that the PMO will manage the EPM tool for the benefit of the business
- Assuming that the business has a $100 million fiscal year project portfolio
- Assuming a 6 percent ROI on project fraud detection
- Assuming that the business has a need for 750 seat licenses in an EPM tool

Then the benefit of the EPM tool, when deployed to the business, expected to return cost savings, capture early revenue, prevent project rework while raising visibility to project progress that prevents and detects project fraud should cause the following minimal results:

- 10 percent ROI on project portfolio = $10 million
- 6 percent ROI on fraud detection = $6 million

Total ROI to the business resulting from the above yields $16 million in fiscal year or 16 percent return against the fiscal year project portfolio.

Finally, consider that the cost to operate a PMO for the business in any fiscal year at maturity should not expect to exceed $2 million using the parameters in the above example. Therefore, the ratio would become 8 times = $16 million/$2 million. These are direct cost savings and do not include the benefit derived from raised visibility on project fraud prevention and detection among the project delivery teams that leads to workforce compliance to the project fraud management policy.

23.9 Summary

The key to project fraud prevention and detection is improved visibility to project fraud opportunity. This visibility can significantly increase peer pressure on those that might otherwise commit project fraud if this pressure was not present, thereby reducing the opportunity for project fraud. EPM tools are essential business weapons to fight this type of white-collar crime as these tools can bring new visibility to different perspectives of how projects do their work.

It is the fiduciary responsibility of business management to manage business value for the stakeholder and shareholder. This accountability also extends into the nonprofit arena as well. In the time ahead, the need to manage for project fraud will be worldwide and business tools that can help business gain the upper hand will have high value to all.

Questions

23.1 The baseline project schedule establishes the project expectations for delivery achievement. True or false?

23.2 This baseline project schedule visibility to the project team defines satisfactory performance for the project. True or false?

23.3 Which of the following artifacts are NOT typical of an EPM tool repository?
    a. Project charter
    b. Project scope statement
    c. Project management plan
    d. Corporate governance meeting minutes

23.4   Project alignment is the relationship of a project in support of a particular corporate objective, asset, or resource. True or false?

23.5   EPM tools are basically a single-repository systemic group of software processes that collect original data (i.e., project schedules, project artifacts, time-entry data, expenses, etc.) in such a manner that visibility to the impact on a project can be immediate. True or false?

23.6   Key features in EPM tools provide effective support for which of the following project management areas of knowledge?
a. Project integration
b. Scope management
c. Time management
d. Lessons learned

23.7   Risk management capability is a key feature of any EPM tool. True or false?

23.8   Critical pathing project schedules is an essential element of project fraud detection. True or false?

23.9   Types of project fraud scenarios that would NOT be found in the data of an EPM tool repository include:
a. Overestimating work
b. Underreporting work status (avoiding bad news)
c. Working project work not related to the project critical path
d. Personal performance information

24

The Executive Proposal for Sarbanes-Oxley Section 404 Compliance in Detail

The following information is a general proposal template for implementing a project fraud management program in your business that complies with the Sarbanes-Oxley Section 404 federal legislation for improved internal controls. The assumption behind this proposal is that the organization has performed its homework and has prepared and presented a powerful buy-in presentation, utilizing the concepts covered throughout this book.

24.1 Executive Summary/Commitment Letter

This proposal addresses enterprise support required to implement a project fraud management program that is compliant with the federally mandated Sarbanes-Oxley legislation in general and in particular to Section 404 of that code. This proposal also enables improvement in project governance and reporting that effects project and business alignment. This proposal supports the management for project fraud prevention and detection against the return on investment (ROI) in the projects activated to achieve the organization's objectives.

This is a $xx million opportunity (6 percent saved from fraud detected by the program from fiscal year planned spending) for our organization. Getting the right projects completed in the correct expected order far more quickly is key to meeting executive and stakeholder goals. This capability will be accomplished by deploying (further enabling) a project management office (PMO) with the following key objectives:

1. *Produce a corporate governance-sanctioned, prioritized enterprise corporate objectives portfolio.* This portfolio would be governed and visibly supported by the executive corporate governance team. It would be utilized by the workforce to ensure that decisions are made and resources allocated according to executive mandate. Data in this portfolio would emanate from all strategic project investments in all business units. All executives and managers would receive reports to guide decision making and actions from a common base of data.

2. *Build project fraud knowledge and skills to improve delivery performance.* The PMO structure and executive support increases management's ability to meet executive goals through faster and more effective project execution. Managers will effectively utilize progress data within the portfolio and PMO tools to improve delivery performance and manage the constantly changing composition of the portfolio cognitive of the potential for project fraud.

3. *Monitor and improve portfolio performance.* This step provides quick-starting tool utilization to collect, track, and perform project management activities on key project investments while providing strategic and tactical progress data to all stakeholders.

4. *Improve deficient project management processes with standard and best practice tools, methods, and processes.* In order to drive best practices across the organization and be able to share information meaningfully, the organization needs a common language and methodology.

5. *Drive higher value from project management training and skills development.* This step improves project management delivery capability by mapping current skills of the project management community, analyzing the collected data, and creating effective project management training curriculums that focus on key project management weaknesses and that integrate fraud management policies.

6. *Implement PMO help desk.* To obtain consistent, needed executive information on a timely basis, users will need help with the computer-based tools. The PMO data store and PMO help desk will help users with readily available documented procedures and support when required. In

addition, the PMO help desk will collect all insider tips to suspected fraudulent project activities providing another service for whistle-blowers to report misconduct in project delivery.

7. *Comply with Sarbanes-Oxley Section 404 of the code.* Mandated for publicly traded companies by this federal law. Compliance sufficiently improves internal controls.

24.1.1 Section I: Business Case

24.1.1.1 Investment Overview

Implement (further enable) a PMO to improve ROI in the $xx million project portfolio by a minimum of xx percent.

24.1.1.2 Background

The business is seeking to improve its capabilities to deliver projects that are strategic to the vitality of the business and to comply with federal legislation Sarbanes-Oxley (Code Section 404) mandate for improved internal control. The need for this improvement has been demonstrated by the following:

1. Lack of capability across top strategic initiatives to collaborate effectively in avoiding project delivery delays
2. Frequent priority changes, with constant disruption across the organization
3. Inability to complete sufficient projects to counter competitive and economic threats
4. Constant schedule and cost overruns
5. Compliance weakness to federal mandate

24.1.1.3 Objectives

1. Comply with Sarbanes-Oxley Section Code 404
2. Deliver corporate governance capable of creating a balanced project portfolio that the executives believe will meet the organization's goals
3. Put in place processes for managing projects and priorities in the portfolio, data gathering, reporting, tracking, analyzing, and improvement through a subject matter expert PMO
4. Improve delivery of projects in both speed and quality while working to prevent and detect the occurrence of project fraud
5. Allow more projects to be completed with the same resources in the same time or better

6. Provide the information needed to support excellent executive decision making in project investment selection, management, and completion

24.1.1.4 Strategic Corporate Alignment

1. *Internal perspective* — Effective management of organizational capital and opportunities
2. *Operational excellence* — Improve organizational process productivity, leverage strategic technology capabilities with organizational human capital skills
3. *Learning and growth* — Results-oriented leadership and decision making and communicate and share knowledge across the organization that raises visibility to project investment delivery opportunities and threats

24.1.1.5 Opportunity Type

Select the appropriate box to demonstrate the type of opportunity this project investment provides:

☒ Increased revenue ☒ Decreased cost ☒ Regulatory compliance

☒ Increased productivity ☒ Decreased risk ☒ Maintenance

24.1.2 Section 2: Scope

24.1.2.1 Project Scope

1. Identify minimum data requirements for project scheduling
2. Develop, document, and implement a project fraud management policy that is enterprise encompassing
3. Determine minimum data requirements needed for portfolio management
4. Gather, report, and analyze initial portfolio data
5. Support and facilitate first governance meeting
6. Deliver a library of easily accessible user guides for project managers, resource managers, team members, sponsors, and executives that supports project fraud management prevention and detection
7. Develop and implement fraud management processes to enable all project managers to deliver on minimum criteria
8. Add/hire staff to take on roles that provide effective enterprise support through a PMO function
9. Implement necessary training/education/development processes that integrate project management and related skill areas with project fraud policy

Table 24.1   Stakeholder Impact Analysis

Stakeholder	Impact
CEO, CFO, CIO	Executives will have an accurate and current view of how project investments are progressing against corporative objective expectations. All strategic project investments will be prioritized by an approved prioritization model from corporate governance.
PMO	The PMO will own the tactical management of the project fraud management policy under the supervision of internal auditing in compliance with Section 404. The PMO must implement portfolio management processes for corporate objectives, projects, assets, and resources. The PMO will own all project management training curriculum associated with project fraud management.
Internal auditors	Internal auditors will support Section 404 internal compliance efforts through the application of project audits on behalf of the PMO.
Project managers	Are expected to be trained in project fraud policy and to manage their project investments within those guidelines without additional delay in cost and/or time.
Team members	Are expected to be trained in project fraud policy and to manage their project work within those guidelines without additional delay in cost and/or time. Team members will also understand better the relationship of their work toward business alignment.
Resource managers	Resource management will improve through the development of resource portfolio management processes enabled by the PMO and the electronic tools that the PMO provides. This benefit is expected to reduce outside consultant expense by 10 percent year-to-year for the next three years as a result.

24.1.2.2 Impact Analysis

See Table 24.1 for a description of the impact that the project fraud management policy will have on each stakeholder.

24.1.2.3 Critical Success Factors

1. Executive and PMO support across the organization
2. Fraud management policy integration with project management training and skills development at every level of the organization
3. Quality marketing of the PMO, its tools, and support in relation to project fraud management
4. Acquisition/development of quality products to support operational excellence in portfolio management and project management rigor and discipline application to project investment delivery

5. Effective project fraud management training
6. Executive ownership of the corporate objectives portfolio

24.1.3 Section 3: Approach

24.1.3.1 Proposed Solution

A project team, consisting of five senior project managers and five senior internal auditors, will assemble initial data and will select and implement all initial tools and data structures for project fraud management policy implementation. This will allow the project team to focus on the hard and soft tools needed to develop project management delivery rigor and discipline further throughout the organization that will enable project fraud prevention and detection.

24.1.3.2 Alternatives Considered

1. Continue to manage projects as we do now (lack of fraud compliance procedures). This alternative was eliminated because the opportunity represents over 6 percent of $xx million to our organization's bottom line annually.
2. Minimum infrastructure — Begin with one senior project manager, no formal PMO, and no tools. This alternative was eliminated because an optimistic estimate of the amount of work required is several person years. Our organization cannot afford to wait that long for the results.
3. Temporary infrastructure — Build a PMO and disband it once the initial objectives are accomplished. This alternative was eliminated because we believe that the PMO will prove that it will continue to provide outstanding measurable value from improvement in project execution and in project fraud management. The PMO is an essential component to compliance of Section 404 for improved internal controls.

24.1.3.3 Assumptions

1. All project managers will need to attend project management fraud concept courses.
2. All project managers who are managing portfolio projects will buy in to the PMO project fraud guidelines, including using a standard PMO tool suite as the project management tool.
3. All organization units will ultimately use this tool to report status of their projects.
4. PMO tool and other project fraud–related training will be provided for

all users at every level. Executives will be vocal and positive in support of this training.

5. PMO tool functionality will drive certain project processes that integrate essential project governance requirements to comply with federal law.
6. PMO staff will take an executive view of the business, driving project improvements to meet organization goals with compliance to federal law for sufficient internal controls.

24.1.3.4 Obstacles

1. Finding qualified resources to support the project fraud management investment within the PMO
2. Defining the best way to incorporate project fraud management policy into every functional unit's need without sacrificing the need for a common structure
3. Buy-in of functional units to move approach to project management and project fraud management and utilizing the tools made available

24.1.3.5 Stakeholder Expectations

See Table 24.2 for the expectations that each stakeholder group can enjoy.

Table 24.2 Stakeholder Expectations

Stakeholder	Expectations
CEO, CFO, CIO	Minimal impact to budget. Significantly improved internal controls that enable corporate governance to navigate toward business opportunity and away from threat in corporate objectives and related project investments.
PMO	Significantly improved ROI from the PMO year-to-year resulting from incremental process improvement in portfolio information to an annual level that exceeds five times the annualized cost to operate the PMO.
Internal auditor	Significantly improved positioning in the viewing of project investment delivery work that enhances the visibility of active project fraud instances to the internal auditor.
Project manager	Improved business support for his or her project because of the improved business alignment that links the project with a specific corporate objective. Improved work culture from the high levels of vigilance for project fraud.
Team member	Improved work culture that fosters intraproject team trust in work completion.

24.1.3.6 Project Organization

An organization chart for the project is located in Appendix I (include chart for your organization). Core team members and time commitments are identified in the Project Resource Plan in Appendix II (include list of team members and planned commitments for your organization).

24.1.3.7 Procurement Plan

Jane Smith and John Doe have been our primary negotiators from corporate purchasing. We have negotiated a purchase price for PMO software (EPM tool) and have surrounding agreements for maintenance, training, and consulting. In addition, we have a master consulting agreement in place with ALLPMO Network Inc., to provide implementation consulting, training development, and project manager mentoring. We continue to evaluate alternatives in acquiring implementation expertise from external providers as opportunities arise.

24.1.3.8 Communication Plan

On executive authorization, the project investment team will:

1. Develop a welcome packet for project investment participants; include background, expectations, schedule, key contacts, overview of the project investment, etc.
2. Develop training materials and presentation for project management training in the new tools, reporting, and delivery acceleration strategies
3. Conduct training for initial participants
4. Provide weekly communication to project participants; status, results, recommendations for improvement, and request for feedback
5. Provide one-on-one project resource mentoring to discuss experiences and concerns
6. Provide project status updates, portfolio analysis, and recommendations to executive management at critical junctures
7. Hold regular meetings with participants to discuss experiences, concerns, successes, and progress
8. Provide a project summary report for all key audiences
9. Create content for the project investment website regarding the team's activities, end-user testimonials as they use the project fraud management policy deliverables (including FAQs, Issues, etc.)
10. Adapt initial welcome packet to meet the needs of each new group of users; distribute prior to communication

11. Conduct awareness sessions during business unit rollouts
12. Coordinate with business unit contacts to promote the project fraud management policy within their business unit
13. Present project fraud management policy results/findings and future outlook at a project management network meeting
14. Provide a conclusive rollout summary to all key audiences at the end of the project investment implementation

24.1.3.9 Change Control Plan

As potential changes to the project baselined scope, time, and budget are identified, they will be documented by the project manager, logged, distributed to the change control committee and core team, and reviewed weekly (unless urgent). For urgent change matters, an emergency teleconference or meeting will be convened. The change control committee consists of the PMO officer, CIO, and CEO.

The project team will first review changes and escalate questions and recommendations to the project executive sponsor and business unit contacts as appropriate. Once the change has been accepted or denied, the request resolution is documented and the appropriate project documents are updated to reflect any changes. The project manager will be responsible for managing this process.

24.1.4 Section 4: Risk

24.1.4.1 Risk Identification Matrix

See Table 24.3 for a description of the key risks of this project and the approach that the PMO implementation team is planning to take.

24.1.5 Section 5: Costs and Benefits (Insert Appendix for Your Organization's Detailed Cost Benefit Analysis)

24.1.5.1 Project Costs Breakdown

See Table 24.4 for the cost breakdown summary.

24.1.5.2 Project Resource Costs Summary for Executing/Controlling Phases

1. *Project manager* — Project Executing/Control Phase 17 weeks, 100 percent (external), $105,000

Table 24.3 Project Fraud Management Risk Matrix

Description of the Risk	Quantification of the Risk	Risk Response
May have difficulty acquiring the appropriate core team, business unit, and external consultant resources needed for the project.	This is considered a moderate impact risk.	Work closely with resource manager to assess and respond to resource needs.
Too much delay in acquiring and/or assigning resources could result in a delay in critical path activities.		Identify staff needs as far in advance as possible to allow enough lead time for acquisition. Keep sponsor updated on resource issues and escalate as needed.
Project team communication requirements with multiple departments/business units. This could result in communication breakdowns and spreading project team support too thin during pilot and rollout.	This is considered moderate and moderate impact risk.	Detailed marketing and communication plan for how to handle cross-functional unit communication. Align core team members to focus some of their efforts on specific business units.
Project may also be at risk that the PMO tools might not be in alignment with some existing functional unit processes.		Investigate staffing a position to work specifically with business unit configurations and implementations. Conduct regular status meetings with business units.
Lack of agreement over project priorities and resource assignments will also significantly reduce benefits.	This is considered a low probability and moderate impact risk.	Leverage functional unit contacts to uncover concerns/issues and develop a plan to address those at the functional unit level. Leverage executive owner and sponsor to uncover senior management concerns/issues and develop a buy-in presentation. We will not proceed with implementation until we have secured majority executive team support.
Users may also resist cultural changes that would result from policy and tool implementation.		Work with functional unit contacts to uncover cultural change issues and incorporate a plan to address those during the functional unit rollout.

Table 24.4   Cost Breakdown Summary for Project Investment

	Costs			
Cost Category	Year 1	Year 2	Year 3	Year 4
Project costs				
Internal resources	$383,000			
Other project impacts (training)	$100,000			
Total project cash outlay	$483,000			
Ongoing costs				
Internal resources	$150,000			
Equipment (maintenance)				
Total ongoing cash outlay	$150,000			
Total costs	$633,000			

2. *PMO tool strategist lead* — Executing/Controlling Phase 17 weeks, 50 percent (internal), $45,000
3. *Project management integration project leads (2)* — Executing/Controlling Phase 17 weeks, 50 percent each (internal), $33,000 each
4. *Senior auditor* — Executing/Controlling Phase 17 weeks, 100 percent (internal), $54,000
5. *Training/education coordinator lead* — Executing/Controlling Phase 17 weeks, 100 percent (external), $28,000
6. *Portfolio management lead* — Executing/Controlling Phase 17 weeks, 100 percent (external), $51,000
7. *HR and admin/support* — Executing/Controlling Phase 17 weeks, 50 percent (internal), $34,000
8. *Facility, training, and equipment support* — $100,000 (estimated)

24.1.5.3 Project Benefits

See Table 24.5 for a project benefits summary. Benefits can be verified using the following measures:

SUPPORT THE IMPLEMENTATION OF IMPROVED INTERNAL CONTROLS FOR CORPORATE PROJECT MANAGEMENT GOVERNANCE AND REPORTING STANDARDS

According to the Gartner Group (August 1, 2000), projects following a standard life cycle are more often completed on time, on budget, and within scope.

Estimated savings:
# of projects * # of people * average hourly rate * hours saved

Table 24.5   Project Benefits Summary

Benefit Category	Benefits			
	Year 1	Year 2	Year 3	Year 4
Tangibles				
Support the implementation of project fraud management standards		$3,000,000	$3,000,000	$3,000,000
Identify project risks and (resource) constraints		$4,620,000	$4,620,000	$4,620,000
Development cost improvements for seventy projects		$7,000,000	$7,000,000	$7,000,000
Portfolio prioritization		$7,000,000	$7,000,000	$7,000,000
Intangibles				
Total benefits		$21,620,000	$21,620,000	$21,620,000

Example:
25 projects × 10 people × $75/hour × 40 hours/week × 4 weeks = $3,000,000

This example assumes time to market will be reduced by four weeks for twenty-five projects. Of course, the additional revenue that can come from new products delivered to market more quickly can make these benefits pale by comparison.

Verification: Baseline scheduling and cost estimates along with scope definition will be tracked and reported on a monthly basis using critical path scheduling techniques.

IDENTIFY PROJECT RISKS AND (RESOURCE) CONSTRAINTS

PMO tools will require project managers to examine their projects for risks, dependencies, constraints, and impacts on the business. Using rigorous standards to move projects from the planning to execution phase will reduce organizational costs.

Estimated savings:
# of projects ∗ # of people ∗ hourly rate ∗ hours

Example:
14 projects × 10 people × $75/hour × 40 hours/week × 11 weeks = $4,620,000

The Gartner Group estimates that proper risk identification will result in the cancellation of 20 percent of projects before the execution phase. In the example above, savings assumes fourteen projects will be cancelled before execution begins. The time savings are the average for the execution and subsequent phases.

The benefits are actually much greater than portrayed. These resources can be used to execute other projects, which bring far greater value than just the cost savings.

Verification: The PMO will track the number of projects in the project investment portfolio that were cancelled because of risk and impact on the organization.

DEVELOPMENT COST IMPROVEMENT

By the end of 200X, the enterprise will go from tracking less than half of the portfolio projects to more than 90 percent. Payback will occur from having better information to make decisions on the deployment and use of resources and capital. In addition, the significant increase in visibility, cross-functional executive support, and tracking of these projects will enable the portfolio of projects to accelerate their delivery.

Estimated Savings:
Average aggregated budget of (70 active projects) projects in portfolio annualized
= $140,000,000

A 5 percent annual delivery improvement in time and budget for the projects in the portfolio = $7,000,000

Verification: The executive team will recognize delivery improvements as reported in the PMO portfolio reports. These reports will illustrate comparable difference between baseline delivery forecasts and current progress at a summary level to enable management decision action.

PORTFOLIO PRIORITIZATION

The portfolio along with the PMO phase review will answer the question: "Where do high-priority projects stand?" According to the Gartner Group, "Project delivery rates directly impact customer satisfaction, IT's value to the business, the enterprise's competitive edge, market share and profitability. A project portfolio management capability includes a set of organization-specific metrics pertinent to project delivery."

Estimated savings:
Elimination of 7 projects, at an average unsunk cost of $1,000,000
or annualized for a total expected savings of $7,000,000

This assumes that the project portfolio along with the PMO phase review process assists management in making the decision not to implement a portfolio project based on organizational priorities.

Verification: The PMO will use the portfolio management process to review and identify the number of projects that actively follow the life cycle and use the project control tools in the everyday management of the projects.

24.1.6 Section 6 Project Milestones

Project delivery timeline summary:

1. Project planning phase completed by 2/3/200X
2. Project executing/controlling phase completed by 8/6/200X
3. Project closing phase commenced by 9/3/200X
4. Project completed by 10/1/200X

24.2 Summary

The business case for implementing project fraud management policy through a PMO should define the benefits, time, costs, and feature functionality. Once the costs have been identified, the summary cost of the implementation effort (that includes operation expenses for the remainder of the fiscal year) becomes the baseline number that the PMO will be evaluated against for value added to the organization.

Questions

24.1   Explain how a project fraud management policy might bring financial value to any organization through a PMO and portfolio management.

24.2   The executive proposal makes assumptions about why and how the expected benefits would occur. How could you substantiate those assumptions in a real organization?

24.3   Suppose an executive is willing to accept the proposal, but insists that you start with one resource, rather than, for example, five resources. How should you respond?

24.4   Explain the impact that you would expect a PMO to have on executives, project managers, and resource managers who might be resisting.

24.5   What negative impacts from implementing a project fraud policy in his or her project team might a project manager be concerned about? How could a PMO change the project manager's perception?

24.6   Fraud management policy integration with project management training and skills development at every level of the organization is a critical success factor to this business proposal. True or false?

24.7   A key assumption is that not all project managers will need to attend project management fraud concept courses. True or false?

24.8   A key objective is to comply with Sarbanes-Oxley Section 404 of the Code as mandated for publicly traded companies by this federal law. True or false?

24.9   The communication plan does not require that project fraud awareness sessions be conducted during business unit rollouts. True or false?

24.10   This proposal expects significant improved internal controls that enable corporate governance to navigate toward business opportunity and away from threat in corporate objectives and related project investments. True or false?

25

PMO Roadmap for Implementing Sarbanes-Oxley into Project Delivery

The PMO roadmap for implementing Sarbanes-Oxley into project delivery focuses on Section 404 of the Sarbanes-Oxley Code. Once compliance procedures are developed and implemented for utilization by the project delivery workforce, the operational management of these procedures must be monitored within the framework of project management rigor and discipline. It is insufficient for corporate governance to expect the workforce to embrace these new procedures on their own. If the business decides to embark on this type of passive management, the business compliance will be uneven and may be at compliance risk. In the long run, the passive management option is more expensive to manage and operate because the necessary monitoring will be linear and vertical within each business unit and may lead to different levels of emphasis and management and an uneven application of the code. Therefore our recommendation is to enable the PMO at the enterprise or organization level to provide the monitoring and management of Section 404 compliance in an active management style. This approach will lead to reduced project fraud management costs in a manner that as each fiscal year passes, the compliance processes will become more accepted as a way of life within project delivery and become innate in project delivery thinking. Project teams will be motivated to embrace this active management style since it provides the best type of safety net for project delivery success — strategic alignment for projects by corporate objective. This supposition is based on the belief that compliance brings value to the safety of project investments that Section 404 processes are applied to in project work and helps project teams feel more at ease, something that all project teams seek. Therefore, as this behavior is embraced more and more by the project delivery teams, our supposition is that the costs to comply will decrease because project team resistance will decrease as these project teams incorporate project fraud policy into their work routine as a necessary component to job safety in their work.

The following roadmap is listed in a work breakdown structure (WBS) fashion. In Figures 25.1 and 25.2, the WBS depicts a project development plan to operationalize Section 404 code requirements through the PMO. In Figure 25.3 is the operational plan to manage for project fraud through the PMO over the course of a fiscal year supporting project teams, business units, and corporate governance.

ID	Task Name
1	**Implement SOX 404 Processes for Project Fraud Management of Project Delivery Processes**
2	**Business Case Approved**
3	**Initiating Phase**
4	Disclosure Committee formed
5	SOX 404 Steering Committee formed
6	Project manager selected and on board
7	Initial project charter completed
8	Project team formed
9	**Dotted Line Reporting Relationships Approved**
10	Operations
11	Accounting
12	Auditing
13	PMO
14	Conduct project kickoff meeting
15	**Planning Phase**
16	Project charter finalized and approved
17	Project scope statement completed
18	Project Management plan completed
19	Project risk plan completed
20	Project schedule finalized, approved, and baselined
21	Internal auditing approves project planning phase deliverables
22	**Controlling and Monitoring Phase**
23	SOX 404 Steering Committee status meetings
24	Project team status meetings
25	Project life cycle audit review by internal auditing
26	Manage project change management requests

Figure 25.1. Project Development of Section 404 Compliance

ID	Task Name
27	**Executing Phase**
28	**Process Development**
29	**Project Team Focus**
30	Develop workforce prevention process for occupational fraud
31	Develop workforce detection process for occupational fraud
32	Develop project audit process for prevention of overreported and/or unsubstantiated business case
33	Develop project audit process for detection of overreported and/or unsubstantiated business case
34	Develop project audit process for prevention of overreported and/or unsubstantiated project decisions
35	Develop project audit process for detection of overreported and/or unsubstantiated project decisions
36	Develop project audit process for prevention of underreported project life cycle costs (to gain approval)
37	Develop project audit process for detection of underreported project life cycle costs (to gain approval)
38	Develop project audit process for prevention of underreported project maintenance costs (to gain approval)
39	Develop project audit process for detection of underreported project maintenance costs (to gain approval)
40	Develop project audit process for prevention of overreported project schedule progress
41	Develop project audit process for detection of overreported project schedule progress
42	Develop project audit process for prevention of overreported project quality progress
43	Develop project audit process for detection of overreported project quality progress
44	Update as required the project team reporting process to support portfolio management of project fraud prevention and detection
45	Determine utilization of critical path project scheduling techniques within project teams

Figure 25.1. Project Development of Section 404 Compliance (continued)

ID	Task Name
55	**Implement Plan of Record Publishing Process**
56	Develop EPM tool project portfolio reporting process to reflect reporting period progress
57	Develop EPM tool resource portfolio reporting process to reflect reporting period progress
58	Develop EPM tool asset portfolio reporting process to reflect reporting period progress

Figure 25.2. Project Development of Section 404 Compliance

ID	Task Name
59	Develop EPM tool corporate objectives portfolio reporting process to reflect reporting period progress
60	Develop and implement plan of record publishing process
61	Establish PMO project fraud hotline for whistle-blowers
62	Develop conversion plan to implement critical path project scheduling into project teams
63	**Project Fraud Policy Development and Implementation**
64	**Establish project fraud policy support from the PMO for the following entities**
65	**PMO**
66	Perform conversion of project team schedules to critical pathing of project schedules
67	Frequency of reporting
68	Project fraud hot line
69	Communication plan development
70	Revalidate portfolios for critical path by portfolio
71	Project portfolio
72	Resource portfolio
73	Asset portfolio
74	Corporate objectives portfolio
75	**Business Unit**
76	Communication with business units about project fraud program
77	Determine service level agreement requirements with internal auditing
78	Implement service level agreement with internal auditing and other business units for project fraud management as required
79	**Project Management**
80	Determine essential PMBOK standard compliance for project fraud management for project teams
81	**Corporate Governance Support**
82	Corporate objective/project strategic alignment force ranking
83	Plan of record communication development
84	**Training**
85	PMO training to operate project fraud processes
86	Project manager training ready
87	Team member training ready
88	Middle management training ready
89	Executive management training ready
90	Project fraud awareness training ready
91	Turnover to PMO
92	**Project Audit**
93	Internal auditing approves deliverables from project executing phase
94	**Closing Phase**
95	Turn over project work papers to PMO and internal auditing
96	Close project
97	**Project Development End**

Figure 25.2. Project Development of Section 404 Compliance (continued)

ID	Task Name
99	**PMO Project Fraud Management Operational Plan**
100	**Month 1**
101	PMO setup
102	EPM tool process upgrade
103	PMO staff assignments
104	Project fraud policy management support in place
105	Implement plan of record process
106	Publish initial plan of record process
107	**Corporate Governance Support**
108	Distribute plan of record to key stakeholders
109	Manage and administrate PMO data store for data integrity
110	**Conduct Project Fraud Detection Processes Against PMO Data Store**
111	Turn results over to internal auditing
112	Provide project team mentoring
113	Support project help desk
114	**Month 2**
115	Announce project fraud training class schedule
116	Schedule workforce into training classes
117	Produce training participant materials
118	Conduct awareness sessions (multiple)
119	Conduct project management training (multiple)
120	Conduct middle management training (multiple)
121	Publish plan of record
122	**Corporate Governance Support**
123	Distribute plan of record to key stakeholders
124	Support corporate governance meetings
125	Update portfolio alignment results
126	Support internal audit project audits
127	Facilitate project manager portfolio review meetings
128	Facilitate resource manager portfolio review meetings
129	Facilitate asset manager portfolio review meetings
130	Manage and administrate PMO data store for data integrity
131	**Conduct Project Fraud Detection Processes Against PMO Data Store**
132	Turn results over to internal auditing
133	Provide project team mentoring
134	Support project help desk
135	**Subsequent Months (Repetitive)**
136	**Training**
137	Conduct awareness sessions (multiple)
138	Conduct project manager training (multiple)
139	Conduct middle management training (multiple)
140	**Corporate Governance**
141	**Publish Plan of Record**
142	Publish portfolio management results
143	Publish project delivery forecast
144	Distribute plan of record to key stakeholders
145	**Support Corporate Governance Meetings**
146	Update portfolio alignment results

Figure 25.3. Section 404 Operational Compliance Plan for Project Delivery

ID	Task Name
147	Support internal audit project audits
148	Facilitate project manager portfolio review meetings
149	Facilitate resource manager portfolio review meetings
150	Facilitate asset manager portfolio review meetings
151	Manage and administrate PMO data store for data integrity
152	**Conduct Project Fraud Detection Processes Against PMO Data Store**
153	Turn results over to internal auditing
154	Provide project team mentoring
155	Support project help desk
156	**End of Fiscal Year**

Figure 25.3. Section 404 Operational Compliance Plan for Project Delivery (continued)

25.1 Project Development Work Breakdown Structure

The WBS is organized into life cycle phases as defined by the Project Management Institute's PMBOK® standard for project life cycle processes. This includes:

- Initiating phase
- Planning phase
- Controlling and monitoring phase
- Executing phase
- Closing phase

The key premise for the project development WBS model is to develop operational new processes through the PMO that will help prevent and detect project fraud. This will include making use of the PMO data store by adding and updating new processes; additionally, updating the PMO data store data model by possibly adding and/or modifying the data model on how project data is related to corporate objectives, resources, assets, and other project-oriented entities that will support project fraud management by the PMO for the benefit of its internal customers and key stakeholders.

Like most projects that are organized according to the PMBOK® model for projects, this project is organized in a manner that defines the expected project outcomes (planning phase) before any actual project development occurs. Once the development of processes commences (executing phase), this segment will:

- Produce and/or modify PMO processes that:
  1. Review project team information
  2. Analyze portfolio information for projects, resources, assets, and corporate objectives

   3. Creates a plan of record publishing process within the PMO that assesses tactical project progress against the organization corporate objectives portfolio

   4. Creates a project fraud hotline within the PMO (or internal auditing)

   5. Constructs a conversion project schedule that will convert all existing project schedules to critical path techniques

■ Produce the PMO project fraud management policy for role and responsibilities of the:

   1. PMO

   2. Business unit

   3. Project team

   4. Corporate governance

■ Implement fraud management training that increases policy understanding for:

   1. Project managers

   2. Project team members

   3. Middle management

   4. Executive management

   5. Essential awareness seminar

The project team may determine to build these courses in house or solicit a training vendor to deliver the training. The WBS should be modified as required to add work activities for training the trainers on these courses.

As the project development effort ends and the operational compliance plan begins (Figure 25.3), the management approach for operational management is time based on the fiscal year in a month-month fashion. In the first month, operational efforts are to be focused on establishing the operational environment for the PMO, the PMO internal customers, and PMO key stakeholders. This effort is in alignment with the newly constructed project fraud management policy. Subsequent months focus on executing the operations plan. Over the course of the fiscal year, most of this training will be accomplished with the existing workforce. The costs to train the workforce should significantly decrease in the second year unless more changes are applied to the Code. This scenario is very possible.

As each subsequent month passes, the data quality to the project status reporting should improve in the PMO data store. Key to the success of the operational compliance plan is the PMO data store since this data collection is the only place in most businesses that data about project progress can be analyzed on an aggregate level. The overall inspection of how projects are progressing against business expectations and as compared to other projects that may be influencing delivery and project decisions should be of keen interest to those responsible for project fraud prevention and detection policies and processes.

25.2 Summary

Complying with Sarbanes-Oxley Section 404 requires new processes and modifications to existing processes in how projects are managed and delivered for success. In order for any business to gain the most benefit from this action, consideration should be extended beyond building a tool "mind-set." Project fraud is committed by people, not tools. Managing people to motivate them to behave in a manner that the business has deemed proper should be the main focus when complying with the Code. In the project delivery environment and for most businesses, the utilization of the PMO in concert with the PMO data store, corporate governance, and portfolio management is recommended as a very effective compliance solution for project fraud management.

Questions

25.1   Project fraud training classes are normally scheduled to begin the second month of the operational compliance plan. True or false?

25.2   Project fraud management training increases policy understanding the least for:
   a.   Project managers
   b.   Project team members
   c.   Finance department
   d.   Middle management

25.3   Project fraud compliance requires the establishment of corporate governance over corporate objectives relative to project investments. True or false?

25.4   Key to the success of the operational compliance plan is the PMO data store since this data collection is the only place in most businesses that data about project progress can be analyzed on an aggregate level. True or false?

25.5   The project fraud management policy defines roles and responsibilities of the:
   a.   Customers
   b.   Business unit
   c.   Project team
   d.   Corporate governance

25.6   The key premise for the project development WBS model is to develop operational new processes through the PMO that will help prevent and detect project fraud. True or false?

25.7   Internal auditing should conduct a project audit of the developmental project before it closes to validate that expected outcomes were produced. True or false?

25.8   Aggregating project data through the PMO data store from project team status reporting enables the PMO to measure corporate objective achievement progress through portfolio management processes and how the business is progressing against fiscal year expectations. True or false?

25.9   The PMO should always report to internal auditing in every business. True or false?

25.10 A project fraud management policy should NOT include:

    a.   Portfolio information for projects, resources, assets, and corporate objectives

    b.   Human resources department

    c.   Project fraud hotline within the PMO (or internal auditing)

    d.   A conversion project schedule that will convert all existing project schedules to critical path techniques

26

Summary

The essence of this book has been to bring detailed awareness to the value proposition of Sarbanes-Oxley on project investment governance and reporting in general. The fact that Sarbanes-Oxley is a U.S. federal law is notable, but has little impact on our overall message. Our message is global, if not universal. Our message is for all the for-profit and not-for-profit businesses everywhere. Project fraud does not specifically chase American companies, nor does it attack just for-profit businesses. It is everywhere. If you do not believe us, ask yourself if your employer has implemented a fraud management policy. If the answer is no, then project fraud is most likely occurring in your employer's business today.

Our premise is that businesses everywhere have been short on appropriate controls to prevent and detect project fraud. The internal auditors and fraud examiners who seek out fraud for businesses usually do not have the skills to recognize fraud schemes from project delivery that are more complex than normal. This must change. In the project management profession, project managers are lacking essential prevention and detection skills to manage project fraud in their areas. This must change. If corporate governance, internal auditors, fraud examiners, project managers, and middle management can blend together their respective skills in fraud recognition, the business environment will be a safer place to work. Project fraud risks will be significantly reduced (not eliminated) when this occurs. Project fraud will never be eliminated because it is too easy to misrepresent information for personal gain. This will always be so because it is innate to human nature.

Project fraud management is not a silver bullet, nor is this need similar to other fad-like initiatives such as Total Quality Management, ISO, Six Sigma, etc. We must deal with this topic now and forever. Ignoring fraud at any level is dangerous to the livelihood of those who will be impacted by fraud. We must find new project fraud prevention and detection methods that will easily motivate adoption and continuous process improvement by the workforce of businesses everywhere. Project fraud management is not a tool. It is everyone's job. It is a way of life. Project fraud management should be as routine as getting out of bed each day. The problem is that we have not paid attention to the danger.

Today, new ideas are developing within businesses to bring about this type of innovation and motivation. Project management maturity is improving everywhere thanks to the Project Management Institute Association and others like it. Innovation is focusing on the program/project management office (PMO) as a means to improve project fraud management through portfolio management techniques that foster higher levels of tactical progress visibility of project investments. New measurements are emerging from the PMO that assess project investment value in real time when integrated with EPM tools. Soon, people who seek to commit project fraud will have to work much harder for their criminal gain because of the new recognition skills we all will have for project fraud prevention and detection.

Will Sarbanes-Oxley costs hamper the competitive edge of American businesses with their non-American competitors? Many think they already have. We believe that all businesses currently suffer from project fraud across the globe to some degree. We also believe that much of the solution to managing project fraud lays in the improvement of worker conduct and personal willingness to comply with new fraud policies. Personal integrity and vigilance are critical success factors to any project fraud management policy result.

The education in this space is practically nonexistent. American business has a unique business advantage compared to the outside world today. American workers are known for their ability to compete. Once training products are available to help train American workers on managing for project fraud for essential project governance best practices, their business will begin to benefit. Catching the fraudsters is an acquired soft skill.

If your business, your corporate governance board, your business unit, your PMO, your auditing team, your project investment, or your project team is struggling with project fraud management and needs help, contact us. If we cannot help you, chances are very good that we know others who can. Contact Steve Rollins at Steve@pmousa.com or Rich Lanza at Rich@RichLanza.com for assistance in solving your problems.

Finally, we thank you for taking the time to hear our message. We do hope that you will use this book as a reference. We plan to update this material from time to time. In the interim, we encourage you to visit www.jrosspub.com, www.pmousa.com, and www.auditsoftware.net for additional information. Note that downloadable copies of templates discussed in this book can be found at www.jrosspub.com. We welcome all fraud-related stories you care to share with us. Our next editions will feature the best of the stories.

Appendices

Appendix 1:
List of
Sarbanes-Oxley
Act Sections

Below is a list of sections from the Sarbanes-Oxley Act signed into law on July 30, 2002. The entire act is available on the PCAOB's website at www.pcaobus.org.

TITLE I — PUBLIC COMPANY ACCOUNTING OVERSIGHT BOARD
Sec. 101. Establishment; administrative provisions.
Sec. 102. Registration with the Board.
Sec. 103. Auditing, quality control, and independence standards and rules.
Sec. 104. Inspections of registered public accounting firms.
Sec. 105. Investigations and disciplinary proceedings.
Sec. 106. Foreign public accounting firms.
Sec. 107. Commission oversight of the Board.
Sec. 108. Accounting standards.
Sec. 109. Funding.

TITLE II — AUDITOR INDEPENDENCE
Sec. 201. Services outside the scope of practice of auditors.
Sec. 202. Preapproval requirements.
Sec. 203. Audit partner rotation.
Sec. 204. Auditor reports to audit committees.
Sec. 205. Conforming amendments.

TITLE VIII — CORPORATE AND CRIMINAL FRAUD ACCOUNTABILITY

Sec. 801. Short title.
Sec. 802. Criminal penalties for altering documents.
Sec. 803. Debts nondischargeable if incurred in violation of securities fraud laws.
Sec. 804. Statute of limitations for securities fraud.
Sec. 805. Review of Federal Sentencing Guidelines for obstruction of justice and extensive criminal fraud.
Sec. 806. Protection for employees of publicly traded companies who provide evidence of fraud.
Sec. 807. Criminal penalties for defrauding shareholders of publicly traded companies.

TITLE IX — WHITE-COLLAR CRIME PENALTY ENHANCEMENTS

Sec. 901. Short title.
Sec. 902. Attempts and conspiracies to commit criminal fraud offenses.
Sec. 903. Criminal penalties for mail and wire fraud.
Sec. 904. Criminal penalties for violations of the Employee Retirement Income Security Act of 1974.
Sec. 905. Amendment to sentencing guidelines relating to certain white-collar offenses.
Sec. 906. Corporate responsibility for financial reports.

TITLE X — CORPORATE TAX RETURNS

Sec. 1001. Sense of the Senate regarding the signing of corporate tax returns by chief executive officers.

TITLE XI — CORPORATE FRAUD AND ACCOUNTABILITY

Sec. 1101. Short title.
Sec. 1102. Tampering with a record or otherwise impeding an official proceeding.
Sec. 1103. Temporary freeze authority for the Securities and Exchange Commission.
Sec. 1104. Amendment to the Federal Sentencing Guidelines.
Sec. 1105. Authority of the Commission to prohibit persons from serving as officers or directors.
Sec. 1106. Increased criminal penalties under Securities Exchange Act of 1934.

Appendix 2: Capitalization Decision Tree Software Development Projects

Synopsis: The purpose of this document is to provide a decision-tree analysis for the expense and capitalization of software development projects, incorporating all associated fixed asset capitalization standards.

Notes to Decision Tree Analysis

1. To distinguish whether software is used for internal use (software acquired, internally developed, or modified solely to meet the entity's internal needs per SOP 98-1) or a product for sale, refer to the following example (para. 15 from SOP 98-1): "If software is used by the vendor in the production of the product or in providing the service but the customer does not acquire the software or a future right to use it, then it is one for internal use. For example, for a communications company selling telephone services, software included in a telephone switch is part of the internal equipment used to deliver a service but is not part of the product or service actually being acquired or received by the customer." Therefore, the telephone switch would be treated as an internal use software and likewise most applications would be accounted for under

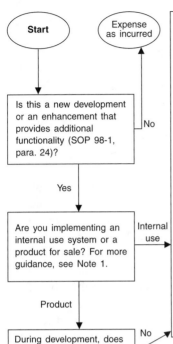

Handle expense/capitalize the following activities as follows:
- ■ (Expense) Business plan for system (EITF 00-2, para. 10)
- ■ (Expense or Capital) Expense all R&D except costs associated with a routine or an on-going effort to improve an existing product or adapt a product to a particular customer's need (FASB 2, para. 12 and FIN 6, para. 7)
- ■ (Expense) Determine the functional and nonfunctional requirements (SOP 98-1, 19)
- ■ (Expense) Formalization, evaluation, and selection of technology alternatives including vendor selection (SOP 98-1, 17)
- ■ (Capital) Design of the chosen path, including software configuration and interfaces (SOP 98-1, 17)
- ■ (Capital) Coding, testing (including parallel processing phase for legacy system), and installation to hardware (SOP 98-1, 17)
- ■ (Capital) Establish data conversion tools (SOP 98-1, 21)
- ■ (Expense) Complete data conversion (SOP 98-1, 22)
- ■ (Expense) Training and maintenance (SOP 98-1, 17)
- ■ (Capital) Initial graphical elements and overall design of web page (EITF 00-2, para. 6)
- ■ (Capital) Web and text content development (no guidance — EITF 00-2 para. 7 noted Task Force will review at a later time)

See Note 3 for all costs to include in the above categories.

Handle expense/capitalize the following activities as follows (see Note 4 for a further description of FASB 86):
- ■ (Expense) Business plan for system (EITF 00-2, para. 10)
- ■ (Expense or Capital) Expense all R&D except costs associated with a routine or an on-going effort to improve an existing product or adapt a product to a particular customer's need (FASB 2, para. 12 and FIN 6, para. 7)
- ■ (Expense) Determine the functional and nonfunctional requirements (FASB 86, para. 3 & 4)
- ■ (Expense) Formalization, evaluation, and selection of technology alternatives including vendor selection (FASB 86, para. 3 & 4)
- ■ (Capital) Design of the chosen path, including software configuration and interfaces (FASB 86, para. 3 & 4)
- ■ (Capital) Coding, testing (including parallel processing phase for legacy system), and installation to hardware (FASB 86, para. 3 & 4)
- ■ (Capital) Establish data conversion tools (FASB 86, para. 3 & 4, SOP 98-1, para. 22)
- ■ (Expense) Complete data conversion (FASB 86, para. 3 & 4, SOP 98-1, para. 17)
- ■ (Expense) Training and maintenance (FASB 86, para. 3 & 4)
- ■ (Expense) Initial graphical elements and overall design of web page (EITF 00-2, para. 6)
- ■ (Capital) Web and text content development (no guidance — EITF 00-2 para. 7 noted Task Force will review at a later time)

See Note 3 for all costs to include in the above categories.

SOP 98-1 vs. FASB 86. Even applications that provide a service for sale would be accounted for under SOP 98-1 as we are not selling them software to own but rather a service to utilize.

2. As to a substantive marketing plan, refer to the following (para. 12 from SOP 98-1): "A substantive plan to market software externally could include the selection of a marketing channel or channels with identified promotional, delivery, billing, and support activities. To be considered a substantive plan, under this SOP, implementation of the plan should be reasonably possible." Note that doing feasibility studies to market would not constitute a substantive plan to market.

3. Costs to include in the software development categories are as follows from SOP 98-1, para. 31: fees paid to third parties, travel expenses incurred, payroll and benefits, additional direct costs (hardware/software), and interest costs (which would be capitalized as part of FASB 34).

4. FASB 86 dictates, for computer software to be sold, leased, or otherwise marketed, that costs to establish technological feasibility should be expensed as incurred (para. 3). Per para. 4, "Technological feasibility is established when the enterprise has completed all planning, designing, coding, and testing activities that are necessary to establish that the product can be produced to meet its design specifications including functions, features, and technical performance requirements. At a minimum, the enterprise should have performed activities in a or b below: (a) The product design and the detail program design have been completed. (b) A product design and a working model of the software product have been completed and such model has been confirmed through testing."

Appendix 3: Project Fraud Management Policy Template

Business: Any Company
Policy No.:
Policy Title: General Operations: Project Fraud Management
Policy Date:
Policy Type: Executive
Page: 1 of X
Prepared By:
Approved By:

I. Policy Statement

This policy addresses how the business will manage for project fraud prevention and detection across the business where project work is being performed. All organizational units are expected to comply with this policy. The organization project management office (PMO) will manage the application of this policy onto all project teams. Internal auditing will assess policy compliance on a prescribed basis in collaboration with organizational management and the PMO. This policy provides guidelines for project team work delivery in project fraud prevention and detection. This policy identifies actions required by business workforce members to minimize project fraud opportunities and to control work issues that might lead to project fraud.

II. Purpose

Members of the business workforce must conduct themselves with unconflicted loyalty to the interests of the business and its customers and workforce. This accountability supersedes any conflicting loyalty, such as loyalty to other nonrelated business activities. Furthermore, no employee shall use their knowledge of company affairs that conflicts in a manner detrimental to the company's best interests.

Nothing in this policy is intended to limit staff's day-to-day responsibility as set forth in the Company Employment Guide, job descriptions, or other policies governing staff conduct, nor is this policy intended to affect the responsibility of the CEO over the conduct of staff in performing any duty regarding the company.

III. Desired Results/Objectives

1. Business staff members will have a clear understanding of the business requirement to minimize and control perceived project fraud events.
2. Business staff members will understand what action they need to take to report project fraud. Those in charge of executing the project fraud management policy will understand their responsibilities and actions to implement this policy.
3. The customer public will have confidence in the business integrity and in the products and services that the business delivers.
4. This policy will minimize the potential for business value to be compromised in the event that project fraud does occur.
5. The implementation of this policy will enable project teams to improve their visibility to work acceleration opportunities and threats, which enables a greater rate of work delivery for the benefit of the business.
6. The implementation of this policy will enable more value toward business transformation resulting from change management in the business.
7. All project investments will be mapped in alignment with corporate objectives that raise visibility for improved business navigational decision making and project fraud detection.

8. The PMO is responsible for the application of this rigor and discipline across the business regarding project delivery work.
9. Internal auditing will oversee the functional compliance to Section 404 of the Sarbanes-Oxley legislation.

IV. Definitions

- *Project fraud* — An employee working as a project team member in the execution of their job that makes a misrepresentation that leads to a negative consequence on the company.
- *Conflict of interest* — A transaction in which an employee becomes a party to and/or beneficiary from actions resulting from their participation that is not approved and that leads to injury to the company. Examples of conflict of interest include:
  1. An employee has a financial interest in a company that would benefit from the output of the group they are working with.
  2. An employee who is also employed with another competing business.
  3. An employee who limits vendor selection or participation because of personal relationship.
- *Misrepresentation* — Knowingly misstating information to influence business decisions that have impact on company business.

V. Persons Affected

All employees and contracted vendors.

VI. Dissemination

- *Internal* — All employees
- *External* — Approved vendors and business partners

VII. Responsibilities

The PMO will oversee policy compliance in the project delivery space for the organization. Internal auditing will recommend approval for the developed policy based on federal law requirements and how the policy enables compliance with the federal requirements and with how the policy supports the business needs.

PMO Role and Responsibilities

The PMO role in managing for project fraud is to enable project support processes that will actively prevent and detect project fraud directly within intra- or interproject team relationships within the organization. These processes include:

1. Portfolio management
   - Corporate objectives portfolio
   - Project investment portfolio
   - Resource portfolio
   - Asset portfolio
2. PMO data store access
3. One hundred percent data integrity with the PMO data store
4. Project delivery mentoring
5. Whistle-blowing help desk (integrated into PMO help desk)
6. Service level agreements with internal auditing and strategic planning
7. Project management standard methods and templates
8. Essential project governance facilitation support at various levels of the organization
9. Project fraud management training
10. Project management training

Internal Auditing Role and Responsibilities

The internal auditing role in managing for project fraud is to support project audits and approved overall project fraud management policy implementation and change management to that policy. In addition, the role is to ensure that the business is meeting federal compliance expectations in part with this policy applied to intra- or interproject team relationships within the organization.

In the execution of the project audit, auditors are to examine project records that are required by this policy and for the presence of policy expectations within the work outputs of the audited project. This includes the following items minimally:

1. Project charter
2. Project scope statement and actions
3. Project management plan and actions
4. Project risk plan and action
5. Project change management plan and actions
6. Project communications plan and actions
7. Project staffing plan and actions

8. Project schedule iterations
9. Utilization of critical path techniques
10. One hundred percent resource labor reported within policy guidelines within the project
11. Project sponsor approvals at the appropriate points

VIII. Procedures

- *Authority* — Unless otherwise specified, the enforcement of this policy requires all employees to abide by the bylaws, policies, rules, requirements, and procedures of the company and will not knowingly engage or assist in activities to compromise the integrity, reputation, property, and/or legal rights of the employee.

- *Disclosure* — Employees, accountable under this policy, must identify those situations where project fraud is occurring or about to occur at the earliest possible time.

- *Disclosure review* — All employees will formally acknowledge once a year, in written fashion to the company, that they have not engaged in activities that are in violation of this policy. In the event this does occur and it becomes determined that the employee did not initially recognized the violation, said employee is to report the policy violation to their immediate supervisor. Apparent violations of this policy, including but not limited to, the failure to make adequate and full disclosure of any policy violation by an employee, will be forwarded to the appropriate employee supervisor for management action.

INDEX